COMPARATIVE MIDRASH
*The Plan and Program of Genesis Rabbah
and Leviticus Rabbah*

Program in Judaic Studies
Brown University
BROWN JUDAIC STUDIES
Edited by
Jacob Neusner,
Wendell S. Dietrich, Ernest S. Frerichs,
Calvin Goldscheider, Alan Zuckerman

Project Editors (Project)

Number 111
COMPARATIVE MIDRASH
*The Plan and Program of Genesis
Rabbah and Leviticus Rabbah*
by
Jacob Neusner

COMPARATIVE MIDRASH
The Plan and Program of Genesis Rabbah and Leviticus Rabbah

by
Jacob Neusner

Scholars Press
Atlanta, Georgia

COMPARATIVE MIDRASH
The Plan and Program of Genesis Rabbah and Leviticus Rabbah

Library of Congress Cataloging in Publication

Neusner, Jacob, 1932–
    Comparative midrash.

    (Brown Judaic studies ; no. 111)
    Includes index.
    1. Midrash rabbah. Genesis—Criticism, interpretation etc. 2.
Midrash rabbah. Leviticus—Criticism, interpretation, etc. I.
Title. II. Series.
BM517.M65N48   1986   296.1'406   85-27669
ISBN 0-89130-958-6 (alk. paper)
ISBN 0-89130-959-4 (pbk.)

For

MANFRED VOGEL

Principal voice in
the unfolding of contemporary
Judaic thought, dear and
loyal friend.

In admiration and thanks.

CONTENTS

Preface

This book carries forward my sustained inquiry into the character of compilations of scriptural exegeses, called *midrashim,* produced in late antiquity by the sages who framed the canon of Judaism. It completes the inquiry begun in *The Integrity of Leviticus Rabbah. The Problem of the Autonomy of a Rabbinic Document* (Chico, 1985: Scholars Press for Brown Judaic Studies).

My work on exegesis of Scripture in the canon of Judaism began with *A History of the Mishnaic Law of Purities. VII. Negaim. Sifra* (Leiden, 1975: E. J. Brill). Studies of the relationship between Scripture and the discrete rules of the Mishnah, Mishnah-tractates one by one, and the Mishnah as a whole, went forward with the further volumes of my *History of the Mishnaic Law of Purities* (Leiden, 1975-1977: E. J. Brill) I-XXII, *History of the Mishnaic Law of Holy Things* (Leiden, 1979) I-VI, *History of the Mishnaic Law of Women* (Leiden, 1979-1980) I-V, *History of the Mishnaic Law of Appointed Times* (Leiden, 1981-1983) I-V, and *History of the Mishnaic Law of Damages* (Leiden, 1983-1985) I-V. Each study of a tractate and of a complete division worked out systematic, and detailed studies of the same problem: the relationship of Mishnah-rules, principles, and tractates, to verses of Scripture on the same subject, and to Scripture as a whole.[1]

Then in *Judaism. The Evidence of the Mishnah* (Chicago, 1981: University of Chicago Press), pp. 167-229, I presented a systematic study of the question of Mishnah-Scripture relationships. That is in the context of the description of the formative document, the Mishnah, in its relationship to Scripture. That is the correct way to ask about the role of scriptural exegesis in Judaism, namely, en route to explaining the role and authority of Scripture in Judaism. For it is

---

[1] The question of which comes first, *midrash* or *mishnah,* meaning exegesis of Scripture or apodictic statement of a law, has never attracted my attention, because I do not understand the issue. I do not know how, in any event, one would settle the question of priority or construct a test to validate or invalidate a theory on it. The best statement on the question known to me is Jacob Z. Lauterbach, "Midrash and Mishnah. A Study in the Early History of the Halakhah," *Jewish Quarterly Review,* n.s., 5, 1914, pp. 503-527, 6, 1915, pp. 23-905, 303-327, and reprinted in Lou H. Silberman, ed., *Rabbinic Essays* (Cincinnati, 1951: Hebrew Union College Press). Since all of the actual evidence in hand derives from the period of the Mishnah, ca. 200, and beyond, I do not know precisely what evidence permit us to investigate the question to begin with. It is important, therefore, that when I phrase the issue of Mishnah-Scripture and Midrash-Scripture relationships, readers understand the question I do not propose to ask at all.

Judaism, that is, in its language, the one whole torah of Moses, our rabbi, that dictated the place and uses of the written component of that one whole Torah. The system absorbed and made use of Scripture. Scripture did not define the system, that is, the one whole Torah, written and oral. The system comes prior to its utilization of, among other things, Scripture. While these propositions seem to me self-evident, I spent a great deal of time, and many books of detailed analysis, in order to demonstrate them.[2] A still more elaborate statement of the main results of detailed analysis is presented in "From Scripture to Mishnah. A Systematic Account," in my *Method and Meaning in Ancient Judaism. Second Series* (Chicago, 1981: Scholars Press for Brown Judaic Studies), pp. 101-214.

A second approach to the question, that of redaction-criticism, occupied me in sequence. It seemed the logical next step, that is, from substance to form. I turned to the study of sages' compilations of exegeses of Scripture viewed as whole documents.[3] That represented a considerable shift in approach, since these compilations of exegeses now are viewed when *not* set into relationship either with a legal conception or with a document of law. That is to say, I had answered the question of the relationship of Scripture to the laws of the Mishnah, viewed one by one, by tractates, and as a whole, thus: Mishnah-Scripture relationships. Now I wanted to know about the relationship of the *heirs* of the Mishnah to Scripture, that is, the same question turned on its head. As I just said, I now asked the question of *systemic* analysis: in the unfolding of Judaism of the one whole Torah of Moses our rabbi, in media both oral and written, what of the place and uses of Scripture?

My way is to start with the documents and work inductively. Further, I approach a document from its outer limits and work my way in, trying to allow the document's own characteristic and definitive traits of plan and program, form and doctrine, to guide me. The first study turned to the whole documents made up of exegeses of Scripture and produced by the Mishnah's authorities in the third and fourth centuries. Here I placed into canonical context the work of compiling exegeses into documents. The result is *Midrash in Context. Exegesis in Formative Judaism..* (That book forms volume I of *The Foundations of Judaism. Method., Teleology, Doctrine* [Philadelphia, 1983-1985: Fortress] I-III.) This work deals mainly with Genesis Rabbah, the taxonomy of its forms, and the relationship between that taxonomy and one that serves the Talmud of the Land of Israel. I have proved that a single taxonomy

---

[2] The contrary proposition -- "Judaism" really restates what is merely the plain sense of Scripture, so it is the one authoritative continuator of Scripture --serves theological purposes as part of the apologetic against Christianity, but rests on no firmer analytical-descriptive and inductive foundations than the Christian view of the "New Testament" as the authoritative continuator of the "Old." For both Judaism and Christianity, faith demands believing despite, not through, the world.

[3] I merely follow the example of my splendid friend, Brevard S. Childs.

serves both documents -- a necessary first step in the comparison of whole documents to one another.

From the issue of context I turned to a particular document, beginning, of course, by confronting its every detail: translating it and so effecting a detailed commentary. I took up Leviticus Rabbah and carried out a complete form-analytical translation of that work.[4] At the same time, having defined the formal traits of the document, I investigated the modes of thought that produced, for the framers, intelligible statements: modes of syllogistic discourse and how they work. The result is *Judaism and Scripture: The Evidence of Leviticus Rabbah* (Chicago, 1986: University of Chicago Press). The upshot was to show how the framers of the canon of Judaism, in theological language, the Oral Torah, not only drew upon verses of Scripture but absorbed into their system an entire biblical book, turning it into a kind of Mishnah-tractate, that is, component of the Oral Torah. This process of systemic analysis and its results are restated in the larger context of the formation of the canon of Judaism in *The Oral Torah. The Sacred Books of Judaism. An Introduction* (San Francisco, 1985: Harper & Row), pp. 88-131. My conclusion is that Leviticus Rabbah presents a deeply *religious* view of Israel's historical and salvific life, in much the same way that the Mishnah provides a profoundly *philosophical* view of Israel's everyday and sanctified existence. So the Mishnah presents the philosophy of the Torah, that is, of Judaism, and Leviticus Rabbah presents the theology of history of the Torah, that is, of that same Judaism.

The next project, which, as I said, defined the question of this one, is *The Integrity of Leviticus Rabbah. The Problem of the Autonomy of a Rabbinic Document* (Chicago, 1985: Scholars Press for Brown Judaic Studies). The present work completes the inquiry begun in *Integrity*, as I shall explain in the introduction. This book rests on my translation of Genesis Rabbah: *Genesis Rabbah. The Judaic Commentary on Genesis. A New American Translation* (Atlanta, 1985: Scholars Press for Brown Judaic Studies) I-III.[5] So this book belongs to on-going research into the literature, character, and context of exegesis of Scripture in the formative age of the Judaism of those sages who produced the Mishnah, the two Talmuds, the compilations of exegeses of Scripture, and the rest of the canon of the one whole Torah of Moses, our rabbi.

---

[4] My translation, a small part of which is used in this book as well, rests on the wonderful text of Mordecai Margulies, *Midrash Wayyikra Rabbah. A Critical Edition Based on Manuscripts and Genizah Fragments with variants and noters* (Jerusalem, 1953-1960) I-V. I further consulted the fine translation of J. Israelstam and Judah J. Slotki, *Midrash Rabbah. Leviticus* (London, 1939: Soncino).

[5] My translation takes up the text of Theodor-Albeck. I made abundant use of the fine translation of H. Freedman, *Midrash Rabbah. Genesis* (London, 1939: Soncino) I-II. Where my translation refers to a page and note with the name, Freedman, it refers to this work.

Let me now turn to the program of the book at hand. It presents a sustained inquiry into theory of comparison (the introduction), then [1] the systematic description of a compilation of exegeses of Scripture (parts I and II) and [2] the consequence of the comparison of one whole compilation of exegeses of Scripture with another whole compilation of exegeses of Scripture: *comparative midrash* the way it should be done (part III). I close with a detailed inquiry (Appendix) into the two former approaches to the same general subject, with a glance also at the methodological confusion displayed in some current work.

Thus, since the first part of the project took up the problem of how to describe a compilation of exegeses of Scripture accomplished by sages of the same group and age that produced the two Talmuds, here I proceed to describe in exactly the same way yet another text and then to compare the two texts, thus, from description of one document to comparison of two documents.

In the Introduction I present a sustained statement of the theory and method of the matter, explaining the question of this book and the method by which I propose to answer it.

In Part I of this book I describe Genesis Rabbah in accord with the same procedures through which I earlier described Leviticus Rabbah. We thus begin with the description, along exactly the same lines of inquiry, of a second document.

In Part II I review the relevant results of my description of Leviticus Rabbah.

In Part III I compare the two compilations. Having proved that the two documents do fall into the same genus, I claim that, at that point but not before, the work of *comparative midrash* can begin.

This is in two aspects, first, the editorial plan of one compared with that of the other (Chapter Six section ii), second, the theological program of one compared with that of the other (Chapter Six, sections iii and iv). I conclude (Chapter Six, section v) with a fleeting gesture outward, from the comparison of two congruent texts to remarks on incongruent texts, drawn from other Judaisms than the one at hand. That gesture is meant only to point to the possibility of results entirely different from those at hand, so to show that likeness is as unlikely as unlikeness.

I should not want to ignore other peoples' definitions of the same problem. So in the Appendix I include comments on the way in which the work of comparison has been done and explain briefly how former work, from the theoretical viewpoint spelled out in detail in the Introduction, is hopelessly flawed. I print the two principal statements of the theory of *comparative midrash* in its earlier versions, those of René Bloch and Geza Vermes. I do not know any others of rigor and sustained importance in any language. At the end, to show the parlous state of the theory of the matter, I cite an unfortunate example of utter confusion in method: someone who has in two successive monographs done things one way, that is, improperly, then in another way, that is, (from a theoretical viewpoint) properly -- without apparently remarking on his own shiftings and turnings.

In working on the problem of this book I had the advantage of daily conversations with my dear colleagues Ernest S. Frerichs, Calvin Goldscheider, and Wendell S. Dietrich, as well as with my co-workers William Scott Green, Baruch A. Levine, and Jonathan Z. Smith. I found their remarks stimulating and revised more than a few proposition in response to them. Working with them every day makes life an on-going circus: pure fun.

Jacob Neusner

Program in Judaic Studies
Brown University
Providence, Rhode Island

14 Tishre 5746
September 29, 1985

Introduction

i. Defining the Terms of this Book: (1) Midrash

This book investigates what it means to compare *midrash* to *midrash*. So the first question before us is the meaning of the title of the book, hence, first, of the word *midrash*. The second, to come in due course, is the meaning of the word *comparative*, what we do when we compare one thing to something else.

The word *midrash* stands for many things, but, in the main, is used in three ways. First of all, *midrash* refers to the processes of scriptural exegesis carried on by diverse groups of Jews from the time of ancient Israel to nearly the present day. Thus people say, "He produced a *midrash* on the verse," meaning, "an exegesis." A more extreme usage produces, "Life is a *midrash* on Scripture," meaning that what happens in the everyday world imparts meaning or significance to biblical stories and admonitions. It is difficult to specify what the word *midrash* in Hebrew expresses that the word *exegesis* in English does not. It follows that quite how "exegesis" in English differs from *midrash* in Hebrew, or why, therefore, the Hebrew will serve better than the more familiar English, I do not know. Some imagine that *midrash* for Jewish exegetes generically differs from *exegesis* for non-Jewish ones. What hermeneutics characterizes all exegeses produced by Jews, but no exegeses produced by non-Jews, who presumably do not produce *midrashim* on verses but do produce exegeses of verses of the same Hebrew Scriptures, no one has said. Accordingly, the first usage seems so general as to add up to nothing. That is to say, *midrash*, a foreign word, simply refers to the same thing -- the activity or process or intellectual pursuit -- as exegesis, an English word. The word *midrash* bears no more, or less, meaning than the word *exegesis*.

The other two usages will detain us considerably less, since they bear a precision lacking in the first. The word *midrash* further stands for [2] a compilation of scriptural exegeses, as in "that *midrash* deals with the book of Joshua." In that sentence, *midrash* refers to a compilation of exegeses, hence the statement means, "That compilation of exegeses deals with the book of Joshua." *Compilation* or composite in the present context clearly serves more accurately to convey meaning than *midrash*. I use both words in this book. The word *midrash*, finally, stands for [3] the written composition (e.g., a paragraph with a beginning, middle, and end, in which a completed thought is laid forth), resulting from the process of *midrash*. In this setting *a midrash* refers to a paragraph or a unit of exegetical exposition, in which a verse of the Hebrew

Scriptures is subjected to some form of exegesis or other. In this usage one may say, "Let me now cite the *midrash*," meaning, a particular passage of exegesis, a paragraph or other completed whole unit of exegetical thought, a composition that provides an exegesis of a particular verse. I use the word composition in this sense.

Accordingly the word bears at least three distinct, if related, meanings. If someone says "the *midrash* says," he may refer to [1] a distinctive *process* of interpretation of a particular text, thus, the hermeneutic, [2] a particular compilation of the results of that process, thus, a book that is the composite of a set of exegeses, or [3] a concrete unit of the working of that process, of scriptural exegesis, thus the write-up of the process of interpretation as it applies to a single verse, the exegetical composition on a particular verse (or group of verses).

It follows that for clear speech the word *midrash*, standing by itself, bears no meaning. In the Appendix we deal with how some have used the word for a particular purpose, in a discrete context, e.g., to mean saying or story, or "tradition." There, in reporting others' usages of the word, we shall accede to the common confusion. But elsewhere, in this book as in my others, in place of the word *midrash*, I prefer to use three words:

[1] exegesis, for *midrash* in the sense of an exegesis (of indeterminate character) of a verse of Scripture;

[2] composite, or compilation of exegeses (or occasionally, compilation of *midrashim*), for *midrash* in the sense of a sustained and sizable set or sequence or group of exegeses or even for a whole book made up of exegeses of Scripture;

[3] and unit of discourse, unit of thought, whole or completed unit of thought, composition, or similar expressions, for *midrash* in the sense of a single paragraph or a single fully spelled out essay of exegesis of a given verse or group of verses.

Since I have not studied the hermeneutics at hand -- the processes or principles of exegesis -- I have no reason to make a point of introducing a commonly used word in place of *midrash* in the sense of an allegedly distinctive hermeneutic for the interpretation of Scripture or the exegesis of a given verse of Scripture.

ii. Defining the Terms of this Book: (2) Toward a Theory of Comparison

Having defined the critical word of the title of this book, *midrash*, let me turn to the program at hand. The reason that we began as we did, with close attention to the word that signifies the classification of writing under study, now attains exposure. I am trying at the outset to clarify what we compare when we *compare midrash[im]*. Explaining what in general should be done, and comparing what I contend the work requires with what people actually do, is the purpose of this book.

Specifically, in Part Three, having described two compilations of exegeses in accord with a single program of description, I compare one *midrash* to another *midrash* , meaning, one compilation of exegeses, its plan and program, with another compilation of exegeses, its plan and program also having been systematically described in the same categories and methods. I execute comparison of both literary plan and theological program. So I do the work the way I think, in strict logic, it must begin.

Then in the Appendix I review other peoples' conceptions of the same work. Readers can then compare my proposed program for *comparative midrash* with the proposals of others, two theories and two examples of the execution of those contradictory theories (both, amusingly, by a single person). As we shall see, the inquiry of *comparative midrash* today encompasses three distinct activities. People may mean that they wish to compare [1] processes or methods of exegesis of Scripture (e.g., hermeneutics), [2] compilations of exegeses of Scripture (but this is uncommon), or [3] specific exegeses of a given verse of Scripture with other exegeses of the same verse of Scripture (this being the most commonplace activity of the genre). Let me now clarify the inquiry into comparison and place the work on firmer epistemological and methodological foundations. For when colleagues reflect on what they are doing, they may well find reason to redefine and reorder their agenda of inquiry. So we come to a theory of comparison, necessary at the outset of any work such as this.

When we compare, we seek, first, perspective on the things compared. Second, we look for the rule that applies to the unfamiliar thing among the things compared. The unknown thing is *like* something else, therefore falls under the rule governing the known thing to which it is likened, or it is *unlike* something else, therefore falls under the opposite (or, at least, another) rule. So comparison always entails the claim of likeness and requires the demonstration, at the same time, of difference: comparison and contrast at one and the same time. We compare, third, so as to discover the context for interpreting the things compared. How so? Through comparison we uncover traits that are unique to one thing and therefore also those that are shared among the things compared.

In these three as well as in other ways the labor of comparison and contrast forms the foundation of all inquiry into the description, analysis, and interpretation of otherwise discrete and unintelligible data. Without [1] perspective, [2] knowledge of the applicable rule, and [3] a conception of the context, we understand only the thing itself -- and therefore nothing at all. For not described, analyzed, and interpreted, the thing is unique -- by definition. And what is unique, also by definition, is beyond all rational comprehension. The reason is that we understand what is not yet known by reference to metaphors supplied by the things already understood. Their perspective, the pertinent rule governing them, the understanding of them gained in knowledge of their context -- these form the bridge between the known and the unknown. The work of comparison and contrast, classification and interpretation of discrete data, therefore defines all rational inquiry. The sole alternative, the claim of *a priori* understanding of things otherwise incompletely known, requires no attention. Why not? That claim lies outside of rational inquiry, for we have no way of falsifying, therefore verifying, *a priori* allegations concerning knowledge.

So we come to "comparative *midrash*" in particular. What, precisely, do we compare when we compare *midrash[im]* ? The answer will derive from asking how properly to compare one thing with something else, in this case one *midrash* with another *midrash*. The reader will immediately wonder which of the three meanings I have found in the word *midrash* defines the question of this book.

Do I mean comparing hermeneutics, one mode of exegesis of Scripture with some other, for example, comparing the methods of *midrash*/exegesis of Matthew with the methods of *midrash*/exegesis of the Essene writers of Qumran's library?

Do I mean comparing the redactional and formulary plans and theological programs, the definitive traits of one compilation of exegeses/*midrashim* with another such compilation, for example, Matthew Chapter Two with an equivalent composition of the Habakkuk commentary or with an equivalent passage of the Sifre to Numbers?

Or do I mean comparing the substantive results -- the treatment of a given verse of Scripture/*midrash* in one compilation of exegeses/*midrashim* with the treatment of that same verse or theme of Scripture/*midrash* in another compilation of exegeses/*midrashim*?

Since the phrase, "comparative *midrash*," applies quite comfortably to all three types of comparison, the answer to my question cannot emerge from common usage. Common usage is confused. Here I propose to clarify and purify that usage.

I do so by arguing that, to begin with -- but only to begin with -- the work of comparative *midrash*, should commence with [2] compilations, whole documents, and not [1] with modes of exegesis of Scripture occurring here, there, and everywhere, and also not with [3] discrete parts of documents . What should be compared at the outset is [2] whole to whole, document to document, and only later on [3] the constituent element of one document with the constituent element of another document, and last of all [1] the exegetical techniques, policies, or issues of one document with those of a second document.

Why begin with the entirety of a composite of exegeses [2], rather than with [1] techniques or modes of exegesis, on the one side, or [3] the results of exegesis, on the other? The reason is simple. Comparison begins in the definition of things that are to be compared. That means we must know *that* things fall into a common genus, and only then shall we be able to ask *how* things are different from one another. We cannot be sure that a detail, e.g., the result of exegesis of a given verse of Scripture on the part of two or more parties, defines a common genus because the same verse is at hand. We all the more so cannot be certain that an approach to exegesis permits comparison of two or more principles. But we have the possibility of comparing something so concrete as a document with an equivalent thing, another document. Very little subjectivity enters into such a comparison.

Why so? Because when we take up the outermost layer of an exegetical exercise, -- the document that presents exegeses, and not the mode or result -- we describe the context that contains the other two layers of the same exercise. So, I maintain, on the basis of logic we first of all must determine the context -- the two or more documents at hand -- and their respective roles in imparting to the materials contained within those documents the characteristic and consistent preferences in matters of both style and viewpoint. Only when we know the impact of the documentary context upon the materials in a document can we take up an individual item from that document and set it into comparison and contrast with a discrete item drawn out of some other, also carefully delineated and defined, document. At the point at which we can define the traits distinctive to one documentary context we may ask about traits of an item that occur in other documentary contexts in which that item makes its appearance. Then we may inquire into the comparison and contrast of one detail, drawn from one document, with what we conceive to be a parallel or intersecting detail, drawn from another.

Why do I argue, therefore, that we must first start with the definition of the documentary context, the whole of a compilation of exegeses? The documentary context stands first in line because it it is what we know for sure. When we describe a document, we know as fact that [1] a given method of exegesis has yielded [3] a given exegetical comment on a verse of Scripture, the result of which is now in [2] *this particular document.* Since we know the wonderfully simple facts of what is found in which document, we can begin the work of describing the traits imparted by [2] that document to the [3] exegetical result of [1] the exegetical method at hand. Traits characteristic of [2] the documentary setting likewise emerge without a trace of speculation. To state matters more concretely, if a document routinely frames matters in accord with one repertoire of formal conventions rather than some other, and if it arranges its formal repertoire of types of units of discourse in one way, rather than some other, and if its compilers repeatedly propose to make one point, rather than some other, we can easily identify those traits of the passage under study that derive from the larger documentary context.

Accordingly, we begin with the document because it presents the first solid fact. Everything else then takes a position relative to that fact. What then are some of the documentary facts? Here are some: this saying or story occurs here, bears these traits, is used for this larger redactional and programmatic purpose, makes this distinct point in its context (or no point at all). One may readily test these allegations and determine their facticity. These facts therefore define the initial context of interpretation. The facts deriving from the documentary setting define the context in which a given trait shared or not shared among the two discrete items to be compared. In Parts One and Two I show for Genesis Rabbah what this work of entirely inductive description entails, just as I did in the *Integrity of Leviticus Rabbah*.

In laying emphasis on the document as the correct first point of comparison, I exclude as the appropriate point of departure for comparative studies two others, namely, [1] modes of exegesis, hence, comparative hermeneutics, and [3] results of exegesis, hence, comparison of the exegesis of a verse in one document, deriving from one period and group of authorities, with the exegesis of that same verse in some other document, deriving from a completely different sort of authorities and a much earlier or much later period. (In the Appendix Vermes and the first of the two Fraades in Fraade vs. Fraade serve as examples of this approach.) In both cases I maintain that the context for comparison is improper, with the result that the work of comparison produces mere information, but no insight.

What is the insight we miss? Let me ask the question more broadly: what do we *not* know if at the outset of comparing things we ignore what I regard as the first and fundamental issue, the plan and program of the document in which an item appears? If we ignore as unimportant the characteristic traits of the documentary locations of an exegesis of a verse of Scripture or of a story occurring in two or more documents, or if we treat as trivial the traits characteristic of those locative points, we do not know the rule governing both items subject to comparison. We establish no context that imparts meaning to the work of comparison. Why not? Because, in simple words, we have no perspective on the similarities and differences among two or more things that are compared with one another. These similarities and differences may prove merely adventitious. But we shall never know. Points of likeness may constitute mere accidents of coincidence, e.g., of internal logic of the statement of the verse of Scripture at hand. But we cannot tell.

Let me offer a silly possibility of argument. If people in different places, times, or groups concur that a verse means one thing and not some other thing, it may be that that is because the meaning on which diverse groups concur is the only meaning the verse can yield. How do we know that that meaning, shared among diverse groups, is the only possible meaning? It is proved by the fact of broad concurrence among different groups (!). What is the upshot of this marvelously circular mode of reasoning? The claim that, because the items are alike -- say the same thing, for example, about the same verse -- therefore we know something we otherwise would not know about [1] hermeneutics, [2] documentary context, or [3] the history and meaning of the exegesis of the verse at hand, does not permit us to invoke processes of falsification or verification.

Why not? Because, not knowing the context of likeness or difference, we also do not know the meaning of likeness or difference. That is why the definition of the context in which discrete data make their appearance demands attention first of all. But -- I repeat -- it is only first in sequence. Rightly done, comparative midrash in sequence also will take up questions of [1] shared or different techniques and also [3] shared or different exegetical results in discrete settings. These two define further points of interest. But we must start at the largest and most general stage of description, the one resting on no speculation as to the facts, that is, therefore, the stage of establishing context: defining the genus as a matter of context prior to comparing the species differentiated in that same context.

Up to now, as we shall note in the Appendix (Vermes), we have the results of comparison of [3] *results* of exegesis. These results derive from observations made wholly out of documentary context. But comparing what has not been shown comparable yields mere information, in the category of such a statement as this: apples are different from Australians. Out of context that information proves not merely trivial but mindless. How so? Apples and Australians are alike and may be compared and contrasted because they both begin with an A. Or it is because they both thrive on the same vast island-continent. Now anyone who has visited Sydney knows that in general Australians, living in the South Pacific sun, are ruddy. Everyone knows that all apples have stems. It furthermore is true that not all apples have rosy cheeks, for some are green or yellow, and no Australians are known to have stems and grow on trees. So apples are like Australians in that they come from Australia, and apples are not like Australians in that they have stems. Australians are like apples in that they come from Australia, but they are not like apples in that they all have ruddy cheeks. We can go on making such perspicacious observations. But so what? That information leads us deep into a unending wonderland of odd information.

Lacking all context, the generality of results of *comparative midrash* as presently practiced compares apples to Australians. That is to say, masses of information gained by comparing what may or may not prove consequential when compared or even comparable at all fills books lacking all particular program. One can produce a great many such books without explaining what is at stake in any one of them. That explanation demands an answer to the question, *what else* do we know if we know the result of this inquiry? Comparing what different people happen to say about the same verse of Scripture has yet to yield a compelling answer to "so what?"

In other words we must be able to state what is at stake in observing that apples differ from Australians. True, it is because Australians have ruddy cheeks and some apples are green, on the one hand, apples have stems and Australians do not, on the second hand, and both apples and Australians are known to thrive in Australia, on the third hand. But nothing is at stake in these observations, which, therefore, are inane. Logic demands that inquiry rest upon a point of interest, a hypothesis, a theory, a mode of validation and invalidation. We must know what we know -- which is to say, what *else* we know -- if we know the result at hand: this is like that, this is not like that.

Comparison and contrast depend, in strict logic, upon prior identification of appropriate commonalities. The genus comes before the species. When we know that in consequential ways things are alike, we then can discover in what ways they are not alike. We further can derive further insight from the points in common and the differences as well. We cannot ask how things differ if we do not know that there is a basis for the question of comparison and contrast. And the point of distinction between one thing and another thing must be shown to make a difference.

If we do not ask the question concerning, in Jonathan Z. Smith's phrase, what difference a difference makes,[1] then we are comparing apples to Australians. Only when we can demonstrate that diverse objects fall into a single appropriate genus -- are all apples, for example, or are all Australian -- can we differentiate the species of the appropriately-defined genus, apple from apple, Australian from Australian. And that point of differentiation -- the distinction at hand -- must make a difference, must tell us something else about either apples or Australians. Knowing that apples and Australians have in common a point of origination on the same great continent tells us a point in common that yields no more useful insight than that both begin with the letter A. The distinctions we draw then also make no difference. We learn no "something else." In my view beginning at layer [3], namely, the results of exegesis of the same verse by diverse groups, sets the comparative study off on the wrong course. There is no *what else*, no answer to the question: so what?

The proponents of *comparative midrash* in its present formulation argue quite reasonably that they too begin with a premise of shared traits. They compare not apples and Australians but apples and apples Perhaps so, but then they select the wrong traits for comparison, and therefore they do not describe the right things at all. They describe and then compare [3] the results of exegesis of a given verse in one document with [3] the results of exegesis of that same verse in another document. But the context of description is not established. Let me spell out my objection to the comparison of what different people say about a given verse without reference to the documents in which what they say is preserved. That is the crux of matters.

When practitioners of *comparative midrash* compare not [2] document to document, but [3] exegetical result to exegetical result, their articles and books produce information of this sort: on a given verse, X says this and Y says

---

[1]   Jonathan Z. Smith, "What a Difference a Difference Makes," in J. Neusner and E. S. Frerichs, eds., *"To See Ourselves as Others See Us." Christians, Jews, "Others" in Late Antiquity*   (Atlanta, 1985: Scholars Press Studies in the Humanities), pp. 3-48.

something else. The Appendix will prove I do not misrepresent. That, sum and substance is the result of their study of *comparative midrash*. What then defines that shared foundation that makes possible comparison and contrast? It is [3] the object of *midrash*, namely as verse of Scripture.

So the proponents of *comparative midrash* invoke the continuity of Scripture in defense of comparing and contrasting only [3] the results of exegesis. They maintain that what one party says about a given verse of Scripture surely is comparable with what another party says about that same verse of Scripture. So they compare and contrast what two or more parties say about a given verse or story of Scripture. That seems to me entirely correct and proper, -- but only in its appropriate setting. And what is that setting at which it is quite proper to undertake comparison of [3] results of exegesis and even [1] modes of exegesis? It is when we know the setting in which people reached one conclusion and not some other. That is to say, when we know the issues exegetes addressed and the intellectual and political and theological setting in which they did their work, then the fact that they said one thing and not something else will illuminate *what* they said and may further explain their rejection of what they did *not* say. Since, moreover, we deal not with the gist of what people said but with a given version in one set of words rather than some other, a message captured in particular language governed by conventions of form, comparison of modes of expression and conventions of language and form proceeds apace. So comparing what people said demands that we notice, also, the different ways in which they may (or may not) have said the same thing (or the opposite things). Formal traits, involving use of language and highly formalized expression, define part of the task of interpreting what is like and what is unlike.

Everything we propose to examine finds its original place in some document, rather than in some other (or in two or three documents and not in ten or twenty others). Have the framers or compilers of one document selected an item merely because that item pertains to a given verse of Scripture? Or have they chosen that item because it says what they wish to say in regard to a verse of Scripture they have identified as important? Have they framed matters in terms of their larger program of the formalization of language, syntax and rhetoric alike? Have their selection and formalization of the item particular relevance to the context in which they did their work, the purpose for which they composed their document, the larger message they planned to convey to those to whom they planned to speak? These questions demand answers, and the answers will tell us the *what else*, that is, what is important about what people say in common or in contrast about the verse at hand. Without the answers provided by analysis of circumstance and context, plan and program, of the several documents one by one and then in comparison and contrast with one another, we know only what people said about the verse. But we do not know why they said it, what they meant by what they said, or what we learn from the fact *that* they said what they said about the verse in hand. The answers to these questions constitute that "what-else?" that transforms catalogues of pointless facts into pointed and important propositions.

The question about the precipitant of exegesis, namely, whether it is the literary and theological context, as I maintain, or principally the verse subject to exegesis,[2] as proponents of *comparative midrash* in its present formulation hold, brings us to the crux of the matter.

The premise of all that I have said is that Scripture serves a diversity of purposes and therefore cannot establish a single definitive plane of meaning, the frame of reference against which all other things constitute variables. Scripture constitutes the neutral background, not the variable. Exegetes tell us what verses of Scripture matter and what we should learn from those verses. Scripture dictates nothing but endures all things. What people tell us about the meaning of Scripture (points [1] and [3] in what has gone before) represents the outcome of the work of exegetes, not the inexorable result of the character or contents of Scripture. The issue for debate as I think it should be argued is this:

1. Does Scripture dictate the substance of exegesis?

2. Or do exegetes dictate the sense they wish to impart to (or locate in) Scripture?

If the former, then the ground for comparison finds definition in a verse of Scripture. What X said, without regard to circumstance or even documentary context, compared with what Y said, viewed also with slight attention to canonical context and concrete literary circumstance, matters.

If the latter, then canon and its components take pride of place, and what diverse persons said about a given verse of Scripture defines only a coincidence, unless proved on the basis of circumstance and context to constitute more than mere coincidence.

So I think the question must be framed. The answer to the question lies spread across the surface of the reading of Scripture in the history of the scriptural religions of the West, the Judaisms and the Christianities in perpetual contention among and between themselves about which verses of Scripture matter, and what those that matter mean. That remarkably varied history tells the story of how diverse groups of believers selected diverse verses of the Hebrew Scriptures as particularly important. They then subjected those verses, and not other verses, to particular exegetical inquiry. The meanings they found in those verses answer questions they found urgent. Scripture contributed much but dictated nothing, system -- circumstance and context-- dictated everything and selected what Scripture might contribute in *midrash*. In this context, *midrash*

---

[2] That is the single most common mode of study of comparative midrash. The supposition is that traits of the verse subject to exegesis lead people to make one comment rather than some other. I cannot imagine a less likely possibility -- in real life. But it is a common staple of research for those who *compare-midrashim*.

means the whole extant repertoire of exegeses of verses of Scripture we possess in [2] various compilations of exegeses of Scripture, made up of [3] compositions of exegesis of verses of Scripture, guided by [1] diverse hermeneutical principles of interpretation of Scripture. Since in *midrash* as just now defined, system, *hence canon*, comes first, prior to exegeses of particular verses of Scripture, all the more so prior to the hermeneutics that guides the work of exegesis, the documents that constitute the canon and contain the system form the definitive initial classification for comparative *midrash*. System must be compared to system, not detail to detail, and, therefore, to begin with, we compare [2] compilation of exegeses to the counterpart, thus document to document. So comparison of the repertoire of verses people chose and those they ignored yields the governing insight. Before we know the answers, we have to understand the questions people addressed to Scripture. Why so? Because a group chose a repertoire of verses distinctive to itself, rarely commenting on, therefore confronting, verses important to other groups. When we deal with different groups talking about different things to different groups, what difference does it make to us that, adventitiously and not systematically, out of all systemic context, we discover that someone reached the same conclusion as did someone else, of some other group? What else do we know if we discover such a coincidence? Parallel lines never meet, and parallel statements on the same verse may in context bear quite distinct meaning.

For instance, Pharisees appear to have found especially interesting verses in Leviticus and Numbers that failed to attract much attention from the Evangelists. Evangelists found unusually weighty verses of Scripture that the Pharisees and their heirs tended to ignore. Accordingly, Scripture forms the neutral ground. It is the constant -- the letter A or the continent of Australia, in our earlier analogy. Merely because both apples and Australians originate in Australia and begin with the letter A (among much else they have in common), we know nothing else than that apples and Australians originate in Australia and begin with an A. Contending groups selected verses of Scripture important to the larger programs that, to begin with, brought them to the reading and interpretation of particular verses of Scripture. In context they may have reached the same conclusions as did other groups. But so what? Do we therefore learn what that verse of Scripture must mean? No one can imagine so. We learn little about Scripture, and little about the diverse groups whose views, on a given verse of Scripture, happened to coincide. What is neutral conveys no insight, only what is subject to contention. That is why the choice of a given verse of Scripture for sustained inquiry comes prior to inquiry into the meaning or message discovered in that verse of Scripture. And that choice derives not from the neutral repertoire of Scripture but the polemical program of the group that makes the choice. So we must describe the program and the system, and that means the canon, item by item: the documents in their canonical context, the exegeses of verses in their documentary context, then the results of exegesis.

Scripture itself forms the undifferentiated background. It is the form, not the substance, the flesh, not the spirit. The fact that a single verse of Scripture generates diverse comments by itself therefore forms a statement of a merely formal character. It is a sequence of facts that may or may not bear meaning. That statement hardly differs in logical status from the one that Australians are different from apples because all apples have stems and no Australians have stems. True enough, but so what? What *else* do we know, when we know that apples and Australians, alike in some ways, differ in the specified way? The stress in *comparative midrash* as presently done on the (mere) formality that everyone is talking about the same thing yields long catalogues of information about what different people say about the same thing. What is at stake in making these lists, what syllogism or proposition we prove by compiling information, rarely, comes to expression. More often than not, the list is the thing.

To conclude: the correct thing to describe and compare first of all is [2] the document that contains the results of the exegesis of diverse verses of Scripture with [2] another such document. For comparison begins with the system as a whole, dealing with the system through its canon, so one whole document compared with another document, described in the way the first has been described. We have to describe documents one by one, then in relationship to one another: description first, then analysis through comparison and contrast. Description begins with the whole of the thing described, thus documents, one at a time, then documents in comparison with one another. Later on we turn to details of documents, their contents, viewed first in their respective documentary contexts, then alongside one another.

iii. Comparing Whole to Whole: The Centrality of the Canon and its Documents

The work of analysis rests upon establishing the genus first, and only then the species,. Comparing one species of one genus with another species of a different genus proves parlous indeed. For when we deal with a species distinct from the genus which defines its traits and establishes the context of those traits, we do not really know what we have in hand. Why not? The context of a definitive trait not having been established, we cannot know the sense and meaning of a given detail, indeed, even whether the detail by itself defines and distinguishes the species of which it is a part. It is the genus which permits us to describe and analyze the species of that genus. When, therefore, we propose to undertake a work of comparison and contrast, we must begin at the level of the genus, and not at any lesser layer. What that means is simple. The work of description, prior to analysis and so comparison and contrast, begins with the whole, and only then works its way down to the parts. The work of analysis, resting on such a labor of description, proceeds once more, as I have proposed, from the whole, the genus, to the parts, the species.

iv. The Peripatetic Saying and the Argument of *The Integrity of Leviticus Rabbah*

In my study of Leviticus Rabbah I proposed to demonstrate in the case of that compilation of exegeses of Scripture that a rabbinic document constitutes a text, not merely a scrapbook or a random compilation of episodic materials. A text is a document with a purpose, one that exhibits the traits of the integrity of the parts to the whole and the fundamental autonomy of the whole from other texts. I showed that the document at hand therefore falls into the classification of a cogent composition, put together with purpose and intended as a whole and in the aggregate to bear a meaning and state a message. I therefore disproved the claim, for the case before us, that a rabbinic document serves merely as an anthology or miscellany or is to be compared only to a scrapbook, made up of this and that. In that exemplary instance I pointed to the improbability that a document has been brought together merely to join discrete and ready-made bits and pieces of episodic discourse. A document in the canon of Judaism thus does not merely define a context for the aggregation of such already completed and mutually distinct materials. Rather, I proved, that document constitutes a text. So at issue in my study of Leviticus Rabbah is what makes a text a text, that is, the textuality of a document. At stake is how we may know when a document constitutes a text and when it is merely an anthology or a scrapbook.

The first half of this study, on Leviticus Rabbah, is relevant to the present exercise because it answers the question on which all comparison rests: how to describe a document whole. Before we can compare, we have to describe the things we propose to compare with one another. In *Integrity* I so framed the question as to show the way to do so. I dealt in a very specific instance, with two problems of broad and general interest, one in literature, the other in the study of religion.

The first is what makes a text a text. I dealt with the textuality of a text, the issue of whether a given piece of writing hangs together and is to be read on its own

The second is what makes a group of texts into a canon, a cogent statement all together. At issue is the relationship of two or more texts of a single, interrelated literature to the world-view and way of life of a religious tradition viewed whole.

The problem of *Integrity* is whether or not a rabbinic document to begin with stands by itself or right at the outset forms a scarcely differentiated segment of a larger uniform canon. Since people rarely wonder why a given composition should not be described by itself, let me spell out the basis for the contrary view. The reason one might suppose that, in the case of the formative age of Judaism, a document does not exhibit integrity and is not autonomous is simple. The several writings of the rabbinic canon of late antiquity, formed from the Mishnah, ca. A.D. 200, through the Talmud of Babylonia, ca. A.D. 600, with numerous items in between, share materials -- sayings, tales, protracted discussions.   Some of these shared materials derive from explicitly-cited documents.   For instance, passages of Scripture or of the Mishnah or of the Tosefta, cited verbatim, will find their way into the two Talmuds. But sayings, stories, and sizable compositions not identified with a given, earlier text and exhibiting that text's distinctive traits will float from one document to the next.

This brings us to the problem of peripatetic sayings and stories, that is, materials shared in common among two or more documents and their implications for the comparison of exegeses of the same verse and compilations of exegeses. The fact that the same saying may recur in diverse documents has so impressed students of the rabbinic canon as to produce a firm consensus of fifteen hundred years' standing. It is that one cannot legitimately study one document in isolation from others, describing its rhetorical, logical, literary, and conceptual traits and system all by themselves. To the contrary, all documents testify to the Torah, or, in secular language, contribute to a common literature, and religion, Judaism.   In the investigation of matters of rhetoric, logic literature, and conception, whether of law or of theology, all writings join equally to give testimony only about the whole. For the study of the formative history of Judaism, therefore, the issue transcends what appears to be the simple, merely literary question at hand: when is a text a text?

v. The Textuality of a Text

When I frame matters in terms of the problem of the rabbinic document, I ask what defines a document as such, the text-ness, the textuality, of a text. How do we know that a given book in the canon of Judaism is something other than a scrapbook? The choices are clear. One theory is that a document serves solely as a convenient repository of prior sayings and stories, available materials that will have served equally well (or poorly) wherever they took up their final location.   In accord with that theory it is quite proper in ignorance of all questions of circumstance and documentary or canonical context to compare the exegesis of a verse of Scripture in one document with the exegesis of that verse of Scripture found in some other document.

The other theory is that a composition exhibits a viewpoint, a purpose of authorship distinctive to its framers or collectors and arrangers.   Such a characteristic literary purpose -- by this other theory -- is so powerfully particular to one authorship that nearly everything at hand can be shown to have been (re)shaped for the ultimate purpose of the authorship at hand, that is, collectors and arrangers who demand the title of authors. In accord with this other theory context and circumstance form the prior condition of inquiry, the result, in exegetical terms, the contingent one.

To resort again to a less than felicitous neologism, I thus ask what signifies or defines the "document-ness" of a document and what makes a book a book. I therefore wonder whether there are specific texts in the canonical context of Judaism or whether all texts are merely contextual. In framing the question as I have, I of course lay forth the mode of answering it. . We have to confront a single rabbinic composition, and ask about its definitive traits and viewpoint.

But, as I said, that is why we have also to confront the issue of the "sources"[3] upon which the redactors of a given document have drawn. By "sources" I mean simply passages in a given book that occur, also, in some other rabbinic book. Such "sources" -- by definition prior to the books in which they appear -- fall into the classification of materials general to two or more compositions and by definition not distinctive and particular to any one of them. The word "source" therefore serves as an analogy to convey the notion that two or more sets of authors have made use of a single, available item. About whether or not the shared item is prior to them both or borrowed by one from the other at this stage we cannot speculate. These shared items, transcending two or more documents and even two or more complete systems or groups, if paramount and preponderant, would surely justify the claim that we may compare exegeses of verses of Scripture without attention to context. Why? Because there is no closed context defined by the limits of a given document and its characteristic plan and program. All the compilers of documents did is collect and arrange available materials.

Therefore we must ask about the textuality of a document -- is it a composition or a scrap book? -- so as to determine the appropriate foundations for comparison, the correct classifications for comparative study. Once we know what is unique to a document, we can investigate the traits that characterize all the document's unique and so definitive materials. We ask about whether the materials unique to a document also cohere, or whether they prove merely miscellaneous. If they do cohere, we may conclude that the framers of the document have followed a single plan and a program. That would in my view justify the claim that the framers carried out a labor not only of conglomeration, arrangement and selection, but also of genuine authorship or composition in the narrow and strict sense of the word. If so, the document emerges from authors, not merely arrangers and compositors. For the same purpose, therefore, we also take up and analyze the items shared between that document and some other or among several documents. We ask about the traits of those items, one by one and all in the aggregate. In these stages we may solve for the case at hand the problem of the rabbinic document: do we deal with a scrapbook or a cogent composition? A text or merely a literary expression, random and essentially promiscuous, of a larger theological context? That is the choice at hand.

---

[3] I use that word only because it is commonplace. In fact it is a misleading metaphor. In *Integrity* I pursued the possibility of characterizing the shared stories in such a way as to claim, as a matter of hypothesis, that they derive from a source, that is, a single common point of origin. The materials I examined in no way suggest that there was a single point of origin.

vi. The Relationships among Documents of the Canon of Late Antique Judaism

Since we have reached a matter of fact, let me state the facts as they are. I describe the relationships among the principal components of the literature with which we deal. The several documents that make up the canon of Judaism in late antiquity relate to one another in three important ways.

First, all of them refer to the same basic writing, the Hebrew Scriptures. Many of them draw upon the Mishnah and quote it. So the components of the canon join at their foundations.

Second, as the documents reached closure in sequence, the later authorship can be shown to have drawn upon earlier, completed documents. So the writings of the rabbis of the talmudic corpus accumulate and build from layer to layer.

Third, as I have already hinted, among two or more documents some completed units of discourse, and many brief, discrete sayings, circulated, for instance, sentences or episodic homilies or fixed apothegms of various kinds. So in some (indeterminate) measure the several documents draw not only upon one another, as we can show, but also upon a common corpus of materials that might serve diverse editorial and redactional purposes.

Now back to the question of the peripatetic sayings, the materials shared among two or more compilations. The extent of this common corpus can never be fully known. We know only what we have, not what we do not have. So we cannot say what has been omitted, or whether sayings that occur in only one document derive from materials available to the editors or compilers of some or all other documents. That is something we never can know. We can describe only what is in our hands and interpret only the data before us. Of indeterminates and endless speculative possibilities we need take no account. In taking up documents one by one, do we not obscure their larger context and their points in common? In fact, shared materials proved for Leviticus Rabbah not many and not definitive. What is unique to that text predominates and bears the message of the whole. To date I have taken up the issue of homogeneity in a limited and mainly formal setting, for the matter of how sayings and stories travel episodically from one document to the next.[4] The real issue is not the traveling, but the unique, materials: the documents, and not what is shared among them. The variable -- what moves -- is subject to analysis only against the constant: the document itself.

vii. The Integrity of a Document in the Canon of Judaism

To describe and analyze documents one by one violates the lines of order and system that have characterized all earlier studies of these same documents. Until

---

[4] This preparatory study is *The Peripatetic Saying. The Problem of the Thrice-Told Tale in Talmudic Literature* (Chico, 1985).

now, just as people compared exegeses among different groups of a given verse of Scripture without contrasting one circumstance to another, so they tended to treat all of the canonical texts as uniform in context, that is, as testimonies to a single system and structure, that is, to Judaism. What sort of testimonies texts provide varies according to the interest of those who study them. That is why, without regard to the source of the two expositions of the same verse, people would compare one *midrash,* meaning the interpretation of a given verse of Scripture, with another *midrash* on the same verse of Scripture. As I have argued, however, comparison cannot be properly carried out on such a basis. The hermeneutical issue dictated by the system overall defines the result of description, analysis, and interpretation.

Let me give a single probative example. From the classical perspective of the theology of Judaism the entire canon of Judaism ("the one whole Torah of Moses, our rabbi") equally and at every point testifies to the entirety of Judaism. Why so? Because all documents in the end form components of a single system. Each makes its contribution to the whole. If, therefore, we wish to know what "Judaism" or, more accurately, "the Torah," teaches on any subject, we are able to draw freely on sayings relevant to that subject wherever they occur in the entire canon of Judaism. Guided only by the taste and judgment of the great sages of the Torah, as they have addressed the question at hand, we thereby describe "Judaism." And that same theological conviction explains why we may rip a passage out of its redactional context and compare it with another passage, also seized from its redactional setting. In the same way *comparative midrash* as presently practiced moves freely across the boundaries of systems and documents alike. But the theological *apologia* for doing so has yet to reach expression; and there can be no other than a theological *apologia.* In logic I see none; epistemologically there never was one.

In fact documents stand in three relationships to one another and to the system of which they form part, that is, to Judaism, as a whole. The specification of these relationships constitutes the principal premise of this inquiry and validates the approach to *comparative midrash* I offer here.

1. Each document is to be seen all by itself, that is, as autonomous of all others.

2. Each document is to be examined for its relationships with other documents universally regarded as falling into the same classification, as Torah.

3. And, finally, in the theology of Judaism (or, in another context, of Christianity) each document is to be allowed to take its place as part of the undifferentiated aggregation of documents that, all together, constitute the canon of, in the case of Judaism, the "one whole Torah revealed by God to Moses at Mount Sinai."

Simple logic makes self-evident the proposition that, if a document comes down to us within its own framework, as a complete book with a beginning, middle, and end, in preserving that book, the canon presents us with a document on its own and not solely as part of a larger composition or construct. So we too see the document as it reaches us, that is, as autonomous.

If, second, a document contains materials shared verbatim or in substantial content with other documents of its classification, or if one document refers to the contents of other documents, then the several documents that clearly wish to engage in conversation with one another have to address one another. That is to say, we have to seek for the marks of connectedness, asking for the meaning of those connections. It is at this level of connectedness that we labor. For the purpose of comparison is to tell us what is like something else, what is unlike something else. To begin with, we can declare something unlike something else only if we know that it is like that other thing. Otherwise the original judgment bears no sense whatsoever. So, once more, canon defines context, or, in descriptive language, the first classification for comparative study is the document, brought into juxtaposition with, and contrast to, another document.

Finally, since the community of the faithful of Judaism, in all of the contemporary expressions of Judaism, concur that documents held to be authoritative constitute one whole, seamless "Torah," that is, a complete and exhaustive statement of God's will for Israel and humanity, we take as a further appropriate task, if one not to be done here, the description of the whole out of the undifferentiated testimony of all of its parts. These components in the theological context are viewed, as is clear, as equally authoritative for the composition of the whole: one, continuous system. In taking up such a question, we address a problem not of theology alone, though it is a correct theological conviction, but one of description, analysis, and interpretation of an entirely historical order.

In my view the various documents of the canon of Judaism produced in late antiquity demand a hermeneutic altogether different from the one of homogenization and harmonization, the ahistorical and anti-contextual one definitive for *comparative midrash* as presently practiced. It is one that does not harmonize but that differentiates. It is a hermeneutic shaped to teach us how to read the compilations of exegeses first of all one by one and in a particular context, and second, in comparison with one another.

viii. From Leviticus Rabbah to Genesis Rabbah

Let me now differentiate the study of the integrity of Leviticus Rabbah from the present work. In connection with Genesis Rabbah I first undertake the same exercises that permitted me to examine the textuality of Leviticus Rabbah. In this way I validly compare the one to the other, for both will have been described in precisely the same way. In Part One (Chapters One through Three) of this book, therefore, I subject Genesis Rabbah to the analyses already performed on Leviticus Rabbah, and in Part Two (Chapter Four) I rehearse the results for Leviticus Rabbah. In both cases, therefore, these are the stages of the work.

Then in Part Three (Chapters Five and Six) I turn to the issue at hand, which is the comparison of one compilation of exegeses of Scripture with another such compilation, that is, Leviticus Rabbah and Genesis Rabbah. The comparison follows two lines of inquiry, one the plan of the two documents, viewed in literary terms, the other, the program of the two documents , described and compared in theological ones.

Let me spell out the method I applied to both Rabbah-compilations. It is not complicated and rests upon what seem to me self-evident premises. I have to prove that the document at hand rests upon clear-cut choices of formal and rhetorical preference, so it is, from the viewpoint of form and mode of expression, cogent. I have to demonstrate that these formal choices prove uniform and paramount. So for both compilations I analyze three large *parashiyyot* to show their recurrent structures. These I categorize. Then, I proceed to survey all *parashiyyot* and find out whether or not every *parashah* of the entire document finds within a single cogent taxonomic structure suitable classification for its diverse units of discourse. If one taxonomy serves all and encompasses the bulk of the units of discourse at hand, I may fairly claim that Leviticus Rabbah or Genesis Rabbah does constitute a cogent formal structure, based upon patterns of rhetoric uniform and characteristic throughout.

My next step, for both documents, is to ask whether the framers of the document preserved a fixed order in arranging types of units of discourse, differentiated in accord with the forms I identified. In both documents I am able to show that, in ordering materials, the framers or redactors paid much attention to the formal traits of their units of discourse. They chose materials of one formal type for beginning their sustained exercises of argument or syllogism, then chose another formal type for the end of their sustained exercises of syllogistic exposition. This seems to me to show that the framers or redactors followed a set of rules which we are able to discern. In this way I answer the question, for the documents under study, of whether or not we deal with texts exhibiting traits of composition, deliberation, proportion, and so delivering a message on their own. Since we do, then Leviticus Rabbah and Genesis Rabbah demand description, analysis, and interpretation first of all on their own, as autonomous statements. Each then requires comparison and contrast with other compositions of its species of the rabbinic genus, that is to say, to be brought into connection with, relationship to, other rabbinic compositions of its type. And on that basis, comparison -- Part III (Chapters Five and Six) -- becomes possible.

Part One

LITERARY STRUCTURES OF GENESIS RABBAH

Chapter One

Recurrent Literary Structures of Genesis Rabbah

i. Introduction

A literary structure is a set of rules that dictate recurrent conventions of expression, organization, or proportion that are *extrinsic* to the message of the author. The conventions at hand bear none of the particular burden of the author's message, so they are not idiosyncratic. They convey in their context the larger world-view expressed within the writing in which they are used, so prove systemic and public. That is because a literary structure conforms to rules that impose upon the individual writer a limited set of choices about how he will convey whatever message he has in mind. Or the formal convention will limit an editor or redactor to an equally circumscribed set of alternatives about how to arrange received materials. These conventions then form a substrate of the literary culture that preserves and expresses the world view and way of life of the system at hand.

On the basis of what merely appears to us to be patterned or extrinsic to particular meaning and so entirely formal, we cannot allege that we have in hand a fixed, literary structure. Such a judgment would prove subjective. Nor shall we benefit from bringing to the text at hand recurrent syntactic or grammatical patterns shown in other texts even of the same canon of literature to define conventions for communicating ideas in those other texts. Quite to the contrary, we find guidance in a simple principle: *A text has to define its own structures for us.* This its authors do by repeatedly resorting to a given set of linguistic patterns and literary conventions and no others.. On the basis of inductive evidence alone we testify the thesis that the authors at hand adhere to a fixed canon of literary forms. If demonstrably present, we may conclude that these forms will present an author or editor with a few choices on how ideas are to be organized and expressed in intelligible -- again, therefore, public -- compositions.

So internal evidence and that alone testifies to the literary structures of a given text. When, as in the present exercise, we draw together and compare two distinct documents, each one to begin with has to supply us with evidence on its own literary structures. It follows that the adjective "recurrent" constitutes a redundancy when joined to the noun "structure." For we cannot know that we have a structure if the text under analysis does not repeatedly resort to the presentation of its message through that disciplined structure external to its message on any given point. And, it follows self-evidently, we do know that we have a structure when the text in hand repeatedly follows recurrent conventions of expression, organization, or proportion *extrinsic* to the message of the author.

Like Leviticus Rabbah, Genesis Rabbah comprises large-scale literary structures. How do we know that fact? It is because, when we divide up the undifferentiated columns of words and sentences and point to the boundaries that separate one completed unit of thought or discourse from the next such completed composition, we produce rather sizable statements conforming to a single set of syntactic and other formal patterns. As we shall see later in this chapter, three large-scale patterns emerge from the entirety of the opening *parashah* of Genesis Rabbah. The patterns find definition in entirely formal and objective facts: the placement of the key-verse subject to discussion in the composition at hand, the origin of that verse: placement at the start or at the end, origin in the book of Genesis (for Leviticus: the book of Leviticus) or some other book of the Hebrew Scriptures). No subjective or impressionistic judgment intervenes.

A few comparative observations on the role of formalization and patterning of language in a variety of texts produced by the sages of Judaism may prove illuminating. These patterns of formulating ideas in Genesis Rabbah and in Leviticus Rabbah prove capacious, encompassing many more sentences, a great many more words, than is the case in patterned language in the Mishnah. On the other hand, in comparing the dimensions of completed units of discourse in Leviticus Rabbah to those in the Yerushalmi or the Bavli, we find in the former less sustained, less protracted discourse than in the latter. That is to say, a unit of thought or analysis in one of the two Talmuds in the average will be made up of a great many more subunits or components than we find in the smallest formalized whole units of thought in Genesis Rabbah. On the other hand, these components of large-scale analytical units of discourse in the Bavli and Yerushalmi will appear autonomous of the larger composition in which they occur. They will not prove cogent within that composition. By contrast, while units of discourse in Genesis Rabbah and Leviticus Rabbah tend not to run on as do those of the two Talmuds, the components prove cogent with the larger discourse which they serve.

What these facts mean is that, in Genesis Rabbah as in Leviticus Rabbah, the repeated patterns follow protracted but fixed orbits, covering a sizable volume of material. As I have stressed, the patterns are large in scale. We deal not with small-scale syntactic formalization, such as the Mishnah's authors use to good effect, for example three or five sentences made up of parts of the speech arranged in exactly the same way. But we do deal with a stylized mode of discourse, unlike the Tosefta's rather miscellaneous style in conveying its authors' ideas. Were we to be guided by either the Yerushalmi's or the Bavli's writers, further, we should look for rigid but abbreviated rhetorical patterns, signals conveyed by little more than recurrent and formulaic parts of speech so set forth as to convey the purpose and sense of sizable discussion. We should be disappointed were we to ask the authors at hand in Genesis Rabbah and Leviticus Rabbah to demonstrate their equivalent skill at the use of rhetoric to lend structure and impart sense to otherwise unformed sentences. Where those authors excel, it is at holding in the balance a rather substantial composite of materials, some of them miscellaneous, systematically and patiently working their way from point, and only at the end drawing the whole to an elegant and satisfying conclusion.

So we look for large-scale patterns and point to such unusually sizable compositions as characteristic. Why? Because they recur and define discourse, *parashah* by *parashah*. Indeed, as we shall now see, a given *parashah* is made up of a large-scale literary structure, which in a moment I shall describe in detail. In all, what I mean when I claim that Genesis Rabbah, like Leviticus Rabbah, is made up of large-scale literary structures is simple. When we divide a given *parashah*, or chapter, of Genesis Rabbah into its sub-divisions, we find these sub-divisions stylistically cogent and well-composed, always conforming to the rules of one out of three possible formal patterns.

How shall we proceed to identify the structures of the document before us? It seems to me we had best move first to the analysis of a single *parashah*. We seek, within that *parashah*, to identify what holds the whole together. The second step then is to see whether we have identified something exemplary, or what is not an example of a fixed and formal pattern, but a phenomenon that occurs in fact only once or at random. For the first exercise, we take up *Parashah* One, and for the second, numbers Four and Nineteen. As we proceed, of course, we shall then examine all one hundred of the *parashiyyot* of Genesis Rabbah and see the extent to which the patterns exhibited in one *parashah*, then in two others, in fact characterize the entire lot.

ii. Genesis Rabbah Parashah I:I.1

We first review our sample passage in its entirety, then analyze its formal traits. On the basis of our sample we shall define a form and in due course compare further passages to the formal traits at hand.

I:I.

1. A. "In the beginning God created" (Gen. 1:1):

B. R. Oshaia commenced [discourse by citing the following verse:] "'Then I was beside him like a little child, and I was daily his delight [rejoicing before him always, rejoicing in his inhabited world, and delighting in the sons of men]' (Prov. 8:30-31).

C. "The word for 'child' uses consonants that may also stand for 'teacher,' 'covered over,' and 'hidden away.'

D. "Some hold that the word also means 'great.'

E. "The word means 'teacher,' in line with the following: 'As a teacher carries the suckling child' (Num. 11:12).

F. "The word means 'covered over,' as in the following: 'Those who were covered over in scarlet' (Lam. 4:5).

G. "The word means 'hidden,' as in the verse, 'And he hid Hadassah ' (Est. 2:7).

H. "The word means 'great,' in line with the verse, 'Are you better than No-Ammon?' (Nah. 3:8). This we translate, 'Are you better than Alexandria the Great, which is located between rivers.'"

2. A. Another matter:

B. The word means "workman."

C. [In the cited verse] the Torah speaks, "I was the work-plan of the Holy One, blessed be he."

D. In the accepted practice of the world, when a mortal king builds a palace, he does not build it out of his own head, but he follows a work-plan.

E. And [the one who supplies] the work-plan does not build out of his own head, but he has designs and diagrams, so as to know how to situate the rooms and the doorways.

F. Thus the Holy One, blessed be he, consulted the Torah when he created the world.

G. So the Torah stated, "By means of 'the beginning' [that is to say, the Torah] did God create..." (Gen. 1:1).

H. And the word for "beginning" refers only to the Torah, as Scripture says, "The Lord made me as the beginning of his way" (Prov. 8:22).

Before we proceed to analyze the formal traits of the composition, we have to identify the units with which we deal. Accordingly, we ask first of all whether Nos. 1 and 2 constitute two distinct units of thought, or whether we must treat them as a single formal composition. The answer on the surface proves ambiguous. On the one hand, if we read No. 1 by itself -- that is, out of all relationship to the exegesis of Gen. 1:1 -- what do we see? It is a systematic explanation of the several meanings of the letters of the word at hand. Each meaning bears its own proof-text. All together, the several lexicographical entries bear no relationship at all to Gen. 1:1. So if we confronted No. 1 in some setting other than the present one, we should classify it as an essay in lexicography, pure and simple. On the other hand, when we come to No. 2, we find ourselves deep in the inquiry into the sense of Gen. 1:1. Then one of the meanings adduced for the letters at hand serves to clarify the sense of the verse of Scripture. In the present context, No. 2 of course is integral and meaningful.

Let me then phrase the questions before us. Do Nos. 1 and 2 form a single, sustained unit of thought? Or should we regard them as a composite and analyze their formal traits out of all relationship to the present setting -- that is to say, the setting of the exegesis of the book of Genesis, verse by verse? What compels us to regard No. 1 as incomplete without No. 2? On the one hand the paragraph on its own is comprehensible. But one detail in No. 2 adds to the proposition announced at No. 1, the interest in the meaning of the letters at hand. No. 1 provides four meanings for the word under study, No. 2, the fifth.

So No. 2 provides the missing detail, the further sense of the letters at hand --
"workman" -- omitted in No. 1. That omission matters. Why? Because the
announced program of No. 1 is to review the senses to be imputed to the letters
'MN, and, as we see, a complete list demands No. 2's information.

It follows that whoever wrote the composition before us planned to review
all of the meanings of the word before him. He set matters apart, using the
device of "another matter," so that his climactic observation, at No. 2, would
enjoy prominence. He laid out his meanings in such a way as to end, at No. 2,
with the one that carries decisive weight for the interpretation of the base verse,
the meaning that delivered the message: God looked into the Torah to create the
world. Viewed in the setting of Genesis Rabbah, therefore, Nos. 1 and 2
therefore constitute a single unitary composition, even though bits and pieces
can have circulated on their own. We may go a step further. The passage as we
have it has been so formulated as to serve the purpose of a systematic exegesis
of Gen. 1:1. Materials serviceable in a variety of settings clearly have been
reworked for the present, and only for the present, one.

Our description of the forms at hand may now proceed. What in fact do we
have before us? I see two distinct formal units, to be classified as follows.

1. Redactional Stich

A redactional stich is a phrase -- invariably, drawn from a verse of the book
of Genesis -- external to the composition that follows. The phrase functions
solely for the redactional purpose of linking a completed composition to the
larger redactional setting of a *parashah* of Genesis Rabbah. We know that the
phrase serves redactional and not substantive purposes because the phrase bears
no weight or meaning in what is to follow and is not cited in an integral way in
what follows. The following provides a good example of the formal and
redactional traits of a redactional stich.

I:I.

1. A. "In the beginning God created" (Gen. 1:1):

The opening statement serves only to link what follows to the redactional
setting of the whole, that is, to establish the proposition that we deal with a
verse-by-verse exegesis of the book of Genesis. The succeeding sentences do not
refer to the redactional stich but ignore it. Nothing that is said carries forward
the cited verse; the focus of discourse is upon a different verse entirely. Without
the cited verse, the composition that unfolds would be, and is, completely
comprehensible in its own terms. Accordingly, as I said, the phrase before us
serves redactional and not substantive purposes, hence is to be classified as a
redactional stich. In point of fact, the verse at hand plays a role only at the end
of I:I.1-2. There it serves as the climax and the point of the whole. Prior to
that point, it is not only irrelevant but confusing. On these grounds we must
regard the citation of Gen. 1:1 at I:I.1.A. as solely redactional in purpose.

Of course our document presents something quite different from such a verse-by-verse treatment of the book of Genesis. How so? A scan of Genesis Rabbah shows us that the framer of the whole has gathered a wide range of materials. He then has organized those materials in the order of the verses of the book. But there is no pretense at explaining verses, one by one, in anything like a systematic commentary upon words and phrases. Rather, a wide variety of materials has been assembled to impart meaning to stories of the book of Genesis. As we shall see, only a small portion of what is assembled directly clarifies the meanings of words and phrases. A vast proportion deals with the sense and meaning of whole stories. So citing words or phrases serves no purpose internal to the composition but only holds together what is already chosen -- hence carrying out a redactional and extraneous function. So, as is clear, the redactional stitch must be regarded as external to the composition, providing the link in the book of Genesis for what is to follow -- Oshaia's discourse.

2. The Intersecting Verse-Base Verse-Form: X commenced + intersecting verse + exposition of intersecting verse in its own terms+exposition of intersecting verse in terms of the base verse

The first important form consists of four elements:

A. *The attributive: X commenced (occasionally, X said)*

An authority is named. What he is to say will be joined to his name by the verb PTH, commenced. Then what he commences with is invariably a verse other than the redactional stitch or base-verse.

B. *Citation of a verse other than the verse of the book of Genesis that will be subject to exposition*

The intersecting verse will be chosen in accord with a variety of criteria, and sometimes we shall not find self-evident the reason that verse has proved illuminating or suggestive.

C. *Systematic exposition of the intersecting verse in terms other than those set by the base verse*

The intersecting verse will be explained "in its own terms," meaning along lines dictated by its distinctive substance, and not the theme, proposition, or detailed contents of the base verse.

D. *Exposition of the intersecting verse in terms of the base verse -- and vice versa*

Now at the climax the intersecting verse will be read in terms of the base verse, and, more commonly, the base verse will be read in terms of the intersecting verse. The reciprocal process of exposition of the one in terms of the other forms the purpose of the whole. Whether the materials of exposition of the intersecting verse contribute at all is not important; sometimes they do, sometimes they do not.

At this point the composition always ends.

So to review: the form as a whole is defined on entirely formal grounds:

1. Attribution + joining language + intersecting verse

2. Exposition of the intersecting verse

3. Reciprocal exposition of the base verse and the intersecting verse

Let us now examine the way in which the form works.

3. X commenced

I:I.

1. B. R. Oshaia commenced [discourse by citing the following verse:] "Then I was beside him like a little child, and I was daily his delight [rejoicing before him always, rejoicing in his inhabited world, and delighting in the sons of men]' (Prov. 8:30-31).

We take up first of all the joining-word, "commenced" (PTH). Does that word form an integral component of the conventional structure at hand? I think not. The formal, hence the structural, traits of the composition are unaffected by the choice of the word "commenced." If the author had stated simply, Oshaia *said*, the formal outcome would have been unchanged: the intersecting verse would have followed, just as it does, and the secondary discussion of the intersecting verse would have proceeded normally. On the other hand, in the present segment of Gen. R., the author invokes the word "commence" prior to the introduction of the intersecting verse. So the attributive particle, "commenced," really does form part of the formal program. It signals the coming of an intersecting verse.

4.   Intersecting verse + exposition of intersecting verse in its own terms

I:I.

1. B. R. Oshaia commenced [discourse by citing the following verse:] "Then I was beside him like a little child, and I was daily his delight [rejoicing before him always, rejoicing in his inhabited world, and delighting in the sons of men]' (Prov. 8:30-31).

C. "The word for 'child' uses consonants that may also stand for 'teacher,' 'covered over,' and 'hidden away.'

D. "Some hold that the word also means 'great.'

E. "The word means 'teacher,' in line with the following: 'As   a teacher carries the suckling child' (Num. 11:12).

F. "The word means 'covered over,' as in the following: 'Those who were covered over in scarlet' (Lam. 4:5).

G. "The word means 'hidden,' as in the verse, 'And he hid Hadassah ' (Est. 2:7).

H. "The word means 'great,' in line with the verse, 'Are you better than No-Ammon?' (Nah. 3:8). This we translate, 'Are you better than Alexandria the Great, which is located between rivers.'"

Once the intersecting verse is introduced. we see secondary discussion of that verse. In the present instance that discussion involves a word in the verse and proofs of various meanings imputed to that word, four in all. An exegete of Genesis Rabbah as a document would then take as the task the explanation of how Prov. 8:30-31 would be explained in accord with the diverse meanings of the key-word at hand. But so far as formal analysis is concerned, we complete the description of the form when we observe that we deal with an intersecting verse and its exposition in its own terms and framework.

5. Exposition of intersecting verse in terms of the base verse

I:I.

2. A. Another matter:

B. The word means "workman."

C. [In the cited verse] the Torah speaks, "I was the work-plan of the Holy One, blessed be he."

D. In the accepted practice of the world, when a mortal king builds a palace, he does not build it out of his own head, but he follows a work-plan.

E. And [the one who supplies] the work-plan does not build out of his own head, but he has designs and diagrams, so as to know how to situate the rooms and the doorways.

F. Thus the Holy One, blessed be he, consulted the Torah when he created the world.

G. So the Torah stated, "By means of 'the beginning' [that is to say, the Torah] did God create..." (Gen. 1:1).

H. And the word for "beginning" refers only to the Torah, as Scripture says, "The Lord made me as the beginning of his way" (Prov. 8:22).

I see no way in which the present composition formally differs from the foregoing. That is to say, just as at I:I.1.C, E, F, G, and F, we have "the word means," so at 2.B we find the same mode of commencing discourse. But what follows, 2.D, does vary the foregoing, because now we have not only the statement of the meaning the verse, but also an exposition, in terms of the sense of the matter, of that meaning. Then, beyond the secondary expansion of the meaning through the cited parable, 2.D-E, we come to the point at which the intersecting verse imposes a deeper meaning upon the base-verse. This is made explicit at 2.F-H.

iii. Systematic Formal Analysis of Genesis Rabbah Parashah I

Pursuing our work of inductive analysis, we seek evidence of formal compositions besides the one we now have identified. We proceed to review the remainder of Parashah I, seeking evidence of further formal constructions. I following the numbering and order of Theodor-Albeck, hence we continue with I:V.1.A.

1.   I:V.1:Intersecting verse-Base Verse

I:V.

1. A. R. Huna in the name of Bar Qappara commenced [discourse by citing the following verse]: "'Let the lying lips be made dumb [which arrogantly speak matters kept secret against the righteous]' (Ps. 31:19).

B. "[Translating the Hebrew word for dumb into Aramaic one may use words meaning] 'bound,' 'made dumb,' or ' silenced.'

C. "Let [the lying lips] be bound,' as in the following verse: 'For behold, we were binding sheaves' s(Gen. 37:7).

D. "'Let the lying lips be made dumb,' as in the usage in this verse: 'Or who made a man dumb ' (Ex. 4:11).

E. "'Let them be silenced' bears the obvious meaning of the word."

F. "Which arrogantly speak matters kept secret against the righteous" (Ps. 31:19):

G.. "...which speak against the Righteous," the Life of the Ages, matters that he kept secret from his creatures [Freedman: the mysteries of creation].

H. "With pride" (Ps. 31:19):

I. That is so as to take pride, saying, "I shall expound the work of creation."

J. "And contempt" (Ps. 31:19): Such a one treats with contempt the honor owing to me.

K. For R. Yose b. R. Hanina said, "Whoever gains honor through the humiliation of his fellow gains no share in the world to come.

L. "For one does so through the honor owing to the Holy One , blessed be he, how much the more so!"

M. And what is written after the cited verse [Ps. 31:19]?

N. How abundant is your goodness, which you have stored away for those who revere you" (Ps. 31:20).

O. Rab said, "Let one [who reveals the mysteries of creation] not have any share in your abundant goodness.'

P. "Under ordinary circumstances, if a mortal king builds a palace in a place where there had been sewers, garbage, and junk, will not whoever may come and say, 'This palace is built on a place where there were sewers, garbage and junk,' give offense? So too, will not whoever comes and says, 'This world was created out of chaos, emptiness, and darkness' give offense?"

Q. R. Huna in the name of Bar Qappara: "Were the matter not explicitly written in Scripture, it would not be possible to state it at all: 'God created heaven and earth' (Gen. 1:1) -- from what? From the following: 'And the earth was chaos' (Gen. 1:2). [Freedman: God first created chaos and emptiness, and out of these he created the world, but this is not to be taught publicly.]"

A new intersecting verse is presented. The formal traits prove consistent with those that we saw at I:I.1. Once more it is clear that we deal with a unified and cogent statement, so that A-I and J to the end, while on the surface distinct from one another, are formed to make a single, exceedingly surprising point, which comes only at the end. That I:I and I:V follow a single pattern is quite clear. The exposition of the intersecting verse takes place in stages, with a philological exercise on the meaning of a fundamental word at hand, followed by a secondary expansion on the sense of the verse as a whole. It is not possible to view the whole as an artificial construct; it seems to me clear that it is a cogent and pointed statement, beginning, middle, and end, even though bits and pieces of available materials may have served the author.

So before us, thus far, is a remarkably cogent composition, making a single point through the selection and organization of distinct materials. Despite the original impression of prolixity and diversity the composition hangs together so cogently as it does only because it depends for sense and deep meaning on the base verse itself. Out of contact with the statement, "In the beginning God created...," the two compositions -- both I:I and I:V -- make little sense.

2. I:VI.1-2: Intersecting Verse-Base Verse (+ 3,4: Miscellanies)

I:VI.

1. A. R. Judah bar Simon commenced discourse [by citing the following verse:] "'And he reveals deep and secret things' (Dan.2:22).

   B. "The word for deep things refers to Gehenna, as it is written, 'But he does not know that the shades are there, that in the depths of the nether world are her guests' (Prov. 9:18).

   C. "And the word for 'secret things' speaks of the Garden of Eden, as it is written, 'And for a refuge and for a hiding place' (Is. 4:6). [This hiding place, using the same word, is taken to mean the Garden of Eden]."

2. A. Another matter:

   B. "And he reveals deep and secret things" (Dan. 2:22):

   C. This refers to deeds performed by the wicked [which God brings out into the open], as it is said, "Woe to the ones who try to hide their plans from the Lord" (Is. 29:15).

   D. "He knows what is in the darkness" (Dan. 2:22):

   E. This refers to deeds performed by the wicked, as it is written, "And their works are in the darkness" (Is. 4:6).

   F. "But the light dwells with him" (Dan. 2:22):

   G. This refers to deeds performed by the righteous, as it is said, "Light is sown for the righteous" (Ps. 97:11).

3. A. Said R. Abba of Sarangayya, "'Light dwells with him' (Dan. 2:22) refers to the messiah-king."

4. A. Said R. Judah bar Simon, "To begin with, when the world was being created, 'He reveals deep and secret things,' for it is written, 'In the beginning God created the heaven (Gen. 1:1).' But the matter was not spelled out.

   B. "Where then was it spelled out?

C. "Elsewhere: 'Who stretches out the heaven as a curtain' (Is. 40:22).

D. "'....and the earth' (Gen. 1:1). But this matter, too, was not then spelled out.

E. "Where then was it spelled out?

F. "Elsewhere: 'For he says to the snow, "Fall on the earth"' (Job 37:6).

G. "And God said, Let there be light' (Gen. 1:3).

H . "And this too was not spelled out.

I. "Where then was it spelled out?

J. "Elsewhere: 'Who covers yourself with light as with a garment' (Ps. 104:2)."

The construction familiar from I:I and I:V -- an intersecting verse leading us back to the clarification of the base-verse -- is not followed here. Rather, we have a more sustained inquiry into the cited verse (we cannot call it an intersecting verse), namely, Dan. 2:22. The first interpretation has no direct relevance to our inquiry at all. The second -- the moral interpretation about how God reveals what the wicked do -- likewise bears no point of relevance. If the passage at hand were to have begun at I:VI.4, however, we should have precisely the familiar construction, that is, an intersecting verse -- Dan. 2:22 -- followed by the base verse, Gen. 1:1. Then the exposition continues. But it is not in terms of the intersection of the intersecting verse and the base-verse. Rather, we have the introduction of several other verses, that is, Is. 40:22, Job 37:6, Gen. 1:3, and Ps. 104:2. None of this has any bearing on the exposition of Dan. 2:22. What it spells out is how in respect to creation, Gen. 1:1, God reveals deep and secret things, Dan. 2:22.

3.   I:VII.1: Syllogistic Composition

We come to an unfamiliar mode of expressing an idea. Let me first introduce the traits of what we shall see is a fixed form, then take up the first instance of it. The composition at hand proposes to prove a point or to state a proposition subjected to systematic argumentation and demonstration. Hence I call it a syllogistic composition.

A syllogistic composition makes a point autonomous of the verse at hand (Gen. 1:1), or , indeed, of any other verse. The purpose of citing verses of Scripture is to prove a point distinct from all of the cited verses. In this type of composition,therefore, the point of interest is in the *proposition* that is subject to demonstration, the proofs of course deriving from verses of Scripture. So the proofs comprise facts, and Scripture supplies those facts, as much as, in philosophy, nature does. So I stress: no one in the passage before us proposes to construct a simple clarification of a single verse, let alone the exposition of one verse in terms of another, that is, of the base-verse in terms of the intersecting- verse. These constitute essentially different modes of construction entirely. The superficial resemblance to the a base verse-intersecting verse form in particular will quickly fall away.

I.VII.

1.   A.   R. Isaac commenced [discourse by citing the following verse]: "'The beginning of your word is truth [and all your righteous ordinance endures forever]' (Ps. 119:16)."

B.   Said R. Isaac [about the cited verse], "From the beginning of the creation of the world, 'The beginning of your word was truth.'

C.   "'In the beginning God created' (Gen. 1:1).

D.   "''And the Lord God is truth '(Jer. 10:9).

E.   "Therefore: 'And all your righteous ordinance endures forever' (Ps. 119:16).

F.   "For as to every single decree which you lay down for your creatures, they accept that degree as righteous and receive it in good faith, so that no creature may differ, saying ' , 'Two powers gave the Torah, two powers created the world.'

G.   "[Why not?]' Because here it is not written, 'And gods spoke,' but rather, 'And God spoke' (Ex. 20:1).

H.   "'In the beginning [gods] created is not written, but rather, 'in the beginning [God] created' [in the singular]."

What we have is a syllogism that there are not two gods or two dominions. Our base-verse supplies a fact for the proof of that syllogism. Here (to state matters negatively) the purpose of the intersecting verse is *not* to conduct an inquiry into the intersecting verse leading to the exposition of the base verse . Rather the interest is in a proposition, namely, that matters are so formulated as to give the lie to those who hold there are two powers or dominions. That is proven by a number of verses, e.g., Ex. 20:1, and not only by Gen. 1:1. Therefore the purpose of the construction is to make the theological point that is expressed, namely, to prove that there is only a single dominion. The exposition of Gen. 1:1 is not at the center of interest. It follows that the formal trait of the passage at hand is not to be classified in the same category as I:I and I:V.

We should take note that the syllogistic composition makes use of of verses of Scripture in a distinctive way, no less striking than the other two forms. Later on we shall confront compositions that formally are miscellaneous but that prove points or demonstrate syllogisms. These are not to be treated as formal or patterned compositions at all, and I assign them their own distinctive mark, as composite A. In no way do such formal miscellanies fall into the classification defined here.

4.   I:II.1: A Syllogistic Composition

I.II.

1.   A.   R. Joshua of Sikhnin in the name of R. Levi commenced [discourse by citing the following verse]: "'He has declared to his people the power of his works, in giving them the heritage of the nations' (Ps. 111:6).

B.   "What is the reason that the Holy One, blessed be he, revealed to Israel what was created on the first day and what on the second?

C. "It was on account of the nations of the world. It was so that they should not ridicule the Israelites, saying to them, 'Are you not a nation of robbers [having stolen the land from the Canaanites]?'

D. "It allows the Israelites to answer them, 'And as to you, is there no spoil in your hands? For surely: "The Caphtorim, who came forth out of Caphtor, destroyed them and dwelled in their place" (Deut. 2:23)!

E. "'The world and everything in it belongs to the Holy One, blessed be he. When he wanted, he gave it to you, and when he wanted, he took it from you and gave it to us.'

F. "That is in line with what is written, '....in giving them the heritage of the nations, he has declared to his people the power of his works' (Ps. 111:6).. [So as to give them the land, he established his right to do so by informing them that he had created it.]

G. "He told them about the beginning: 'In the beginning God created...'' (Gen. 1:1)."

The purpose of the passage is to demonstrate Israel's right to the land. The point at hand is that God informed Israel of his power (Ps. 111:6) so as to give them a valid claim on the Land of Israel. Gen. 1:1 is cited only to validate the claim at hand, so the joining of Ps. 111:6 to Gen. 1:1 is for the purpose of expounding the principle of divine ownership of the Land -- that is, Israel's valid claim -- and not the meaning of either verse. For the purposes of an exegetical compilation on the book of Genesis, Gen. 1:1 is essential. It serves to join the syllogism to the present context. But without Gen. 1:1 the passage makes its point quite amply, and its principal verse is Deut. 2:23 aligned with Ps. 111:6. I would therefore be inclined to see Gen. 1:1 as the sole completely redactional contribution to the whole -- that, and, of course, the selection of the completed entry for the present context.

5. I:III.1-3:   Intersecting Verse-Base Verse Construction (Flawed)

I.III.

1. A. R. Tanhum commenced discourse, "For you are great and do wonderful things, you alone are God "(Ps. 86:10).

   B. Said R. Tanhum b. R. Hiyya, "As to a skin, if it has a hole as small as the eye of a needle, all of the air will escape for from it.

   C. "But as to a human being, a person is made with many apertures and holes, but the spirit does not go forth through them.

   D. "Who has done it in such a way? 'You alone are God' (Ps. 86:10)."

2. A. When were the angels created?

   B. R. Yohanan said, "On the second day of creation [Monday] were they created.

   C. "That is in line with this verse of Scripture: 'Who lays the beams of your upper chambers in the waters' (Ps. 104:3), after which it is written, 'Who makes the spirits of your angels' (Ps. 104:4). [The waters were divided into upper and lower parts, and on that same day the angels were created.]"

D. R. Hanina said, "They were created on the fifth day of creation [Thursday]. For it is written, 'Let fowl   fly above the earth' (Gen. 1:20), and it is written, 'And with two did the angel fly' (Is. 6:21). [Freedman, p. 5, n. 3: Thus angels too fall within the category of beings that fly and were created on the same day as all flying creatures.]"

E. R. Luliani b. R. Tabari in the name of R. Isaac: "Both from the viewpoint of R. Hanina and from that of R. Yohanan, there is agreement that nothing at all was created on the first day.

F. "That is so that you will not reach the false conclusion that Michael was there, stretching out the heaven at the south, with Gabriel at the north, and the Holy One, blessed be he, measuring from the middle.

G. "Rather: 'I the Lord do everything by myself, stretching out the heaven on my own and spreading forth the earth by myself' (Is. 44:24).

H. "'By myself' is written [in Scripture, as if to mean, 'who is with me?'] [That is, God asks, 'Who was my partner in creating the world?'

I. "In ordinary affairs when a mortal king is honored by a province the nobles of the province are honored with him.   Why? Because they bear the burden with him.

J. "But that is not how it is with the Holy One, blessed be he.

K. "But he on his own created his world, so he on his own is glorified in his world."

3 .   A. Said R. Tanhuma, "'For you are great and do wonderful things' (Ps. 86:10).

B. "Why so? Because: 'You alone are God' (Ps. 86:10).

C. "You by yourself created the world.

D. "'In the beginning God created' (Gen. 1:1)."

The opening two units bear no clear relationship to the exposition of Gen. 1:1. But if we omit reference to No. 2 and take account of only Nos. 1 and 3, we see a quite different picture. Now No. 1 expounds Ps. 86:10, and No. 3 does the same. That leaves one question before us. Why was No. 2 inserted? Clearly 2.J links the entire construction to the theme at hand. That is to say, God did things all by himself, and that is the point stressed at No. 3. So we may posit that No. 2 was joined to No. 3, to which it does belong, before Nos. 2 and 3, all together, were joined to No. 1. That speculation allows us to make sense of the insertion of No. 2.

6.   I:IV, I:VIII, I:IX: Syllogistic Composition
I.IV.

1 .   A. ["In the beginning God created" (Gen. 1:1):] Six things came before the creation of the world, some created, some at least considered as candidates for creation.

B. The Torah and the throne of glory were created [before the creation of the world].

C. The Torah, as it is written, "The Lord made me as the beginning of his way, prior to his works of old" (Prov. 8:22).

D. The throne of glory, as it is written, "Your throne is established of old" (Ps. 93:2).

E. The patriarchs were considered as candidates for creation, as it is written, "I saw your fathers as the first-ripe in the fig tree at her first season" (Hos. 9:10).

F. Israel was considered [as a candidate for creation], as it is written, "Remember your congregation, which you got aforetime" (Ps. 74:2).

G. The Temple was considered as a candidate for creation], as it is written, "You, throne of glory, on high from the beginning, the place of our sanctuary" (Jer. 17:12).

H. The name of the Messiah was kept in mind, as it is written, "His name exists before the sun" (Ps. 72:17).

I. R. Ahbah bar Zeira said, "Also [the power of] repentance.

J. "That is in line with the following verse of Scripture: 'Before the mountains were brought forth' (Ps. 90:2). From that hour: 'You turn man to contrition and say, Repent, you children of men' (Ps. 90:3)."

K. Nonetheless, I do not know which of these came first, that is, whether the Torah was prior to the throne of glory, or the throne of glory to the Torah.

L. Said R. Abba bar Kahana, "The Torah came first, prior to the throne of glory.

M. "For it is said, 'The Lord made me as the beginning of his way, before his works of old' (Prov. 8:22).

N. "It came prior to that concerning which it is written, 'For your throne is established of old' (Ps. 93:2)."

2. A. R. Huna, R. Jeremiah in the name of R. Samuel b. R. Isaac: "Intention concerning the creation of Israel came before all else.

B. "The matter may be compared to the case of a king who married a noble lady but had no son with her. One time the king turned up in the market place, saying, 'Buy this ink, inkwell, and pen on account of my son.'

C. "People said, 'He has no son. Why does he need ink, inkwell, and pen?'

D. "But then people went and said, 'The king is an astrologer, so he sees into the future and he therefore is expecting to produce a son!'

E. "Along these same lines, if the Holy One, blessed be he, had not foreseen that, after twenty-six generations, the Israelites would be destined to accept the Torah, he would would never have written in it, 'Command the children of Israel.' [This proves that God foresaw Israel and created the world on that account.]"

3. A. Said. R. Benaiah, "The world and everything in it were created only on account of the merit of the Torah.

B. "'The Lord for the sake of wisdom [Torah] founded the earth' (Prov. 3:19)."

C. R. Berekiah said, "It was for the merit of Moses.

D. "'And he saw the beginning for himself, for there a portion of a ruler [Moses] was reserved' (Deut. 33:21)."

4. A. R. Huna in the name of Rab repeated [the following]: "For the merit of three things was the world created, for the merit of dough-offerings, tithes, and first fruits.

B. "For it is said, 'On account of [the merit of] what is first, God created...' (Gen. 1:1).

C. "And the word 'first' refers only to dough-offering, for it is written, 'Of the first of your dough' (Num. 15:20).

D. "The same word refers to tithes, as it is written, 'The first fruits of your grain' (Deut. 18:4).

E. "And the word 'first ' refers to first fruits, for it is written, 'The choicest of your land's first fruit' (Ex. 23:19)."

I:VIII.

1. A. R. Menahem and R. Joshua b. Levi in the name of R. Levi: "One who builds requires six things: water, dust, wood, stones, canes, and iron. And should you say that [since God] is rich, he will not need canes [which are used only in hovels], lo, he requires a cane for measuring, for it is written, 'And a measuring reed in his hand' (Ez. 40:3).

B. "The Torah came before those six things [as indicated by Prov. 8:22]." [Freedman: The idea is that six expressions of precedence are employed in reference to the Torah]: 'the first,' 'of old,' 'from everlasting,' 'from the beginning,' and 'or ever,' which stands for two such usages as at Prov. 8:22: 'The Lord made me...the first of his works of old, I was set up from everlasting, from the beginning or ever the earth was' (Freedman, p. 8, n. 3).]

I:IX.

1. A. A philosopher asked Rabban Gamaliel, saying to him, "Your God was indeed a great artist, but he had good materials to help him."

B. He said to him, "What are they?"

C. He said to him, "Unformed [space], void, darkness, water, wind, and the deep."

D. He said to him, "May the spirit of that man [you] burst! All of them are explicitly described as having been created by him [and not as pre-existent].

E. "Unformed space and void: 'I make peace and create evil' (Is. 45:7).

F. "Darkness: 'I form light and create darkness' (Is. 45:7).

G. "Water: 'Praise him, you heavens of heavens, and you waters that are above the heavens' (Ps. 148:4). Why? 'For he commanded and they were created' (Ps. 148:5).

H. "Wind: 'for lo, he who forms the mountains creates the wind' (Amos 4:13).

I. "The depths: 'When there were no depths, I was brought forth' (Prov. 8:24)."

We have yet another clear picture of the pattern of laying out a syllogism. Part of the pattern follows clear formal conventions. Then there are appended materials, in no way affected by the redactional requirements of the syllogism-form. So in what follows, A and B constitute formal conventions, the rest not:

A. *Statement of a syllogism or proposition*

B. *Verses of Scripture that prove or illustrate that syollogism, listed in a catalogue of relevance evidence*

C. *Secondary expansion: miscellanies (e. g., stories) on the syllogism, providing further illustration.*

In the passage before us we have a set piece exposition of the opening proposition, that is, the six things preceding the creation of the world. That topic, and not the exposition of Gen. 1:1, explains the composition at hand. We begin with the necessary catalogue of the six things and proceed at No. 2 to a secondary exposition of the same matter. Then we introduce creation for the sake of the Torah, followed by a complementary proposition on other things for the sake of which the world was created. Here is the point at which Gen. 1:1 serves as a proof-text. No. 4 is an autonomous unit, built on the notion that wherever we find the word "first/beginning," we have reference to the proposition before us. The reason for the inclusion of I:VIII is self-evident if we look back at I:IV.1.A, the allusion to six things. Now we have six more things of the same classification. So the compositor has now gathered a set of materials congruent to the theme introduced at the outset. In the coming pericope we have yet another such entry. As is clear, I:IX simply carries forward the interest of I:IV and I:VIII.

7. I:X-XI: Syllogistic Composition

I:X.

1. A. ["In the beginning God created" (Gen. 1:1):] R. Jonah in the name of R. Levi: "Why was the world created with [a word beginning with the letter] B?

B. "Just as [in Hebrew] the letter B is closed [at the back and sides but] open in front, so you have no right to expound concerning what is above or below, before or afterward."

C. Bar Qappara said, "'For ask now of the days past which were before you, since the day that God created man upon the earth' (Deut. 4:32).

D. "Concerning the day *after* which days were created, you may expound, but you may not make an exposition concerning what lies before then.'

E. "'And from one end of the heaven to the other' (Deut. 4:32).

F. "[Concerning that space] you may conduct an investigation, but you may not conduct an investigation concerning what lies beyond those points."

G. R. Judah b. Pazzi gave his exposition concerning the story of creation in accord with this rule of Bar Qappara.

2. A. Why with a B?

B. To tell you that there are two ages [this age and the age to come, for the letter B bears the numerical value of two].

3. A. Another matter: Why was the world created [with a word beginning with the letter] B?

B. Because that is the letter that begins the word for blessing.

C. And why not with an A?

D. Because that is the first letter of the Hebrew word for curse.

4. A. Another matter: Why not with an A?

B. So as not to give an opening to the *minim* to claim, "How can the world endure, when it has been created with a word meaning curse!"

C. Rather, said the Holy One, blessed be he, "Lo, I shall write it with a letter standing for the word 'blessing,' and may the world endure!"

5. A. Another matter: Why with a B?

B. Because the letter B has two points, one pointing upward, the other backward, so that [if] people say to it, "Who created you?" it will point upward.

C. It is as if to say, "This one who is above has created me."

D. "And what is his name?" And it points for them with its point backward: "The Lord is his name," [pointing to the first letter in the alphabet, backward from the second, which is the A, standing for the One].

6. A. R. Eleazar bar Abinah in the name of R. Aha: "For twenty-six generations the letter A made complaint before the Holy One, blessed be he, saying to him, 'Lord of the world! I am the first among all the letters of the alphabet, yet you did not create your world by starting with me!'

B. "Said the Holy One, blessed be he, to the A, 'The world and everything in it has been created only through the merit of the Torah. Tomorrow I am going to come and give my Torah at Sinai, and I shall begin only with you: "I [beginning with the A] am the Lord your God" (Ex. 20:1).'"

7. A. Bar Hutah said, "Why is it called '*alef*'? Because that is the word for a thousand: 'The word which he commanded for a thousand [*elef*] generations' (Ps. 105:8)."

I:XI.

1. A. R. Simon in the name of R. Joshua b. Levi: "[The fact that the letters] M, N, S, P, and K [when appearing at the end of the word have a form different from that used when they appear at the beginning or the middle of a word] is a law revealed to Moses at Sinai."

B. R. Jeremiah in the name of R. Hiyya bar Abba: "It is that which seers ordained.

2. A. Once on an overcast day, on which sages did not come into the assembly house, there were children there. They said, "Let's take up [the topic of the final form of the letters as these have been ordained by] the seers."

B. They said, "What is the reason that there are two forms for the writing of the letters M, N, S, P, and K?

C. "From Word to word [the word at hand begins with M], from Faithful to faithful [the word begins with N], from Righteous one to righteous one [with an S], from Mouth to mouth [with a P], from Hand to hand [with a K].

D. "From the hand of the Holy One, blessed be he, to the hand of Moses."

E. Sages took note of who these children were, and great sages in Israel emerged from that group.

F. There are those who hold that these were R. Eliezer, R. Joshua, and R. Aqiba.

G. They recited in their regard the following verse: "Even a child is known by his doings" (Prov. 20:11).

Formally we have a set of miscellaneous compositions, each pursuing its own pattern. The entire composition draws together a set of alphabet-sayings, pertinent, of course, to the exposition of the first word of the verse under discussion. The passage over all exhibits a certain cogency. There is no pretense of interest in Gen. 1:1. But the composition has been formed into an aggregate on its own terms, for it in no way follows a conventional pattern in the formulation and presentation of the materials at hand. I:XI is inserted because it carries forward the topical program of I:X. That is to say, I:X and I:XI formed a single composite before the whole found its place here. Then those who selected the composite did not remove a passage not relevant to their interests. They preserved what they used without intervening and revising. Where they were prepared to make changes, it is clear, was at the beginning and end of completed compositions, but not in the middle. That of course tells us how they treated what we have before us, not what we do not have.

8.   I:XII-XIII:1:   Formal Miscellany

I:XII.

1. A. ["In the beginning God created..." (Gen. 1:1):] R. Yudan in the name of Aqilas: *"This* one it is appropriate to call God. [Why so?]

B. "Under ordinary circumstances a mortal king is praised in a province even before he has built public baths for the population or given them private ones. [God by contrast created the world before he had received the praise of humanity, so it was not for the sake of human adulation that he created the world.]"

2. A. Simeon b. Azzai says, "'And your modesty has made me great' (2 Sam. 22:36).   A mortal person mentions 'his name and afterward his title, for example, 'Mr. So-and-so, the prefect,' 'Mr. Such-and-such, and whatever title he gets.' But the Holy One, blessed be he, is not that way.

B. "Rather, only after he had created what was needed in his world did he make mention of his name, thus,, 'In the beginning, created...,' and only afterward: ' God.'"

I:XIII.

1. A. R. Simeon b. Yohai taught, "How [on the basis of Scripture] do we know that one should not say, 'For the Lord, a burnt offering,' 'For the Lord, a meal-offering,' 'For the Lord, a peace-offering.'

B. "Rather one should say, 'A burnt-offering for the Lord,' 'A meal-offering for the Lord,' 'A peace-offering for the Lord'?

C. "Scripture says, "An offering for the Lord' (Lev. 1:2).

D. "And lo, this produces an argument *a fortiori* :

E. "If in the case of one who is planning to declare something sanctified, the Torah has said that one should make use of the name of Heaven only in connection with an offering [that has already been sanctified by being designated],

F. "those who blaspheme, curse, and worship idols, all the more so that they should be blotted out of the world."

Both No. 1 and No. 2 make the same point, but No. 2 links the point more explicitly to the base-verse than does No. 1. The exposition of Gen.1:1 takes center-stage again. The order of the words produces the double statement of the same message, first at No. l, and then at No. 2. What follows will pursue the theme of I:XII.l, namely, proper titles, but the point at hand will not undergo further articulation. So here again the aggregate has taken shape in its own terms and only afterward been utilized for the amplification of Gen. 1:1. I do not see how the whole has been made up around the exposition of Gen. 1:1. Rather, the relevant passage, No. 2, has provoked selection of the entire composite. I:XIII.1 carries forward the theme of the right use of God's name. The absence of distinctive formal traits, whole or in part, then yields that formal miscellany that we noted earlier.

9. I:XIII:2-3, I:XIV: Exegesis of a Verse of Scripture

What follows presents us with yet another form, specifically one in which a given verse of Scripture is analyzed in its own terms. The basic requirement of the form will be simple:

A. *Citation of the base-verse (which will always be a verse chosen from the larger passage of the book of Genesis that is subject to interpretation, not a verse chosen from some other book of the Scripture)*

B. *Comment of a given rabbi.*

There will then be appended materials, commonly of a miscellaneous character, just as in the case of the syllogism-form.

In the following the base-verse is not cited but clearly is implied. Why may we be certain? Because without Gen. 1:1 Rabbis' comment makes no sense, for it stands in a redactional vacuum. So while the statement to begin with may or may not have focused upon Gen. 1:1, the redactor assuredly has presupposed the presence of Gen. 1:1 in including the composition here.

I:XIII.

2. A. ["...the heaven and the earth" (Gen. 1:1):] Rabbis said, "When a mortal builds a building, if the building goes as planned, he may continue to broaden the structure as it rises, but if not, he has to make it broad at the bottom but narrow at the top.

   B. "But that is not how things are for the Holy One, blessed be he. But: '...*the* heaven' meaning that very form of heaven as it had come to mind, first, and then: '...and *the* earth...,' as it had originally been planned."

3. A. R. Huna in the name of R. Eliezer, son of R. Yose the Galilean: "Even those concerning which Scripture states, 'For behold, I create a new heaven' (Is. 65:17) were in fact created from the six days of creation.

   B. "This is in line with the following verse: 'For as the new heaven remains before me' (Is. 66:22), not 'new,' but '*the new.*'" [Freedman, p. 12, n. 5: The definite article implies the specific new heavens, those created aforetime.]

I:XIV.

1. A. ["...the heaven and the earth" (Gen. 1:l):] R. Ishmael asked R. Aqiba, saying to him, "Because you served Nahum of Gimzo as disciple for twenty-two years, [learning from him the exegetical principles that] the words 'except' and 'only' are to be interpreted as exclusionary, and the accusative particle '*eth*' and 'also' serve as inclusionary words [indicating that more is covered by the

statement at hand than that which is explicitly mentioned in it], as to the accusative particle in the verse before us [Gen. 1:1], what is the exegesis that that usage applies?"

B. [Ishmael] said to [Aqiba], "If it were stated, 'In the beginning created God [without the accusative particle], heaven, and earth, ' we might have taken the view that heaven and earth are divine. [Without the accusative particle, we might have understood the words 'heaven' and 'earth' to be subjects of the verb 'create,' along with God. Thus we might have thought that the world was made by three: God, heaven, and earth. So the accusative particle is not inclusionary but has its own purpose.]"

C. [Aqiba] said to [Ishmael], "'For it is no empty thing from you,' (Deut. 32:46) means that if the Torah seems empty, it is from you [and your own fault], specifically because you do not know how to expound Scripture.

D. "Rather, the accusative particle prior to the word 'heaven' serves to include the sun, moon, stars, and planets, and the accusative particle prior to the word 'earth' serves to encompass trees, grass, and the Garden of Eden."

What we have now is an explanation of the base-verse, hence, as is clear, a simple exegesis, with the base verse cited or implied, followed by a discussion of a point found relevant by the exegete. The formal grounds for assigning to the present composition the status of an example of a conventional structure are simple. But the criterion is to be stated with appropriate emphasis: *the citation, explicit or implied, of the base verse always will come at the beginning of the composition, followed by whatever secondary exegetical material the exegete wishes to contribute.* So a conventional judgment on form has dictated to the author the arrangement of his materials.

To state the exegetical form very simply:

A. *a verse is cited*

B. *the verse is then explained, ordinarily within the limits of its own contents.*

What follows, by contrast, is formally miscellaneous. XIII:2, 3 proceed to new materials. No. 2 draws a lesson from the word-order at Gen. 1:1. No. 3 makes a distinct point of its own, on why the definite article is used. I:XIV bears a close tie to the foregoing, though, of course, on its own it does supply an exposition of the formulation of Gen. 1:1, just as much as I:XIII.2-3 have done. The polemic is against the view that God had help in creating the world. Because of the present interest in the concluding words of the opening verse, the following is tacked on.

10.   I:XV: Syllogistic Composition

I:XV.

1. A. ["...the heaven and the earth" (Gen. 1:1):] The House of Shammai say, "The heaven was created first."

B. The House of Hillel say, "The earth was created first."

C. In the view of the House of Shammai the matter may be compared to the case of a king who first made a throne for himself and afterward the footstool for the throne, as it is said, "The heaven is my throne, and the earth the dust of my feet" (Is. 66:1).

D. In the view of the House of Hillel the matter is to be compared to the case of a king who built a first palace for himself. Only after he had built the bottom floor did he build the upper floor, for so it is written, "On the day on which the Lord God made earth and [only then] heaven" (Gen. 2:4).

E. Said R. Judah bar Ilai, "The following verse of Scripture supports the view of the House of Hillel: 'Of old you laid out the foundations of the earth..., ' and afterward, '...and the heavens are the work of your hands' (Ps. 102:25).

F. Said R. Hanin, "On the basis of the verse of Scripture that supports the position of the House of Shammai the House of Hillel find evidence to reject that same view: 'The earth was...' (Gen. 1:2), meaning that it had already come into being."

G. R. Yohanan [said] in the name of sages, "As to the act of creation, heaven came first. As to the process of finishing off creation, the earth came first."

H. Said. R. Tanhuma, "I shall supply a verse of Scripture to support that statement. As to creation, the heaven came first: 'In the beginning God created [the heaven, then the earth]' (Gen. 1:1). But as to the process of finishing off creation, the earth came first: 'On the day on which the Lord God made heaven and earth' (Gen. 2:4)."

I. Said R. Simeon, "I should be surprised if the fathers of the world disputed concerning this matter. For both of them were created only as are the pot and its lid [which is to say, in a single act]. In this regard I recite the following verse of Scripture: '[My hand established the earth, and my right hand spread out the heaven.] When I call them, they stand up together' (Is. 48:13)."

J. Said R. Eleazar b. R. Simeon, "According to this opinion of my father, why is it that sometimes heaven comes before earth, sometimes earth comes before heaven. But what it teaches is that the two of them are equal [having been created at the same instant].

2. A. [T. Ker. 4:14 adds: R. Simeon says,] "In every place Scripture gives precedence to Abraham over Isaac, and to Isaac over Jacob. But in one passage Scripture says, 'And I remembered my covenant with Jacob [...Isaac and Abraham...]' (Lev. 26:42).

B. "This teaches that the three of them are equivalent to one another.

C. "In every passage Scripture accords precedence to Moses over Aaron, but in one place Scripture states, 'That is Aaron and Moses' (Ex. 6:26).

D. "This teaches that the two of them are equivalent to one another.

E. "In every passage Scripture gives precedence to Joshua over Caleb, but in one passage it says, 'except for Caleb, the son of Jephunneh the Kenizzite, and Joshua, the son of Nun' (Num. 32:12).

F. "This teaches that the two of them are equivalent to one another.

G. "And in every passage Scripture gives precedence to the honor owing to the father over the honor owing to the mother, while in one place it says, 'A man must fear his mother and his father' (Lev. 19:3), teaching that the two of them are equal to one another."

In a syllogistic composition all verses provide facts to prove the proposition at hand. What we might call the base verse (Gen. 1:1) takes no greater role than any of the other proof-texts at hand. The present composition furthermore provides a good example of the difference between an exegesis of a verse and a syllogistic composition. In the one, attention focuses on the verse, which, on its own terms, dictates the unfolding of discourse. In the other, attention centers on the proposition, not on any verse, and the verses that are cited are subordinate to the proposition that is to be proved by them.

As to the matter at hand, the conglomerate, Nos. 1, 2, has been inserted because of the obvious relevance of No. 1. But No. 2 scarcely belongs here, and it follows that Nos. 1 and 2 were joined before the whole found its way into our setting. The order of the words, heaven and earth, is introduced in No. 1 as evidence for the dispute of the Houses on the order of creation. The focus of interest then is not the exposition of the cited verse, Gen. 1:1, but rather the proposition subject to the Houses' debate, which further forms part of a much larger and cogent composition on the point made by the placing of names in a given order.

iv.   Conclusion: Hypothesis on the Three Formal Conventions of Genesis Rabbah

Differentiating literary forms requires formal, not substantive, criteria. We identify recurrent formal patterns, first of all describing how things are done, then seeking recurrent examples of that same mode of organizing thought. Beginning with a blank page, we therefore have turned to the opening *parashah* and analyzed the formal traits of its successive smallest completed units of thought.

These whole units of thought we have differentiated in a simple way. Where a topic starts, we know that discourse has begun; where the overall theme or topic changes, we know that discourse has concluded and so we have in hand a completed unit of thought. The signification of a topic for its part posed no complexity. Such a topic identifies itself because of the presence of either a verse of the book of Genesis, or a verse of another book of Scripture than Genesis, or a proposition of an abstract (essentially non-exegetical) character. The three formal modes of composition therefore aim at conveying propositions, and the formal traits dictate whether the topic at hand is (I) the interplay of the base verse with some other verse, (II) the meaning of the base verse, or (III) the proof of a proposition abstracted from the context established by the base verse (that is, the book of Genesis) in particular. Our formal criterion for differentiating the first two forms is been the placement of a verse, e.g., at the beginning or at the end of a passage. The criterion for identifying form III is no more subjective, since anyone can tell that verses derive from a variety of books of Scripture and equally serve as proof for a proposition distinct from them all. So to review:

Form I: when a verse from a biblical book other than Genesis occurs at the beginning of the passage, a single formal pattern follows: exposition of that other verse, which I have called the intersecting verse, followed by juxtaposition of the intersecting verse with a verse of the book of Genesis.

Form II: when a verse from the book of Genesis occurs at the beginning of the passage, then the focus of discourse will rest upon the exposition of that verse alone.

Form III: when a given syllogism comes to expression at the beginning of a passage, followed by a broad range of verses, made up ordinarily as a list exhibiting fixed syntactic preferences, then the focus of discourse will require proof of the syllogism, not exposition of the verses cited in evidence for the facticity of that syllogism.

On the basis of these three purely formal criteria, we have differentiated among the patterns of syntax and structure at hand.

To review the results, we have identified three forms, which, for the sake of convenient reference, I identify by the Roman numerals I, II, and III, as follows:

I.   The   Intersecting Verse-Base Verse-Form

1. Attribution + joining language + intersecting verse

2. Exposition of the intersecting verse

3. Reciprocal exposition of the base verse and the intersecting verse

II.   Exegesis of a Verse of Scripture

A. Citation of the base-verse (which will always be a verse chosen from the larger passage subject to interpretation, not a verse chosen from some other book of the Scripture)

B. Comment of a given rabbi. The comment is formulated in diverse ways

C. secondary, miscellaneous materials will be appended.

III.   Syllogistic Composition

A. statement of a syllogism or proposition

B. Verses of Scripture that prove or illustrate that syllogism, listed in a catalogue of relevance evidence

C. Secondary expansion: miscellanies (e. g., stories) on the syllogism, providing further illustration.

The formal requirement invariably is the composition of a list, a repertoire of facts ordinarily formulated in a single syntactic pattern. A syllogistic composition makes a point autonomous of the verse at hand. In this type of composition, the point of interest is in not the exposition of a verse but the proposition that is subject to demonstration, the proofs of course deriving from various verses of Scripture. Now that our hypothesis on the forms of Genesis Rabbah has taken shape, we test it against two further *parashiyyot*, chosen more or less at random. Then, in Chapter Three, through a series of charts we shall survey the entirety of Genesis Rabbah.

Chapter Two

Testing the Form-Analytical Hypothesis

i. Introduction

My hypothesis that Genesis Rabbah in the main, though not wholly, comprises three recurrent literary structures, I. base verse-intersecting verse, II. exegetical, and III. syllogistic, now requires testing. For that purpose we turn to two further *parashiyyot* and undertake exactly the same procedure that produced our original hypothesis. While the procedure may prove tedious, we have no choice. We may ascertain whether analysis of a single *parashah* provides results that may be duplicated through applying the same procedure to others only by examining other *parashiyyot*. If the proposed formal repertoire encompasses the bulk of what is before us, then we find justification to proceed to a survey of the entirety of the document. My comments on the selected *parashiyyot* focus upon form-analytical issues: why do I think a given unit of thought falls into one of the three classifications adduced to date. The upshot of what is to follow had best be stated at the outset. We shall see that our original hypothesis does encompass most of the materials of the two *parashiyyot* under study.

We do, however, find yet another principle of formulation and organization -- gross aggregation -- of materials, this one in no way pertinent to formal expression. Let me spell this out. While in *Parashah* I most units of thought conform to one of three patterns of formal and conventional modes of expressing ideas, in *Parashah* IV that is not the case. We shall see a long and interesting composition in which diverse completed materials -- whole and comprehensible units of thought -- flow together not for formal reasons but only because they speak to a common theme. In no way do they conform to a single pattern of formulating ideas on that common theme. The way in which redactors have selected and organized materials does not relate to the way in which these materials express their ideas. While in the three forms we have identified there is a correspondence between syntactical preference and mode of organizing and expressing ideas, in materials to follow we shall not identify such a concern.

Hence, very rapidly, we must identify a new species of literary principle, in addition to the formal one. This other classification is redactional, and not a matter of formal composition at all. It rests on the notion that framers have collected materials on a common theme, perhaps even offering a single syllogism or proposition, but have not imposed upon those materials a disciplined linguistic pattern. Thus we are moving into a somewhat complicated situation. We have three examples of literary structures. But we also find a formally miscellaneous but thematically cogent mode of organizing materials, one resting solely on the presence of a shared theme. That is quite another matter, so we assign to this other mode of conglomeration its own symbol. Since it cannot fall into the existing classification -- form **I**, form **II**, form **III** - - it will receive a letter symbol, as non-formal principle of conglomeration **A**.

For easy reference, I indicate at the head of each unit of thought the classification to which I assign what follows. Thus **IV:I.** -- **I** will signify that I regard IV:I as an example of form I. So too, **IV:II-V** -- **A** will signify, as just stated, that the materials at hand conform to no formal rules but do form an aggregate composed in accord with a shared theme. Whether, within the materials, there also is a common proposition seems to me too subjective an issue to allow useful speculation.

ii. Parashah Four.

IV:I. -- I

1 .   A. "And God said, 'Let there be a firmament in the midst of the waters'" (Gen. 1:6):

B. It is written, "Who roofs your upper chambers with water" (Ps. 104:3).

C. Under ordinary circumstances, when a mortal king builds a palace, he will roof it over with stones, timber, and earth.

D. But the Holy One, blessed be he, made a roof over his world only with water, as it is said, "Who roofs your upper chambers with water" (Ps. 104:3).

E. Thus: "And God said, 'Let there be a firmament' " (Gen. 1:6).

The intersecting verse, Ps. 104:3, clarifies the substance of the base verse. The intersecting verse then supplies the theme for what follows, which is the relationship between the upper and lower water. But at this point I see no further interest in the clarification of the base verse.

IV:II-V: -- A.

The Empty Space between Heaven and Earth

As I explained in the introduction to this chapter, what follows does not fall into the available categories. For the correct classification of the literary principle at hand is not formal. The intent of the compositor was simply to create a conglomerate on a subject. A single preference on syntax and morphology, whether exhibited overall or only at the beginning, does not emerge. The framer of the protracted passage has gathered diverse materials that treat a single theme. What follows for the study of the literary structures of Genesis Rabbah? It is that the following passage presents us with a new category, not in the genus of formal ones, rather, one that must be called a *redactional preference*.

Here, in what follows, we see no formal characteristics common among the compositions before us. The syntactic patterns are diverse, even at the opening of each unit, at which point, in general, we should expect to see the intervention of the hand of editors or authors interested in formal cogency. The framer of the document, IV:II-V, has drawn together a composite of materials on a single general topic. Calling the result a formally disciplined composition would constitute a gross overstatement of what is in hand. For we see a mere miscellany on a theme, not a syllogistic argument bound by considerations of form, let alone of a formally-structured argument. That is why we have to regard the present protracted passage as illustrative of yet another type of composition (again, we no longer can use the word "form" or even "literary structure"), namely, a formal miscellany on a cogent theme. The reason I dwell on the matter is that in Leviticus Rabbah I did not confront an equivalent problem; nearly all the materials collected in that compilation exhibit marks of formalization or patterning.

IV:II. -- A

1. A. ["And God said, 'Let there be a firmament...'" (Gen. 1:6):] Rabbis state the matter in the name of R. Hanina, R. Phineas, R. Jacob bar Bun in the name of R. Samuel bar Nahman: "At the moment at which the Holy One, blessed be he, said, 'Let there be a firmament in the midst of the water,' the middle layer became solid, and the lower heavens and the upper heavens were made [by the residual water]."

B. Rab said, "The works of creation were in liquid form, and on the second day they solidified: 'Let there be a firmament' is as if to say, 'Let the firmament be strengthened.'"

C. R. Judah bar Simon said, "Let a lining be made for the firmament [Freedman], in line with the following verse of Scripture: 'And they did beat the gold into thin plates' (Ex. 39:3)." [The word for "beat" uses the same letters as the word for "firmament."]

D. Said R. Hanina, "Fire came forth from above and licked at the face of the firmament."

E. When R. Yohanan would reach reach the following verse, "And by his breath the heavens were smoothed over" (Job 26:13), he would say, "Well did R. Hanina teach me."

F. Said R. Yudan bar Simeon, "Fire came forth from on high and licked at the face of the firmament. "

2. A. R. Berekhiah, R. Jacob bar Abina in the name of R. Abba bar Kahana: "The story of the creation of the world serves to teach a lesson concerning the account of the giving of the Torah, and the same story itself is clarified : 'As when fire burns through into parts' (Is. 64:1), that is to say, they divided [Freedman: between the upper and the nether waters].

B. "When, in fact, did the fire divide between the upper and the lower realms? Was it not in the giving of the Torah?

C. "That was how it was when the world was created."

IV:III.

1. A. R. Phineas in the name of R. Hoshayya: "Like the empty space that lies between the earth and the firmament is the empty space between the firmament and the upper water.

B. "[That is in line with the verse]: 'Let there be a firmament in the midst of the waters' (Gen. 1:6), that is to say, right in the middle, between [the water above and below]."

C. Said R. Tanhuma, "I shall cite proof from a verse of Scripture. If the verse had stated, 'And God made the firmament and divided between the water.. which is upon the firmament,' I should have concluded that it is directly upon the body of the firmament that the water is located. But when Scripture states, 'between the water which is upon the firmament, ' this indicates that the upper water is suspended by a word [for the formulation, '*from* above,' which is used, bears a different meaning from the formulation, 'above.' The latter would mean, 'directly above,' while the former, which is used, bears the meaning, 'suspended above.']"

D. Said R. Aha, "It is like the flame of a lamp, and the produce [of the water dripping through the flame] is the rain."

IV:IV.

1. A. A Samaritan asked R. Meir, saying to him, "Is it possible that the upper water is suspended merely by a word?"

B. He said to him, "Indeed so."

C. He said to him, "Bring me a syringe [Freedman, citing Levy]." He handed him a syringe. He put a gold plate over the aperture, and the water was not stopped up. He put a silver plate over the aperture, and the water was not stopped up. When he put his finger over it, the water was stopped up.

D. [The Samaritan] said to [Meir], "You put your finger over it [and stopped it up. But that is not comparable to holding back the upper water merely by a word.]"

E. He said to him, "Now if I, a mere mortal, am able to stop up the water just by putting my finger [over the aperture], as to the finger of the Holy One, blessed be he, how much the more so! This proves that the upper water is suspended by a word."

F. He said to him, "Is it really possible that he concerning whom it is written, 'The heaven and the earth do I fill' (Jer. 23:24) should have talked with Moses between the two horns of the ark?"

G. He said to him, "Bring me a convex mirror, which makes things look big." He handed him a convex mirror. He said to him, "Look at your mirror-image." He saw that it was big.

H. "Now bring me a concave mirror, which makes things look little." He brought him a concave one. He said to him, "Look, at your mirror-image." He saw that it was little.

I. He said to him, "If you, a mere mortal, can change your appearance however you will, he who spoke and brought the world into being -- how much the more so! One must therefore say that, when he wills, is it not the case that 'Do I not fill the heaven and the earth'? But when he wills, he may speak with Moses between the horns of the ark."

2. A. Said R. Anya bar Sussai, "There are moments in which the world and all that is in it cannot hold his glory, and there are times at which he speaks with a human being from among the hairs on his head.

B. "That is in line with the following verse of Scripture: 'Then the Lord answered Job out of the whirlwind' (Job 38:1). [The word for whirlwind can be read the hair, meaning that he spoke with him] from among the hairs on his head."

3. A. [Resuming the conversation of Meir and the Samaritan, the Samaritan] said to him, "Is it possible that 'the river of God has been full of water' (Ps. 65:10) from the six days of creation and as yet has not lost any [water]?"

B. He said to him, "Go in and take a bath. But weigh yourself before you go in, and then weigh yourself after you come out [having lost the sweat that is on your body]." He went and weighed himself [as instructed] and found that he had not lost any weight.

C. He said to him, "Did not all that sweat that went forth not come out of you?"

D. He said to him, "Indeed so."

E. He said to him, "Now while you, a mere mortal, found that nothing had gone forth from your fountain [since despite the loss of your sweat, now removed in the bath, your original weight remained the same], as to the Holy One, blessed be he, how much the more so!

F. "Thus it follows that while 'the river of God has been full of water' from the six days of creation, it has not lost any water at all since that time."

4. A. Said R. Yohanan, "The Holy One, blessed be he, took all of the water present at the creation of the world and put half of the water into the firmament, and the other half into the Ocean.

B. "That is in line with this verse: 'The river...,' and the word for 'river' stands also for 'half.'"

IV:V.

1. A. The firmament is like a lake, and above the lake is an arch, and on account of the evaporation of the lake, the arch drips water. It exudes thick drops, which pass through the salty water and are not mixed up with that water.

B. Said R. Yonah, "Do not let such a matter surprise you. The Jordan river passes through the Sea of Tiberias and is not mixed up with the sea.

C. "There is a miracle in a matter such as this [that the water passes through the sea but is not made salty]. If a person sifts wheat or stubble in a sieve, before the droppings have fallen two or three fingerbreadths, they are mixed together. But these flow together for many years and are not mixed together."

D. R. Yudan b. R. Simeon says, "It is because he brings them down in measure: 'For he draws away the drops of water' (Job 36:27). The word for 'draw away' is used in the sense of the word as it occurs in the following verse: 'And an abatement shall be made from your valuation' (Lev. 27:18). [Freedman: The sense is, 'an abatement that is calculated,' and the same sense is meant here.]"

2. A. As is the thickness of the earth, so is the thickness of the firmament: "It is he who sits above the circle of the earth" (Is. 40:22), "And he walks in the circuit of the heaven" (Job 22:14).

B. The use of the word for circle or circuit in both contexts serves to establish a comparison [between heaven and earth, with both measurements being the same].

C. R. Aha in the name of R. Hinena said, "It is as thick as a metal plate."

D. R. Joshua b. R. Nehemiah said, "It is as thick as two or three fingers."

E. Ben Pazzi said, "The upper water is more in volume than the lower water by thirty *xestes* [pints]: 'Between water and water' (Gen. 1:6) [provides for an additional L before the second appearance of the word for 'water,' and the L bears a numerical value of] thirty."

F. Rabbis say, "Half and half [that is, the volume of the water is equal, above and below]."

At IV:II the theme of the base verse, but not the language or specific allegations, accounts for the present construction. No. 1 makes its own point, on what exactly happened when the firmament was brought into existence in the midst of the water. No. 2 then carries forward the interest and theme of No. 1. But its point is critical: the Torah was given just as the world was created, so that the language used for the story of the one clarifies the language used for the description of the other. IV:III carries forward the general cosmological interest of IV:II.The reason for the inclusion of IV:IV.1-3, with No. 4 tacked on because of its relevance to the proof-text, lies in No. 1 which deals with the theme of the foregoing composition. The entire set, therefore, was composed prior to insertion here.Both components of the passage at IV:V deal with description of the firmament. These materials are not framed as exegeses of any verse. Rather, by themselves they constitute syllogisms on the science of the firmament, with the texts of Scripture providing scientific facts for the description of the matter under discussion. But they form part of a larger composition, which, overall, does not fall into form III, for reasons amply spelled out. It 6remains to note that no further examples of the present phenomenon will come before us in *parashiyyot* IV or XIX.

IV:VI-- II

1. A. "And God made the firmament" (Gen. 1:7):

B. This is one of the verses of Scripture with which Ben Zoma caused an earthquake in the entire world:

C. "[How can Scripture say,] 'And God *made'*? Did he not create the world through a word: 'By the *word* of the Lord were the heavens made, and all the host of them by the breath of his mouth' (Ps. 33:6)! [What sort of work did God have to do, that the word 'made' has been used here?]"

2. A. Why with reference to the creation on the second day is it not written, "And it was good"?

B. R. Yohanan, and it is repeated also in the name of R. Yose b. R. Halafta, "It is because on that day Gehenna was created: 'For Tofet is ordered from yesterday' (Is. 30:33), referring to a day to which there is only a yesterday but no prior day [hence, the second day of creation]."

C. R. Hanina said, "It is because on that day dissension was created: 'And let it divide between the water [setting the upper water apart from the lower water]' (Gen. 1:7). "

D. Said R. Tabyomi, "If, on the occasion of the creation of dissension which is [in the context at hand intended] for the good order of the world, the words, 'and it was good,' are not written, in the case of kinds of dissension which serve only for the confusion of the world, how much the more so [that nothing good can come]!"

E. Said R. Samuel bar Nahman, "It was because the work of making the water was not yet completed. Therefore the words 'it was good' appear two times with reference to the third day. One applies to the work of creating the water [which only now had been completed], and the other to the work of creating the day."

3. A. A noble lady asked R. Yose, "Why in reference to the second day is it not written, 'And it was good'?"

B. He said to her, "Even so, the Scripture goes and encompasses all of the days of creation at the end, for it is said 'And God saw all that he had made, and lo, it was very good' (Gen. 1:31)."

C. She said a parable to him, "If six people come to you, and you give a *mana* to each of the first five of them, and to one you give none, but then, if you go and give all of them a *mana* [shared in common], will not all of them have a *mana* and a sixth, except for this one, who will have only a sixth of a *mana* ? [So the omission of the blessing is not made up by the inclusion of the day at the blessing given for all of the six days of creation.]"

D. He went and stated to her what R. Samuel b. Nahman had said, "It was because on the second day the entire labor of creating the water had not yet been completed. Therefore with reference to the work of the third day, two times is it written, 'For it was good,' one covering the work of creating the water, the other the work of creating the day."

4. A. R. Levi in the name of R. Tanhum bar Hanilai, "It is written, 'Declaring the end from the beginning' (Is. 46:10).

B. "From the very beginning of creating the world, God foresaw Moses, who was called, 'for he was good' (Ex. 2:2), and [God foresaw that] Moses would receive his punishment on account of [water, smiting the rock for water, rather than merely speaking to it], therefore with reference to water, he did not write, 'For it was good.'"

5. A. R. Simon in the name of R. Joshua b. Levi: "The matter may be compared to the case of a king who had a harsh legion. The king said, 'Since this legion is particularly harsh, let my name not be associated with it.'

B. "Along these same lines, the Holy One, blessed be he, said, 'Since this water will punish the generation of Enosh, the generation of the flood, and the generation of division, therefore let the words, 'for it was good' not be written with regard to water.'"

No. 1 provides something of an exegesis for the base verse. We can hardly call Ps. 33:6 an intersecting verse. Rather, what we have is an unanswered question about the formulation of the cited verse. On that basis I am justified in classifying the opening in category II. But what follows seems to me rather miscellaneous, so the arena for formalization encompasses the opening part of the passage alone.

Nos. 2, 3, 4, and 5 all deal with the omitted clause, providing a sequence of answers. What is interesting is the repeated reference to the later narrative of Genesis, e.g., the water through which the generation of the flood would be punished. Still more suggestive is the linking of Moses, "who is good," to the matter at hand. So while the treatment of the issue appears miscellaneous, a broader exegetical program guides the compositors in their selection and arrangement.

IV:VII.-- II

1. A. "And God called the firmament heaven" (Gen. 1:8):

B. Rab said, "The two components of the word for heaven stand for fire and water."

C. R. Abba bar Kahana in the name of Rab: "The Holy One, blessed be he, took fire and water and beat them together, and from the mixture, heaven was made."

2. A. The word for heaven uses the letters that also form the root of the word for weighing, for the heaven weighs the deeds of human beings.

B. If people have merit, "The heaven tells his righteousness" (Ps. 97:6).

C. If not, "The heaven reveals his sin" (Job 20:27).

3. A. The word "heaven" [bears the root of the word for "amazement,"] for human beings express amazement on their account, saying, "Of what is the firmament made up? Is it made of fire? Is it made of water?"

B. R. Phineas in the name of R. Levi: "Scripture itself deals with the question: 'Who lays the beams of your upper chambers in the water' (Ps. 104:3), which indicates that the firmament is made of water."

4. A. [The word for heaven may be compared to the word for] colors, some of which are blue, red, black, or white.

B. Likewise heaven is sometimes blue, red, black, or white.

5. A. R. Isaac said, "The word for heaven, taken apart into its components, yields the meaning, 'Bear water.'

B. "The matter may be compared to a bowl of milk. Before a drop of rennet is put into it, the milk quivers. Once a drop of rennet is put into the milk, the milk immediately congeals and stands firm.

C. "So it is with heaven: 'The pillars of heaven quiver' (Job 26:11).

D. "Once a drop of rennet is put in: 'And there was evening and there was morning, a second day' (Gen. 1:8). "

E. That is in line with Rab's statement, "Creation was like liquid, and only on the second day did it congeal."

The entire passage -- all five components -- is devoted to exegesis of the word heaven. So in formal terms, we have to regard the composition as exegetical.

iii. Genesis Rabbah Parashah XIX

XIX:I.1 -- I

1. A. "Now the serpent was more subtle [than any other wild creature that the Lord God had made]" (Gen. 3:1):

B. "For in much wisdom is much anger, and he who increases knowledge increases sorrow" (Qoh. 1:18).

C. If a person increases knowledge for himself, he increases anger against himself, and because he adds to learning for himself, he adds to anguish for himself.

D. Said Solomon, "Because I increased knowledge for myself, I increased anger against myself, and because I added learning for myself, I added anguish for myself.

E. "Did you ever hear someone say, 'This ass went out and caught "the sun"' [Freedman: ague] or 'caught a fever'?

F. "Where are sufferings located? They are located among men."

XIX:I.2 -- A

2. A. Rabbi said, "A disciple of a sage does not require admonition [that a given act is prohibited, and if he does such an act, he will be penalized. Such a warning is required only for ordinary folk. A disciple of a sage is assumed to know the law and therefore may be penalized without prior admonition. This illustrates the point that learning increases one's exposure to anguish.]"

B. Said R. Yohanan, "He is in the status of fine linen garments that come from Beth Shean. If they are only slightly soiled, they go to waste. But the coarse linen garments that come from Arbela, how much are they worth, and how much money does it take to buy them? [What is more valuable also can produce great loss. What is not valuable also produces no loss.]"

C. R. Ishmael taught, "In accord with the strength of the camel is its load.

D. "In this worldly circumstances, when two men go into a restaurant, one says, 'Bring me roast meat, white bread, and a decent wine.' The other says, 'Bring me bread and beets.' This one eats and gets a bellyache, and that one eats and does not get a bellyache. What follows is that for the one the burden is heavy, and for the other it is not."

E. It was taught in the name of R. Meir, "Because the greatness that the snake had enjoyed was so considerable, so was the depth of his degradation: 'More subtle than all' (Gen. 3:1), 'More cursed than all' (Gen. 3:14). [This makes explicit the point of the foregoing observations.]"

XIX:I.3 -- II

3. A. "And the serpent was more subtle than any other wild creature" (Gen. 3:1):

B. R. Hoshaiah the elder said, "He stood erect like a reed and had feet. [That is what indicated his intelligence.]"

C. R. Jeremiah b. Eleazar said, "He was a disbeliever."

D. R. Simeon b. Eleazar said, 'He was like a camel. This world lost out on a great benefit, for if things had not happened the way they did, a man could send commerce through [a snake], who would come and go [doing his employer's business]."

No. 1 provides an appropriate intersecting verse, in which the advantage of the virtue of intelligence is weighed against the disadvantage. That introduces the discourse at hand, reflections on the futility of learning, as illustrated by the snake, most intelligent, most cursed. No. 2 then underlines the force of the praise bestowed on the serpent. He had much to lose and he lost it all. The composition by itself of course has its own literary integrity; but we know why it has been selected and appended. Nonetheless, I have given it its own classification. That is necessary because No. 3 falls into a different classification of literary form, as indicated: exegetical, pure and simple. No. 3 specifies what sort of ability the serpent had. The exegesis now follows a single line, which is to pursue both the surface-theme, the advantages of the serpent, and the subterranean one, the sorrow of learning. No. 2 joins both themes, in pointing to the serpent's remarkable intelligence as the greatness from which he fell. This is made explicit. 3.C, D underline this same point, specifying two aspects of great intelligence, namely, the power to doubt and the ability to conduct complicated affairs.

XIX:II. -- III

1 . A. "He said to the woman, 'Did God indeed say, "You shall not eat of any tree of the garden?"'" (Gen. 3:2):

B. Said R. Hinena bar Sanesan, "There are four who opened their statements with the word 'indeed' and who perished with the word 'indeed,' and these are they:

C. "The snake, the head baker, the camp of Korach, and Haman.

D. "The snake: 'And he said to the woman, "Did God indeed say..."'" (Gen. 3:2).

E. "The head baker: 'Indeed, I in my dream...' (Gen. 30:16).

F. "The camp of Korach: 'Indeed, you have not brought us...' (Num. 16:14).

G. "Haman: 'Indeed, Esther the queen did let no man come in...' (Est. 5:12)."

The pericope omits the promised other half, the verses in which the word "indeed" opens the statement of the downfall of those named. This is a fine example of formal classification III.

XIX:III. -- II

1 . A. "And the woman said to the snake. 'We may eat of the fruit of the trees[of the garden, but God said, "You shall not eat of the fruit of the tree which is in the midst of the garden, neither shall you touch it, lest you die"']" (Gen. 3:3):

B. Where was man when this conversation was going on?

C. Abba Halpun bar Qoriah said, "He had earlier had sexual relations, and now he was sleeping it off."

D. Rabbis say, "God had taken him and was showing him the whole world, saying to him, 'This is what an orchard looks like, this is an area suitable for sowing grain. So it is written, 'Through a land that no man had passed through, and where Adam had not dwelt' (Jer. 2:6), that is, Adam had not lived there [but there were lands Adam had seen on his tour]."

XIX:III.2 -- I

2 . A. "...of the fruit of the tree which is in the midst of the garden" (Gen. 3:3):

B. That is in line with this verse: "Add not to his words, lest he reprove you, and you be found a liar" (Prov. 30:6). [God had said nothing about not touching the tree, but the woman said they were not to eat of the fruit of the tree or even to touch it.]

C. R. Hiyya taught, "It is that one should not make the fence taller than the foundation, so that the fence will not fall down and wipe out the plants.

D. "So the Holy One, blessed be he, had said, 'For on the day on which you eat from it, you shall surely die' (Gen. 2:17). But that is not what she then said to the snake. Rather: 'God said,"You shall not eat from it *and you shall not touch it*.'" When the snake saw that she was lying to him, he took her and pushed her against the tree. He said to her, 'Have you now died? Just as you did not die for touching it, so you will not die from eating it.'

E. "'Rather: "For God knows that when you eat of it, your eyes will be opened and you will be like God"' (Gen. 3:5)."

No. 1 provides an exegesis for the cited verse, hence falls into classification II, while No. 2 proceeds to introduce an intersecting verse-base verse composition.

XIX:IV. -- II

1. A. Said R. Tanhuma, "This question people asked me in Antioch: "[Could there be more than a single God, in light of the fact that 'knowing good and evil' (Gen. 3:5) is given in the plural, thus,' like gods, knowing' is so constructed as to suggest a plurality of Gods.]

B. "I said to them, 'What is written is not, "For gods know," but rather, "For God knows."'"

2. A. R. Joshua of Sikhnin in the name of R. Levi: "[The snake] began to slander his creator, saying, 'From this tree did God eat and then he created the world. Then he told you, "You shall not eat of it" (Gen. 2:17), so that you should not create other worlds. For everyone hates the competition.'"

B. R. Judah b. R. Simon said, "[This is what he said,] 'Whatever is created in sequence after its fellow rules over its fellow. The heaven came on the first day and the firmament on the second, and does not the firmament bear the weight of heaven [so serving it]? The firmament came on the second day and herbs on the third, and does the firmament not provide water for herbs? The herbs were created on the third day and the great lights on the fourth, the lights on the fourth and the fowl on the fifth.'"

C. R. Judah b. R. Simon said, "The splendor of a clean bird when it flies through the heaven dims the orb of the sun."

D. [Continuing the discourse of B:] "'Yet you were created after everything else, so you should rule over everything that came before. Go ahead and eat before he creates other worlds, which will in sequence rule over you.'

E. "That is in line with the following verse: 'And the woman saw that it was good' (Gen. 3:6).

F. "What she saw was that the statement of the snake [was good]."

No. 1 rests on the citation of the verse and its explanation. Even though in a narrative framework, the formal requirements of the structure at hand are met. The same judgment applies to No. 2. So we have in hand what appears to me to be a variation on the basic composition made up by citing a base verse and explaining its sense or answering a question generated by the cited verse.

XIX:V.1 -- III

1. A. "[So when the woman saw] that the tree was good for food [and that it was a delight for the eyes, and that the tree was to be desired to make one wise]" (Gen. 3:6):

B. R. Eleazar in the name of R. Yose b. Zimra: "Three statements were made concerning the tree, that it was good to eat, a delight to the eyes, and that it added wisdom,

C. "and all of them were stated in a single verse:

D. "'So when the woman saw that the tree was good for food,' on which basis we know that it was good to eat;

E. "'and that it was a delight to the eyes', on which basis we know that it was a delight for the eyes,

F. "'and that the tree was to be desired to make one wise,' on which basis we know that it added to one's wisdom.

G. "That is in line with the following verse of Scripture: 'A song of wisdom of Ethan the Ezrahite' (Ps. 89:1)" [and the root for "song of wisdom" and that for "to make one wise" are the same].

XIX:V.2. -- II

2. A. "She took of its fruit and ate" (Gen. 3:6):

B. Said R. Aibu, "She squeezed some grapes and gave him the juice."

C. R. Simlai said, "She approached him fully prepared [with strong arguments], saying to him, 'What do you think? Is it that I am going to die, and that another woman will be created for you? [That is not possible:] 'There is nothing new under the sun' (Qoh. 1:9).

D. "'Or perhaps you think that I shall die and you will live all by yourself? 'He did not create the world as a waste, he formed it to be inhabited' (Is. 45:18)."

E. Rabbis say, "She began to moan and weep to him."

XIX:V.3. -- II

3. A. The word "also" ['And she *also* gave some to her husband' (Gen. 3:6)] bears the force of a phrase of inclusion, meaning to encompass domesticated beasts, wild beasts, and fowl.

B. Everyone obeyed her and ate of the fruit, except for one bird, which is called the phoenix.

C. For it is written, "Then I shall die with my nest and I shall multiply my days as the phoenix" (Job 29:18).

D. A member of the house of R. Yannai and R. Yudan bar Simeon [debated matters as follows]:

E. A member of the house of R. Yannai said, "It lives for a thousand years, and at the end of a thousand years a fire goes forth from its nest and burns it up and leaves an egg['s bulk of ash], which goes and grows limbs and lives on."

F. R. Yudan bar Simeon said, "It lives for a thousand years and at the end of a thousand years its body dissolves and its wings drop off, but an egg['s bulk] is left and it goes and grows parts and lives on."

Here we see a mixture of forms, III, then II, II. I think the grounds for classifying the statements in the identified forms are self-evident. No. 1 provides an obvious exegesis of the base verse. No. 2 creates a colloquy explaining how the woman persuaded the man to follow her example. No. 3 then moves off in its own direction.

XIX:VI. -- II

1. A. "Then the eyes of both of them were opened" (Gen. 3:7):

B. And had they been blind?

C. R. Yudan in the name of R. Yohanan b. Zakkai, R. Berekhiah in the name of R. Aqiba: "The matter may be compared to the case of a villager who was walking by a glass-maker's stall. In front of him was a basket full of fine goblets and cut glass. He swung his staff and broke them all. The glass-maker went and grabbed him.

D. "He said to him, 'I know full well that I am not going to get anything of value from you [since you are so poor that you cannot pay me back]. But come and let me at least show you how much property of worth you have destroyed.'

E. "So God showed them how many generations they had destroyed [and that is the manner in which their eyes were opened]."

2. A. "And they knew that they were naked" (Gen. 3:7):

B. Even of the single religious duty that they had in hand they were now denuded. [The word "naked" is associated with "being clothed by the merit accruing from the performance of religious duties."]

3. A. "And they sewed fig leaves together and made themselves aprons" (Gen. 3:7):

B. Said R. Abba bar Kahana, "What is not written is 'an apron,' but rather 'aprons.'

C. "The sense of the plural is this: a variety of clothing, such as shirts, robes, and linen cloaks.

D. "And just as these sorts of garments are made for a man, so for a woman they make girdles, hats, and hair nets. [So the plural of the word yields the sense that they clothed themselves in a variety of garments.]"

All three parts present exegesis to the cited verse and exemplify the form quite nicely. Each of the clauses of the verse is subjected to amplification.

XIX:VII.1 -- II

1. A. "And they heard the sound of the Lord God walking in the garden in the cool of the day" (Gen. 3:8):

B. Said R. Hilpai, "We understand from the verse at hand that a sound may move [since the verse refers to the 'sound moving in the garden'], but we have not heard that fire moves.

C. "And how on the basis of Scripture do we know that fire moves? It is in the following verse: 'And the fire travelled down upon the earth' (Ex. 9:23).

XIX:VII.2. -- III

2. A. Said R. Abba bar Kahana, "The word is not written, 'move,' but rather, 'walk,' bearing the sense that [the Presence of God] leapt about and jumped upward.

B. "[The point is that God's presence leapt upward from the earth on account of the events in the garden, as will now be explained:] The principal location of the Presence of God was [meant to be] among the creatures down here. When the first man sinned, the Presence of God moved up to the first firmament. When Cain sinned, it went up to the second firmament. When the generation of Enosh sinned, it went up to the third firmament. When the generation of the Flood sinned, it went up to the fourth firmament. When the generation of the dispersion [at the tower of Babel] sinned, it went up to the fifth. On account of the Sodomites it went up to the sixth, and on account of the Egyptians in the time of Abraham it went up to the seventh.

C. "But, as a counterpart, there were seven righteous men who rose up: Abraham, Isaac, Jacob, Levi, Kahath, Amram, and Moses. They brought the Presence of God [by stages] down to earth.

D. "Abraham brought it from the seventh to the sixth, Isaac brought it from the sixth to the fifth, Jacob brought it from the fifth to the fourth, Levi brought it down from the forth to the third, Kahath brought it down from the third to the second, Amram brought it down from the second to the first. Moses brought it down to earth."

E. Said R. Isaac, "It is written, 'The righteous will inherit the land and dwell therein forever' (Ps. 37:29). Now what will the wicked do? Are they going to fly in the air? But that the wicked did not make it possible for the Presence of God to take up residence on earth [is what the verse wishes to say]."

Once more at No. 1we have an example of form II. While both entries explain the word "walk, No. 2 goes its own way to make a point autonomous of the cited verse.

XIX:VIII. -- II

1. A. Said R. Berekhiah, "Instead of the verb, 'And they heard' ['And they heard the sound of the Lord God walking' (Gen. 3:8)], what it should say is, 'They caused to hear [with the subject of the verb being the trees, as will now be explained].

B. "They heard the sound of the trees saying, 'Lo, the thief who deceived his creator!'"

C. Said R. Hinena bar Pappa, "Instead of 'And they heard,' it should say, 'And they caused to hear.' They heard the voice of the ministering angels saying, 'The Lord is going to those in the garden.'" [This is continued at G.]

D. R. Levi and R. Isaac [concerning what the angels said]:

E. R. Levi said, "[What they heard from the angels was,] 'The one who was in the garden has died.'"

F. R. Isaac said, "[What they heard the angels say is,] 'He is taking a walk.' [Freedman, p. 154, n. 4: When has God declared that disobedience would be followed by death? According to these interpretations the verse is rendered thus: "And they heard the voice of the angels declaring either, "O God, man is dead and gone," or, "God is going to those in the garden to punish them," or, "O God, does man still walk about?"]

G. [Continuing C:] "Said the Holy One, blessed be he, to them, '[He will die] but with the respite of a day [for the Hebrew translated "in the cool of the day"]. Lo, I shall provide him with the space of a day. So did I say to him, 'For on the day on which you will eat it, you will surely die' (Gen. 2:17). But you do not know whether it is one day by my reckoning or one day by your reckoning. Lo, I shall give him a day by my reckoning, which is a thousand years by your reckoning. So he will live for nine hundred and thirty years and leave seventy years for his children to live in their time.' [So God's statement that man would surely die if he ate the forbidden fruit in fact did come to fruition. Adam lived a period of nine hundred thirty years. and each subsequent Adam gets seventy years.]

H. "That is in line with this verse of Scripture: 'The days of our years are threescore years and ten' (Ps. 90:10)."

2. A. "In the cool of the day" (Gen. 3:8):

B. Rab said, "He judged him at the east, for 'at the cool of the day;' refers to the direction from which the day comes up, [which is to say, at the east]."

C. Zabedi b. Levi said, "It was at the west that he judged him. The cool of the day' refers to the direction at which the day goes down, [which is to say, at the west]."

D. In the view of Rab, he treated him harshly, just as, for the time the day rises, it gets hotter.

E. In the view of Zabedi, he treated him leniently, just as, for the time that the day closes, it gets cooler.

3. A. "And the [man and his wife hid themselves from the presence of the Lord God among the trees of the garden]" (Gen. 3:8):

B. R. Aibu said, "[In hiding,] his height shrunk down and he was only a hundred cubits tall."

4. A. "Among the trees of the garden" (Gen. 3:8):

B. Said R. Levi, "This gave a foretaste of the fact that his descendants would be put into wooden coffins."

Once more we have an example of form II. Both entries explain the word "walk. How does the exegesis proceed? The effect of No. 1 is to remove the implication of a corporeal God, now by having the "sound" refer not to God's physical movements but to some other noise. No. 2 produces the same result; it is no longer "the cool of the day," but a figurative statement bearing its own message. Nos. 3 and 4 move forward in the exegesis of the verses at hand.

XIX:IX.1 -- II

1. A. "And the Lord God called to the man and said to him, 'Where are you?'" (Gen. 3:9):

B. [The word for "where are you" yields consonants that bear the meaning,] "How has this happened to you?"

C. [God speaks:] "Yesterday it was in accord with my plan, and now it is in accord with the plan of the snake. Yesterday it was from one end of the world to the other [that you filled the earth], and now: 'Among the trees of the garden' (Gen. 3:8) [you hide out]."

This seems to me nothing more than a routine exegesis of the sense of the verse.

XIX:IX.III

2. A. R. Abbahu in the name of R. Yose bar Haninah: "It is written, 'But they are like a man [Adam], they have transgressed the covenant' (Hos. 6:7).

B. "'They are like a man,' specifically, like the first man. [We shall now compare the story of the first man in Eden with the story of Israel in its land.]

C. "'In the case of the first man, I brought him into the garden of Eden, I commanded him, he violated my commandment, I judged him to be sent away and driven out, but I mourned for him, saying "How..."'[which begins the book of Lamentations, hence stands for a lament, but which, as we just saw, also is written with the consonants that also yield, 'Where are you'].

D. "'I brought him into the garden of Eden,' as it is written, 'And the Lord God took the man and put him into the garden of Eden' (Gen. 2:15).

E. "'I commanded him,' as it is written, 'And the Lord God commanded...' (Gen. 2:16).

F. "'And he violated my commandment,' as it is written, 'Did you eat from the tree concerning which I commanded you' (Gen. 3:11).

G. "'I judged him to be sent away,' as it is written, "And the Lord God sent him from the garden of Eden' (Gen. 3:23).

H. "'And I judged him to be driven out.' 'And he drove out the man' (Gen. 3:24).

I. "'But I mourned for him, saying, "How...".' 'And he said to him, "Where are you"' (Gen. 3:9), and the word for 'where are you' is written, 'How....'

J. "'So too in the case of his descendants, [God continues to speak,] I brought them into the Land of Israel, I commanded them, they violated my commandment, I judged them to be sent out and driven away but I mourned for them, saying, "How...."'

K. "'I brought them into the Land of Israel.' 'And I brought you into the land of Carmel' (Jer. 2:7).

L. "'I commanded them.' 'And you, command the children of Israel' (Ex. 27:20). 'Command the children of Israel' (Lev. 24:2).

M. "'They violated my commandment.' 'And all Israel have violated your Torah' (Dan. 9:11).

N. "'I judged them to be sent out.' 'Send them away, out of my sight and let them go forth' (Jer 15:1).

O. "'....and driven away.' 'From my house I shall drive them' (Hos. 9:15).

P. "'But I mourned for them, saying, "How...."'' 'How has the city sat solitary, that was full of people' (Lam. 1:1)."

No. 2 presents a proposition, not spelled out but nonetheless clear, comparing Adam and Israel. That is why I classify this item as exemplary of form III. From a redactional viewpoint, of course, No. 1 certainly sets the stage for No. 2 and the whole must be regarded as a single, thoughtful composition.

XIX:X. -- II

1. A. "And he said, 'I heard the sound of you in the garden, and I was afraid, because I was naked, and I hid himself.' He said, 'Who told you [that you were naked? Have you eaten of the tree of which I commanded you not to eat?']" (Gen. 3:10-11):

B. Said R. Levi, "The matter may be compared to the case of a woman who wanted to borrow a little yeast, who went in to the house of the wife of a snake-charmer. She said to her, 'What does your husband do with you? [How does he treat you?]'

C. "She said to her, 'Every sort of kindness does he do with me, except for the case of one jug filled with snakes and scorpions, of which he does not permit me to take charge.'

D. "She said to her, 'The reason is that that is where he has all his valuables, and he is planning to marry another woman and to hand them over to her.'

E. "What did the wife do? She put her hand into the jug [to find out what was there]. The snakes and scorpions began to bite her. When her husband got home, he heard her crying out. He said to her, 'Could you have touched that jug?'

F. "So: 'Have you eaten of the tree of which I commanded you not to eat?' (Gen. 3:11)."

The parable serves as an exegesis of the cited verses. At a more sophisticated stage of the work, people may wish to differentiate among the forms and types of exegeses, but, at this stage, it suffices to classify the item as exemplary of form II. Why so? As I see it, the parable spells out the obvious sense of the discourse of Scripture.

XIX:XI. -- III

1. A. "The man said, 'The woman whom you gave to be with me gave me fruit of the tree, and I ate'" (Gen. 3:12):

B. There are four on whose pots the Holy One, blessed be he, knocked, only to find them filled with piss, and these are they: Adam, Cain, the wicked Balaam, and Hezekiah.

C. Adam: "The man said, 'The woman whom you gave to be with me gave me fruit of the tree and I ate" (Gen. 3:12).

D. Cain: "And the Lord said to Cain, 'Where is Abel, your brother?" (Gen. 4:9).

E. The wicked Balaam: "And God came to Balaam and said, 'What men are these with you?'" (Num. 22:9)

F. Hezekiah: "Then came Isaiah the prophet to king Hezekiah and said to him, 'What did these men say?'" (2 Kgs. 20:14).

G. But Ezekiel turned out to be far more adept than any of these: "'Son of man, can these bones live?' And I said, 'O Lord God, you know'" (Ez. 37:3).

H. Said R., Hinena bar Pappa, "The matter may be compared to the case of a bird that was caught by a hunter. The hunter met someone who asked him, 'Is this bird alive or dead?'

I. "He said to him, 'If you want, it is alive, but if you prefer, it is dead.' So: '"Will these bones live?" And he said, "Lord God, you know."'"

The list proves a point, hence a fine instance of form III. Those who turned out to be pisspots did not reply in a humble way.

XIX:XII.1-3 + 4-- I

1. A. ["The man said, 'The woman whom you gave to be with me gave me fruit of the tree, and I ate'" (Gen. 3:12):] That is in line with the following verse of Scripture: "Then would I speak and not fear him, for I am not so with myself" (Job 9:35).

B. Said Job, "I am not like him who said, 'The woman whom you gave to be with me gave me the fruit of the tree' (Gen. 3:21) [and further, 'Because you have listened to the voice of your wife' (Gen. 3:17)]. He obeyed his wife's instructions, but I did not obey my wife." [We shall shortly see a more important contrast between Job and Adam, also showing the degradation of Adam.]

2. A. Said R. Abba bar Kahana, "Job's wife was Dinah, to whom he said, 'You speak as one of the vile women speaks' (Job 9:10). 'What? shall we accept good at the hand of God and shall we not accept evil?'(Job 9:10)."

B. Said R. Abba, "What is written is not, 'I shall receive,' but 'We shall receive.' The sense of the statement then is this: 'Are we going to be fit people when it comes to what is good and not fit people when it comes to what is bad?'"

3 . A. "For all this did not Job sin with his lips" (Job 9:10):

B. Said R. Abba, "With his lips he did not sin, but in his heart he sinned."

4 . A. Said R. Abba, "What is written [at Gen. 3:12] is not, 'and I did eat,' but, 'I did eat and *I will eat* .'"

B. Said R. Simeon b. Laqish, "The first man was separated from the garden of Eden only after he had actually blasphemed and cursed. That is in line with what is written: 'And he looked that it should bring forth grapes, and it brought forth wild grapes' (Is. 5:2)."

XIX:XII.5 -- II

5 . A. "The woman said, 'The serpent beguiled me, and I ate'" (Gen. 3:13):

B. "He incited, incriminated, beguiled me" [Freedman].

C. "He incited me:" "The enemy shall not incite him" (Ps. 89:23).

D. "He incriminated me:" "When you lend to your neighbor" (Deut. 24:10) [making him liable for repayment, here: making me liable to punishment (Freedman, p. 58, n. 2)].

E. "He beguiled me:" "Now therefore let not Hezekiah beguile you" (2 Chr. 32:15).

XIX:XII.1-3 + 4 introduce Job in the clarification of the passage at hand, and the initial phase of the composition follows form I. No. 5 then proceeds to the exegesis of the cited verses, also following a single formal pattern. No. 5 moves on to the next verse. So Nos. -1-4 present an intersecting verse, and those components provide a fairly substantial exposition of the intersecting verse before returning to the base verse. On that basis the opening component of the composition falls into the classification of form I, the concluding, form II (for self-evident reasons).

iv. Conclusion

The three hypothetical forms encompass most, though not all, of the materials of *parashiyyot* IV and XIX. The other items are joined together into classification A: thematic composites, lacking distinctive formal traits. The present result justifies our turning to the document as a whole. We proceed to survey Genesis Rabbah with two questions in hand, one on the literary forms of the work, the other about the organization of the forms in particular order.

Chapter Three

Recurrent Literary Structures
Types of Units of Discourse
and their Order
in Genesis Rabbah as a Whole

i. Sorting Out the Major Units of Discourse

Genesis Rabbah is made up of one hundred *parashiyyot*, and each *parashah* is comprised of from as few as five to as many as fifteen subdivisions. In my translation and explanation of the text, I was able to show that these subdivisions in the main formed cogent statements. That is to say, words joined together to form autonomous statements, sentences. Sentences then coalesced into cogent propositions, paragraphs. Paragraphs then served a larger purpose, forming a cogent proposition of some sort. All together, therefore, discrete words turned into sentences, and sentences into whole thoughts, that we can discern and understand. That is the premise of all that follows. The contrary proposition, that the words of the document, Genesis Rabbah, present us with meaningless statements, pure gibberish, does not require attention. Other documents that reach us from late antique Judaism, for example the writings called "hekhalot," would have to be shown to constitute syllogistic or propositional compositions -- units of thought, as distinct from units of emotive or affective expression of some other than a rational character, But that is not our problem. Every single set of sentences of Genesis Rabbah makes a cogent statement of some sort. So much for the smallest whole units of thought of Genesis Rabbah. They do contain cogent thought. We can discern the ideas presented in the composition at hand. The use of the word "composition" is justified: there is thought, in logical sequence, in proportion, in order, with a beginning, a middle, and an end. Genesis Rabbah then is composed of a long sequence of these smallest whole units of thought, strung together for some purpose or another.

What is important to us is the fact that these smallest whole units of discourse or thought join together for a larger purpose. The document intellectually is more than an anthology of discrete passages. How so? Among all the diverse smaller units of discourse, sayings, stories, exegeses of verses of Scripture, protracted proofs of a single proposition, and the like, ordinarily served a purpose cogent to the whole subdivision of a *parashah*. That is to say, whatever finished materials are present have been made by the compositors -- the authorities who selected the smallest completed units of thought and arranged them as we now have them -- to serve their goals, that is, purposes of the compositors of the larger unit of thought of which the several smallest units of thought now form a part. That is why our form-analysis worked its way from the largest components of the document, the *parashiyyot*, to the next largest, the completed paragraphs signified by a Roman numeral (and in this I follow the convention of the standard critical text and earlier ones as well) and then to the next largest, and so on down -- from whole to parts. Any analysis of the overall structure and organization of the document as a whole, therefore, must begin with the principal divisions, the one hundred *parashiyyot*, specifically to analyze the character of the subdivisions.

What we now wish to know is whether a given *parashah* will be composed of materials that derive from a limited repertoire of patterns of expression. We ask about the patterns of grammar and syntax, word-choice and positioning of citations of verses of Scripture, in the smallest whole units of thought. Do we discern recurrent arrangements -- patterns, forms -- or only miscellaneous and non-recurrent usages individual to the given passages? We further want to know how the materials are arranged. That is to say, if we are able to carry out a taxonomy of the units of discourse, to show that a limited repertoire of patterns or forms governed the way in which ideas were expressed, have these types of units of discourse been arranged in a pattern or not so ordered? Do the authors of the several *parashiyyot* organize in a cogent way the repertoire of materials that they choose to use?

So we are concerned to investigate two things. First we wish to see whether the primary constituents of discourse, the subdivisions of the *parashiyyot*, fall into a limited taxonomic framework. Second, we have to find out whether or not the types of units of discourse -- the subdivisions of the *parashiyyot* -- are arranged in a consistent order. Accordingly, the suggestive results of Chapter One now demand systematic reconsideration, so that the entirety of the data will be subjected to examination. The inquiry encompasses an inductive examination of the whole of Genesis Rabbah. Only then shall we see whether and how Genesis Rabbah follows a disciplined literary plan throughout. The question is: does Genesis Rabbah reveal a literary structure, or, from a formal and rhetorical viewpoint, is it a mere miscellany? The answer to that question will allow us to compare Genesis Rabbah to Leviticus Rabbah.

The types of units of discourse outlined in Chapter One in the main find definition in formal, therefore objective traits. I have tried to avoid any subjective judgment. That is to say, if I call a recurrent mode of organization the base-verse/intersecting-verse construction (form I), all I mean to say is that, in the sort of passage under discussion, (1) a verse of the book of Genesis will be followed by (2) a verse from some other book of the Hebrew Scriptures. The latter (2) will then be subjected to extensive discussion. But in the end the exposition of the intersecting-verse will shed some light, in some way, upon (1) the base-verse, cited at the outset.

If I call a recurrent pattern one of exegesis of a verse (form **II**), all I mean is that, in this type of discourse, a verse of the book of Genesis will be subjected to sustained analysis and amplification, but not with reference to some other intersecting-verse but now, commonly with regard to numerous proof-texts, or to no proof-texts at all. So we deal with a completely formal criterion. It is merely the location of the base-verse and intersecting-verse. In what I called "the base verse-intersecting verse form," the base-verse always comes first, the intersecting-verse follows. That is a logical arrangement, since the focus of analysis will be upon the intersecting-verse. In what I called "the exegetical form," by contrast, the verse subjected to intensive discussion will derive from the book of Genesis and will stand on its own, not in relationship to systematic exegesis of verses from other books of the Scriptures.

Finally, the syllogism-form (form **III**) will cite a variety of verses, drawn from a broad range of books of the Hebrew Scriptures, ordinarily composed in a list of like grammatical and syntactical entries. What follows, therefore, provides a repertoire of judgments based on objective and formal considerations only.

Once the taxonomic exercise has worked its way through Genesis Rabbah, a similarly inductive exercise will take up the correlative question. If the bulk of the materials turn out to fall into a limited set of formal patterns of syntax or arrangement, can we show that these patterns themselves will be ordered in one sequence rather than in some other or in no sequence at all? In section ii we deal with the taxonomy of the composites and of the smallest units of discourse of which they are made up, and in section three we proceed to the issue of the ordering of these types of units of discourse.

ii. Types of Units of Discourse in Genesis Rabbah

We shall now classify among the three forms we have identified in *parashiyyot* I, IV, and XIX all the units of discourse demarcated by Roman numerals. In some instances we shall subdivide, classifying also units of discourse signified by Arabic numerals. Where this is done, it is because one or more of the subunits falls into a different classification from the others. At issue is whether, overall, we are able to classify the bulk of Genesis Rabbah within a single, simple, and cogent system of taxonomy. The answer is that we are.

I:I	I
I:V	I
I:VI	I
I:VII	III
I:VIII	III
I:II	III
I:IV	III
I:VIII	III
I:IX	III
I:X	III
I:XI	III
I:XII	III
I:XIII	III
I:XIV	II
I:XV	III

II:I	I
II:II	II
II:III	II
II:IV	III
II:V	III

III:I	I
III:II	I
III:III	I
III:IV	III(?)
III:V	III
III:VI.1-2	III
III:VI.3-4	II
III:VII	II
III:VIII	III
III:IX	III

IV:I	I
IV:II	A
IV:III	A
IV:IV	A
IV:V	A
IV:VI	A
IV:VII	II

V:I	I
V:II	III
V:III	III
V:IV	III
V:V	III
V:VI	III
V:VII	III
V:VIII	II
V:IX	III

VI:I	I
VI:II	I
VI:III	II
VI:IV	III
VI:V	III
VI:VI	II + A (No. 1 provides an exegesis and the rest is a formal miscellany on a common theme.)
VI:VII	A
VI:VIII	A
VI:IX	II

VII:I	I
VII:II	Appendix to VII:I.
VII:III	II
VII:IV	II (No. 1. The remainder is a formal miscellany tacked on to No. 1.)
VII:V	II

VIII:I	I (+ miscellany on the theme of No. 1.)
VIII:II	I
VIII:III	II
VIII:IV	Continues the foregoing
VIII:V	Continues the foregoing
VIII:VI	Continues the foregoing
VIII:VII	Continues the foregoing
VIII:VIII	Continues the foregoing
VIII:IX	Continues the foregoing.
VIII:X	Continues the foregoing.
VIII:XI	II
VIII:XII	II
VIII:XIII	II

Once we recognize the continuity indicated above, the *parashah* may be seen to move in a stately progression from type I to type II to type III. But this is by no means a consistent pattern.

IX:I	I
IX:II	I
IX:III	II
IX:IV	II
IX:V-XIII	II/III/A. This is a sustained composition on the cited verse, but the common theme accounts for the inclusion of a sizable part of the whole. Yet when we come to the end, we realize that the entire composite aims at making a point in an essentially syllogistic man- ner. So the passage may be classified as to its parts, but also as a whole. Some of its components fall into type II, some into type III, some are joined as part of a common theme of a formally mis- cellaneous character, hence a different classification en- tirely as type A, but the whole, seen all together, may be regarded as *sui generis* (!).

X:I	I
X:II	I
X:III	III
X:IV	II
X:V	II

X:VI	III (Continues the proposi - tion of the foregoing, X:V.3)
X:VII	III (as above)
X:VIII-IX	This composite, viewed whole, serves as an exegesis of Gen. 2:1-2. But it is not formally composed at all, and we cannot confuse the function of exegesis with the exegetical form. So, as a whole, we cannot classify this composition at all, even though, in context, it serves a clear and useful purpose.
XI:I	I
XI:II	II. (But while exegetical in overall form, the composite presents a powerful argument for its syllogism.)
XI:III	II (Continues the foregoing.)
XI:IV	II (But Nos. 2-4 contribute a sequence of stories, not exegeses of the base-verse. These stories to be sure carry forward the proposition and theme of the base-verse and its exegesis.)
XI:V	(Continues the sequence of stories inaugurated at XI:IV.)
XI:VI-VII	A This is a formal miscellany, focused on the substantive theme of the righteousness of the early saints who did not keep the law yet were saved. So we have a thematic composite exhibiting no formal traits of definition.
XI:VIII	II. (This is essentially an exegesis of the base-verse, even though the verse is not cited.)
XI:IX	II
XI:X	II
XII:I	I
XII:II	I
XII:III	III/II. (The exegesis of Gen. 2:4 serves quite well, but it is part of a larger exegetical syllogism.)
XII:IV	II
XII:V	III
XII:VI	III (Same problem as at XII:III. This vast composi - tion in no way illustrates a prevailing interest in formal composition and conglo - meration.)
XII:VII	III
XIII:VIII	III (The purpose is syllogistic, not exegetical.)
XII:IX	II

XII:X	II
XII:XI	III
XII:XII	III
XII:XIII	III
XII:XIV	II (XII:XI-XIII form a single continuing composition, syllogistic in a general way, but reaching a climax with an exegesis of Gen. 2:4.)
XII:XV	II
XII:XVI	II
XIII:I	II
XIII:II	II
XIII:III.1	II
XIII:III.2, IV-VI	A (Anthology on the theme of rain, no clear syllogism at issue, no proposition.)
XIII:VII	II
XIII:VIII	II
XIII:IX-XV	A. (Even though No. 1 appears to introduce an intersecting verse, in fact what we have is an exercise solely focused on the intersecting verse, not on that returns to the base verse. The exercise, more - over, explores a problem in physics. I see no formal policy governing the formulation of the whole, so we have nothing more than a thematic miscellany.)
XIII:XVI	II
XIII:XVII	II
XIV:I	I
XIV:II	II
XIV:III	II
XIV:IV	II
XIV:V	II
XIV:VI	II
XIV:VII	II (+ diverse materials.)
XIV:VIII	II
XIV:IX	III
XIV:X	II
XV:I:1	II
XV:I.2-4	III (This seems to me a thematic composition of a miscellaneous formal charac - ter. Since there is no move - ment from the intersecting verse to the base verse, the whole hardly falls into the category of form I.)
XV:II	II
XV:III	II
XV:IV	II
XV:V	II
XV:VI	II

XV:VII	II (This item bears a rather extensive burden of secondary accretions, none of them formally congruent to the opening component of the composition.)
XVI:I	I
XVI:II	II
XVI:III	II (+ secondary expansion on the same theme)
XVI:IV	III (III-IV form a single large-scale composition, which makes a point as a whole.)
XVI:V	II
XVI:VI	II
XVII:I	A (I see no formal pattern of a recurrent character.)
XVII:II	A (As above. The base verse introduces a theme, for which a proposition is adduced, and the proposition finds proof in diverse verses and other materials. But there is no formalization of any kind that I discern.)
XVII:III	A (As above, a proposition, then secondary, formally miscellaneous, materials on the same theme.)
XVII:IV	II
XVII:V	III
XVII:VI	II
XVII:VII	Continues the theme of the foregoing.
XVII:VIII	This set of colloquies is introduced because of its thematic relevance to the foregoing. But it is in no way formulated to follow a fixed pattern discerned in the present context.
XVIII:I.1	A. The cited base-verse yields to a Mishnah-passage, which in a rather general way clarifies the sense of the base verse.
XVIII:I. 2-3+4	No. 2 clarifies the language of the base verse. No. 3 does the same. I see no formalization in the presentation here. No. 4 then provides an extended exegesis of a proof-text introduced in No. 3.
XVIII:II	III
XVIII:III	II
XVIII:IV	II
XVIII:V.1	A. This is formally a replay of XVIII:I.1.

XVIII:V.2	II
XVIII:V.3	III
XVIII:VI	III
XIX:I.1+2	I. No. 2 is tacked on.
XIX:I.3	II
XIX:II	III
XIX:III	II
XIX:IV	II
XIX:V	II
XIX:VI	II
XIX:VII.1	II
XIX:VII.2	III
XIX:VIII	II
XIX:IX	III (While exegetical, the composition in fact makes a point by proving it through adducing a set of verses in evidence.)
XIX:X	II
XIX:XI	III
XIX:XII	III (Once Job 9:35 is introduced, an extensive comparison of Job and Adam is introduced. I see none of the formal requirements of the base verse-intersecting verse in play here, however. Rather, the purpose is to establish a proposition, not to clarify the base verse on its own terms.
XX:I	I
XX:II	II
XX:III	III
XX:IV	II
XX:V	II
XX:VI	II (+ appended miscellaneous materials)
XX:VII	III
XX:VIII	II
XX:IX	III
XX:X	II
XX:XI	II
XX:XII	II
XXI:I	I
XXI:II	I
XXI:III	III
XXI:IV	A (I am not entirely certain what we have here, but it does seem to me to serve the exegetical purpose defined by the base verse. In formal terms, however, we have not got an example of form II.)
XXI:V	II
XXI:VI	II
XXI:VII	II
XXI:VIIIII	
XXI:IX	III (This is a fine example of form III.)

XXII:I	I
XXII:II	II
XXII:III	II
XXII:IV	III
XXII:V	II (This item bears a sizable appendix.)
XXII:VI	II
XXII:VII	II
XXII:VIII	II
XXII:IX.1	I
XXII:IX.2-7	II
XXXII:X	II
XXII:XI	II
XXII:XII	II
XXII:XIII	II
XXIII:I	I
XXIII:II	II
XXIII:III	II
XXIII:IV	II
XXIII:V	II
XXIII:VI.1	II
XXIII:VI.2	III
XXIII:VII	III
XXIV:I	I
XXIV:II	I
XXIV:III	I
XXIV:IV.1	I
XXIV:IV.2	III
XXIV:V.1-2	II
XXIV:V.3	I. (Clearly the intervening materials have been inserted into what was, to begin with, an intersecting verse-base verse composition.)
XXIV:VI	II
XXIV:VII	II
XXV:I	II
XXV:II	II
XXV:III	III
XXVI:I	I
XXVI:II	I
XXVI:III	II
XXVI:IV.1	III
XXVI:IV.2	II (+ formal miscellanies on a given topic, in classification A)
XXVI:V	II
XXVI:VI	II
XXVI:VII	II
XXVII:I	I
XXVII:II	I
XXVII:III	II
XXVII:IV	II
XXVIII:I	I
XXVIII:II	II
XXVIII:III	II
XXVIII:IV	II

XXVIII:V	II
XXVIII:VI	II
XXVIII:VII	II
XXVIII:VIII	II
XXIX:I	I
XXIX:II	I
XXIX:III	III
XXIX:IV	III
XXIX:V	III
XXX:I	I
XXX:II	I
XXX:III	II
XXX:IV	III
XXX:V	II
XXX:VI	I
XXX:VII	III
XXX:VIII	III
XXX:IX	II
XXX:X	II
XXXI:I	I
XXXI:II	I
XXXI:III	I
XXXI:IV	I
XXXI:V	II
XXXI:VI	II
XXXI:VII	II
XXXI:VIII	III
XXXI:I	II
XXXI:X	II
XXXI:X	II
XXXI:XII	II
XXXI:XIII	II
XXXI:XIV	II
XXXII:I	I
XXXII:II	III (But this passage is continuous with the following, which does carry out the requirements of form I.,)
XXXII:III	I
XXXII:IV	II
XXXII:V	II
XXXII:VI	II
XXXII:VII	II
XXXII:VIII	II
XXXII:IX	II
XXXII:X.1	This is a story tacked on to the base verse.
XXXII:X.2-5	II
XXXIII:I.1-3	I
XXXIII:I.4-5	Stories inserted on account of thematic relevance.
XXXIII:I.6	I. What we have in XXXIII:I is a composite of materials, in which Nos. 1, 6 really do follow the identified form; the rest of the compositions at hand have been inserted

for essentially thematic reasons. From a formal viewpoint they are miscellaneous.

XXXIII:II	I
XXXIII:III.1	I. Here too we have an inserted complex of stories, Nos. 2-6.
XIII:III.7-9	II
XXXIII:IV	II
XXXIII:V	II (No. 4 appends a story.)
XXXIII:VI	II
XXXIII:VII	The base verse serves as a peg on which to cite a passage of the Mishnah. But the passage does contribute to the exegesis of the base verse, and the composite as a whole serves that one purpose and entirely falls into the formal classification at hand.

XXXIV:I	I
XXXIV:II	I
XXXIV:III	I
XXXIV:IV	I
XXXIV:V	I
XXXIV:VI	I. In these several cases, the intersecting verse is not substantially amplified or explained, but only declared to speak about Noah. So we cannot cite the present items as good examples of the form at hand.
XXXIV:VII	II
XXXIV:VIII	II
XXXIV:IX	II
XXXIV:X.1	III
XXXIV:X.2	II
XXXIV:X.3	III
XXXIV:XI	II
XXXIV:XII	II
XXXIV:XIII	II
XXXIV:XIV	III. The passage expounds the laws governing gentiles ("children of Noah") and is in no way narrowly exegetical, let alone formally so.
XXXIV:XV	III

XXXV:I	II
XXXV:II	II, III. While the passage begins with an observation on the meaning of the verse, it moves on to a general thesis.
XXXV:III.1	II
XXXV:III.2	A. The protracted composit-ion bears no relationship to the context.

XXXVI:I	I
XXXVI:II	II
XXXVI:III	II. Note that XXXVI:III.3 presents a proposition, so too No. 5. The remainder follow a fairly standard exegetical form. I further see no formal differences between the syllogistic and the exegetical entries. The form is consistent throughout: citation of a verse, comment on the verse. So what appears to fall into syllogistic form does so only because of the origin of the verses that are cited.
XXXVI:IV	II
XXXVI:V	II
XXXVI:VI	II
XXXVI:VII	II
XXXVI:VIII	II. This composite contains propositional and not exegetical materials, as well as stories, but begins in an appropriately formal manner.

XXXVII:I	II
XXXVII:II,1	II
XXXVII:II,2	I
XXXVII:III	III
XXXVII;IV	II
XXXVII:V	II
XXXVII:VI	II
XXXVII:VII	II
XXXVII:VIII	II

XXXVIII:I	I
XXXVIII:II	I
XXXVIII:III	I
XXXVIII:IV	I
XXXVIII:V	I
XXXVIII:VI	II
XXXVIII:VII	II
XXXVIII:VIII	II
XXXVIII:IX.1	III. This is one of ten passages that refer, etc.
XXXVIII:IX.2-5	II
XXXVIII:X	III
XXXVIII:XI	II
XXXVIII:XII	III
XXXVIII:XIII	II. But what we have is not an exegesis of the verse. Rather it is a protracted and powerful story. But the upshot is to explain the wording and sense of the verse. So from a redactional viewpoint the composition is in good exegetical form, that is to say, citation of a verse plus an explanation of the verse. But ordinarily the explanation is cast not as a

story but as a general
remark.
XXXVIII:XIV.1 II
XXXVIII:XIV.2 III

XXXIX:I   I
XXXIX:II   I
XXXIX:III   I
XXXIX:IV   I. But here the intersecting
               verse is not spelled out,
               only applied to the matter at
               hand.
XXXIX:V   I
XXXIX:VI   I
XXXIX:VII   II
XXXIX:VIII.1 II
XXXIX:VIII.2, 3 I
XXXIX:IX   II
XXXIX:X   III. But the main point is to
               explain a matter having to
               do with the base verse. The
               composite on its own is
               syllogistic.
XXXIX:XI.1-3, 6-10 II
XXXIX:XI.4-5 III
XXXIX:XII.1-2 III
XXXIX:XII.3-5 II
XXXIX:XIII   II
XXXIX:XIV   II
XXXIX:XV   II
XXXIX:XVI   II

XL:I   I
XL:II   I
XL:III   III. Catalogue of ten items.
XL:IV.1, 2   II
XL:IV.3   III
XL:V   II
XL:VI   III. The exposition of the
               base verse makes the point
               that Abraham sets an
               example for Israel later on.
               This is a fine example of the
               form associated with
               syllogistic argument, with
               its indicative characteristic
               of a long catalogue of facts
               (verses of Scripture).

XLI:I   I
XLI:II   II
XLI:III   II
XLI:IV   III. The composition is not
               particular to the cited base
               verse but makes a more
               general point.
XLI:V   II
XLI:VI   II
XLI:VII   II
XLI:VIII   II
XLI:IX   II
XLI:X   III. The verse of Scripture is
               joined to a passage of the
               Mishnah's law. The verse

then serves as a proof text
for the Mishnah's law's
proposition.

XLII:I   I
XLII:II   I
XLII:III   III. This is a syllogistic
               composition of the most
               impressive sort.
XLII:IV   II
XLII:V   II
XLII:VI   II
XLII:VII   I
XLII:VIII   II

XLIII:I   I. But there is no
               systematic exposition of the
               intersecting verse.
XLIII:II.1   I. As above.
XLIII:II.2-5   II
XLIII:III   II. But not all the entries
               conform to the simple
               exegetical form, which
               dictates citing a verse and
               making a comment on it.
               Some of the entries, e.g,
               Nos. 4, 5, cite other verses
               and then show how they
               clarify the base verse. This
               is not the same form that we
               have called exegetical.
XLIII:IV   II
XLIII:V   II

Note that Theodor-Albeck treat
XLIII:VIff. as a new *parashah* . That
division will be important when we take
up the question of the order of the types
of units of discourse.

XLIII:VI.1   I
XLIII:VI.2-6 II
XLIII:VII   II
XLIII:VIII   II
XLIII:IX   II

XLIV:I   I
XLIV:II   I
XLIV:III   I
XLIV:IV   II
XLIV:V   II
XLIV:VI   III
XLIV:VII   II
XLIV:VIII   III
XLIV:IX   III
XLIV:X   II
XLIV:XI   II
XLIV:XII.1-3 II
XLIV:XII.4   III
XLIV:XIII   II
XLIV:XIV   II
XLIV:XV   II
XLIV:XVI   II

XLIV:XVII.1-3 III
XLIV:XVII.4 II
XLIV:XVIII II
XLIV:XIX II
XLIV:XX II
XLIV:XXI II
XLIV:XXII II
XLIV:XIII II

XLV:I.1   I. Here again the inters-ecting verse receives only a casual exposition. It is cited and immediately brawn into relationship with the base verse. So the form is not so disciplined as one might expect.

XLV:II.2-5 II
XLV:II II
XLV:III II
XLV:IV II
XLV:V.1-3, 5-6 II
XLV:V.4 III
XLV:VI II
XLV:VII II
XLV:VIII III
XLV:IX II
XLV:X.1 III
XLV:X.2-3 II

XLVI:I I
XLVI:II I
XLVI:III II
XLVI:IV II
XLVI:V   III. The syllogism bears an eexegetical relevant to the base verse, but there is no resort to exegetical form. Nor does the composition conform to the syllogism-form, for that matter.

XLVI:VI II
XLVI:VII III
XLVI:VIII III
XLVI:I III
XLVI:X III
XLVI:XI   III. The cited verse serves as a proof text for what is to follow, a rule of the Tannaite authority at hand.
XLVI:XII   III. As above.
XLVI:XIIIII

XLVII:I.1 I
XLVII:I.2 II
XLVII:II II
XLVII:III II
XLVII:IV II
XLVII:;V II
XLVII:VI   III. The cited verse serves as a proof text, as above.
XLVII:VII II
XLVII:VIII II
XLVII:IX II

XLVII:X   III. The cited verse serves as a proof text, as above.

XLVIII:I I
XLVIII:II II
XLVIII:III I
XLVIII:IV   I. But as is not uncommon, the intersecting verse by itself does not receive an sustained exegesis. It is cited in clarification of the base verse.
XLVIII:V   I. As above.
XLVIII:VI I
XLVIII:VII II
XLVIII:VIII II
XLVIII:IX II
XLVIII:X   II. To call No. 2 merely exegetical hardly does justice to its sustained and substantial argument, which is formally well-disciplined. It must be regarded as an unusual example of the syllogism-form.
XLVIII:XII III
XLVIII:XI.2-4 II
XLVIII:XII II
XLVIII:XIII II
XLVIII:XIV.1, 2-4 III, II
XLVIII:XV II
XLVIII:XVI II
XLVIII:XVII II
XLVIII:XVIII III
XLVIII:XIX II
XLVIII:XX III

XLIX:I I
XLIX:II II
XLIX:III II
XLIX:IV II
XLIX:V II
XLIX:VI.1 III
XLIX;VI.2-4 II
XLIX:VII III
XLIX:VIII II
XLIX:IX II
XLIX:X   I. Two intersecting verses are adduced to cast light on the base verse, but the intersecting verses do not undergo substantial exegetical development.
XLIX:XI II
XLIX:XII II
XLIX:XIII II
XLIX:XIV II

L:I I
L:II.1   How to classify this item is not obvious. L:II.1 starts with the base verse, cites the intersecting verse, and then introduces a Tannaite

teaching, concluding with the base verse. If the writer has followed the dictates of a formal pattern, I cannot show it.

L:II.2-3	II
L:III	II
L:IV	II
L:V	II
L:VI	II
L:VII	II
L:VIII	II
L:IX	II
L:X	II
L:XI	II
L:XII	II
LI:I	I
LI:II	II
LI:III.1-3	I
LI:III.4	II
LI:IV	II
LI:V	II
LI:VI	II
LI:VII	II (?)
LI:VIII	II
LI:IX	III
LI:X	III
LI:XI	II
LII:I	I
LII:II	I
LII:III	I
LII:IV	II
LII:V	III
LII:VI	II
LII:VII	II
LII:VIII	II
LII:IX	II
LII:X	II
LII:XI.1	III. After the base verse is cited, a Tannaite teaching is introduced, for which the base verse serves as a proof-text.
LII:XII	II
LII:XIII	II
LIII:I	I
LIII:II	I
LIII:III	I
LIII:IV.1-2	I. In several of these instances the intersecting verse is not systematically spelled out.
LIII:IV.3	III
LIII:V	I. As above.
LIII:VI	II
LIII:VII	II
LIII:VIII	II
LIII:IX	II
LIII:X	II
LIII:XI	II
LIII:XII	II

LIII:XIII	II
LIII:XIV.1	Two intersecting verses are cited, but neither is then brought into juxtaposition with the base verse. Formally we do not have the exegetical pattern, but the net effect is to clarify the materials at hand.
LIII:;XIV.2-4	II
LIII:XV	III, II
LIV:I	I
LIV:II	II
LIV:III	III
LIV:IV	II
LIV:V	II
LIV:VI	II
LV:I	I
LV:II	III
LV:III.1	I. But the intersecting verse is not worked out, simply expounded by being set in juxtaposition to the base verse.
LV:III.2	III
LV:IV	II
LV:V	II
LV:VI	II
LV:VII	II
LV:VIII.1	III
LV:VIII.2-5	II
LVI:I	II
LVI:II	II
LVI:III	II
LVI:IV	II
LVI:V	II
LVI:VI	II
LVI:VII	II
LVI:VIII	II
LVI:IX	II
LVI:X	II
LVI:XI	II
LVII:I	I. As before, the inter-secting verse clarifies the base verse, so the formal pattern belies the substantive effect, which is exegetical in a limited sense.
LVII:II	I. As above.
LVII:III	II
LVII:IV.1	I. As Above. Note that No. 2 is simply a long essay on Job, falling into classifica-tion A.
LVIII:I	I
LVIII:II	III
LVIII:III	II
LVIII:IV	II

LVIII:V	II
LVIII:VI	II
LVIII:VII	II
LVIII:VIII	II
LVIII:IX	I
LIX:I	I
LIX:II	I
LIX:III	I
LIX:IV	I
LIX:V	II
LIX:VI	II
LIX:VII	II
LIX:VIII	II
LIX:IX	II
LIX:X	II
LIX:XI	II
LIX:XII	II
LX:I	I
LX:II	II
LX:III	III
LX:IV	III
LX:V.1	III
LX:V.2-3	II
LX:VI	II
LX:VII	III
LX:VIII	II
LX:IX	II
LX:X	II
LX:XI	II
LX:XII	II
LX:XIII	II
LX:XIV	II
LX:XV	II
LX:XVI	II
LXI:I	I
LXI:II	I

LXI:III   II. The verse under discussion does not, however, derive from the book of Genesis. The composition bears a number of illustrative stories. So while the form is reasonably close to the exegetical one, the passage does not constitute an apt example.

LXI:IV	II
LXI:V	II
LXI:VI	II

LXI:VII   A. This item consists of a citation of the base-verse followed by a long story that is attached here because the base-verse recurs in it. I see no form, otherwise used in our document, to which the present composition is to be compared.

LXII:I	I
LXII:II.1	III

LXII:II.2-8   A. The general theme is dealt with through a sequence of exegeses of verses and stories about sages.

LXII:II.9	II
LXII:III	II
LXII:IV	III
LXII:V	II
LXIII:I	I

LXIII:II   III or I. What I see here is a syllogism, dealing with the theme of the base verse. But one may well discern a rather poor example of the intersecting verse-base verse form.

LXIII:III	III
LXIII:IV	II
LXIII:V	I
LXIII:VI	II
LXIII:VII	III
LXIII:VIII	II
LXIII:IX	II
LXIII:X	II
LXIII:XI	II
LXIII:XII.1	III
LXIII:XII.2-4	II
LXIII:XIII	II
LXIII:XIV	II
LXIV:I	I
LXIV:II.1-2	I
LXIV:II.3	III
LXIV:III	II
LXIV:IV	II
LXIV:V	III
LXIV:VI	II
LXIV:VII	II
LXIV:VIII	II
LXIV:IX	II

LXIV:X   II. Note that No. 3 is an inserted story. But otherwise the form is followed.

LXV:I	I
LXV:II	I
LXV:III	I
LXV:IV	II
LXV:V	I
LXV:VI	I
LXV:VII	I
LXV:VIII	I

LXV:IX   III. This passage makes its own point, drawing on diverse materials. But it is not formally syllogistic, in that the verses are not composed into a syntactically uniform list.

LXV:X	II
LXV:XI	II
LXV:XII	III

LXV:XIII	II
LXV:XIV	I
LXV:XV	II
LXV:XVI	II
LXV:XVII	II
LXV:XVIII	II
LXV:XIX	II
LXV:XX	II
LXV:XXI.1, 3	II
LXV:XXI.2	III
LXV:XXII	II
LXV:XXIII	III

LXVI:I	I
LXVI:II	I
LXVI:III	II
LXVI:IV	II
LXVI:V	II
LXVI:VI	Not in text.
LXVI:VII	I

LXVII:I	I
LXVII:II	II
LXVII:	IIIII
LXVII:IV	III
LXVII:V	II
LXVII:VI	II
LXVII:VII	II
LXVII:VIII	II
LXVII:IX	II
LXVII:X	II
LXVII:XI	II
LXVII:XII	II
LXVII:XIII	II

LXVIII:I	I
LXVIII:II	I
LXVIII:III	I
LXVIII:IV	I. Continues the preceding.
LXVIII:V	II
LXVIII:VI	III
LXVIII:VII	II
LXVIII:VIII	II
LXVIII:IX.	III
LXVIII:X	II
LXVIII:XI	II

LXVIII:XII.1-4 A. The syllogism is followed by a set of stories, and the whole in no way conforms to syllogistic form.
LXVIII:XII.5-8 II
LXVIII:XIII II
LXVIII:3-LXVIII:XIII form a single enormous exegesis of the base verse in terms of a sequence of intersecting verses. But the latter in no way form the subject of exegesis. In consequence we have to treat the whole as a rather sizable exercise in the interpretation of the base verse alone.

LXIX:I	I
LXIX:II	I
LXIX:III	II
LXIX:IV.1	III
LXIX:IV.2	II
LXIX:V	II
LXIX:VI	II
LXIX:VII	II
LXIX:VIII	II

LXX:I	I
LXX:II	III
LXX:III	III
LXX:IV	II
LXX:V	II
LXX:VI	III
LXX:VII	II

LXX:VIII-IX II Here again we have a vast exercise in interpreting the base verse in line with a sequence of other verses. But the other verses are not spelled out, but provide only proof-texts for the inter-pretation of the base verse. On that basis we cannot identify the present enormous composition with form I.

LXX:X	II
LXX:XI	II
LXX:XII.1,3-5	II
LXX:XII.2	III
LXX:XIII	II
LXX:XIV	II
LXX:XV	II
LXX:XVI	II
LXX:XVII	II
LXX:XVIII	II
LXX:XIX	II
LXX:XX	II

LXXI:I	I
LXXI:II.1	I
LXXI:II.2-7	II
LXXI:III	III
LXXI:IV	II
LXXI:V	III
LXXI:VI	II, III
LXXI:VII	I, II
LXXI:VIII	II
LXXI:IX	II
LXXI:X	II

LXXII:I	I
LXXII:II	II
LXXII:III	II

LXXII:IV III Citation of the base verse followed by a Mishnah-paragraph. But the purpose is to clarify the latter.
LXXII:V II
LXXII:VI II

LXXIII:I	I
LXXIII:II	II
LXXIII:III	III Here again the intersecting verse is simply read in terms of the topic or theme of the base verse.
LXXIII:IV	II
LXXIII:V.1	III
LXXIII:.V.2	II
LXXIII:VI	II
LXXIII:VII	II
LXXIII:VIII	II
LXXIII:IX	II
LXXIII:X	II
LXXIII:XI	II
LXXIII:XII	II
LXXIV:I	I
LXXIV:II	III
LXXIV:III	II
LXXIV:IV	II
LXXIV:V	II As above, the intersecting verse is simply read in terms of the base verse. In this case the context is a set of exegesis of the base verse, and it is difficult to regard the present passage as other than an exegetical one, following the rough form we have ready identified.
LXXIV:VI	II
LXXIV:VII	III
LXXIV:VIII	I
LXXIV:IX	II
LXXIV:X	III
LXXIV:XI	II
LXXIV:XII	III
LXXIV:XIII	II
LXXIV:XIV.1	III
LXXIV:XIV.2-3	II
LXXIV:XV	II, III
LXXIV:XVI	II
LXXIV:XVII	II
LXXV:I	I
LXXV:II	I
LXXV:III	I
LXXV:IV	II
LXXV:V	II
LXXV:VIII	I
LXXV:IX	II
LXXV:X	II
LXXV:XI	II
LXXV:VI	II
LXXV:VII	II
LXXV:XII	II
LXXV:XIII	II
LXXVI:I	I
LXXVI:II	II
LXXVI:III	III
LXXVI:IV	II

LXXVI:V	II
LXXVI:VI	I
LXXVI:VII	II
LXXVI:VIII	III. Here we have a story attached to the verse. The story alludes in one detail to the contents of the verse. It is easy to explain the redactional principle that has motivated the inclusion of the story, less so to classify the composition as a whole.
LXXVI:IX	II
LXXVII:I	I
LXXVII:II	II
LXXVII:III	II
LXXVIII:I	I. Nos. 1-2 pursue the same object. No. 3 then is appended because it is relevant in theme. No. 4 is an independent composition inserted because of its thematic relevance. So only the opening part of the composite conforms to the theoretical form in service here.
LXXVIII:II	II
LXXVIII:III.1	III
LXXVIII:III.2-3	II
LXXVIII:IV	II
LXXVIII:V	II
LXXVIII:VI	II. The continuation of the passage is not formally congruent.
LXXVIII:VII	II
LXXVIII:VIII	II
LXXVIII:IX	III
LXXVIII:X	II
LXXVIII:XI	II
LXXVIII:XII	II. The continuation of the passage at Nos. 4-5 is made up of stories relevant in theme but not congruent in form.
LXXVIII:XIII	II
LXXVIII:XIV	II
LXXVIII:XV	II
LXXVIII:XVI	II
LXXIX:I	I
LXXIX:II	II. The requirements of the intersecting verse-base verse form, involving a protracted exegesis of the intersecting verse, are not met here.
LXXIX:III	I
LXXIX:IV	II
LXXIX:VI.1, 2, 4	II. No. 3, a story, is appended as an illustration of No. 2.
LXXIX:VII.1-2	III

LXXIX::VII.3 II
LXXIX:VIII II

LXXX:I   A. While the composition begins by citing a base verse and then an intersecting verse, what follows is a story, which, only at the end, refers to the intersecting verse, and, in conclusion, the base verse as well. It would be stretching matters to claim that the passage conforms in more than a general way to the form at hand.
LXXX:II   I
LXXX:III   I
LXXX:IV   II
LXXX:V   II
LXXX:VI   II
LXXX:VII   III
LXXX:VIII   II
LXXX:IX   A. A Tannaite rule is cited in relationship to the base verse.
LXXX:X   II
LXXX:XI   II
LXXX:XII   II

LXXXI:I   I
LXXXI:II   A. After citation of a verse unrelated to the passage at hand, a story is introduced to illustrate the point of the passage as interpreted. Yet another interpretation of the same intersecting verse is given. At the end, however, the main point of the base verse is spelled out. If we had only the intersecting verse as dealt with in No. 3 plus the reversion to the base verse in No. 4, the whole would conform nicely to the requirements of form I.
LXXXI:III.1   II. The sense of the base verse is clarified by citation of a Mishnah-rule.
LXXXI:III.2   II
LXXXI:IV   II
LXXXI:V   II

LXXXII:I   I
LXXXII:II   I
LXXXII:III   II
LXXXII:IV   II
LXXXII:V   II
LXXXII:VI.1/2   III/II.
LXXXII:VII   II
LXXXII:VIII   A. After the base verse is cited, a story is told, in which the base verse figures. The base verse is explained. But there is no formal relationship between this composition and the exegetical form.
LXXXII:IX   II
LXXXII:X   II
LXXXII:XI   III
LXXXII:XII   II
LXXXII:XIII   II
LXXXII:XIV.1   II
LXXXII:XIV, 2, 3   A. No. 2 cites the base verse and attaches a Tannaite statement. No. 3 pursues its own program, out of all relationship to the passage at hand. It may well serve to exemplify form III, though this is not self-evident. In my view all we have is a thematic composition of miscellaneous formal traits.

LXXXIII:I   I
LXXXIII:II   I
LXXXIII:III   II
LXXXIII:IV   II
LXXXIII:V   This little tale makes its point quite clearly. But I see no classification at hand applicable to its formal traits.

LXXXIV:I   I
LXXXIV:II   I. Both entries invoke the intersecting verse to clarify the theme of the base verse, but neither provides an extensive exegesis of the intersecting verse.
LXXXIV:III   II
LXXXIV:IV   II
LXXXIV:V   II
LXXXIV:VI   II
LXXXIV:VII   II
LXXXIV:VIII   II
LXXXIV:IX   II
LXXXIV:X   II
LXXXIV:XI   II
LXXXIV:XII   II
LXXXIV:XIII   II
LXXXIV:XIV   II
LXXXIV:XV   II
LXXXIV:XVI   II
LXXXIV:XVII   II
LXXXIV:XVIII   II
LXXXIV:XIX   II
LXXXIV:XXII   II
LXXXIV:XXI   II
LXXXIV:XXII   II

LXXXV:I	I. We have a set of four exercises in the application of an intersecting verse to the base verse. In all four instances the application of the diverse intersecting verses is critical, and the exegesis of those verses routine and desultory.
LXXXV:II	III. Nos. 2-6 provide exegeses in the model of No. 1's, and only No. 1 pertains to the base verse. The entire composition serves to explain the redactional principle operative in Scripture throughout, not the passage at hand. On that basis, from the perspective of the composition as a whole, we have to classify the passage as an excellent example of form III.
LXXXV:III	II
LXXXV:IV	II
XXXV:V	II. But note that beyond the brief explanation of the base verse we have a Tannaite teaching. Then No. 2 in no way relates to No. 1 except in theme. Nos. 3, 4, 5 fall into the classification of exegetical compositions, pure and simple.
LXXXV:VI	II
LXXXV:VII	II
LXXXV:VIII	II
LXXXV:IX	II
LXXXV:X	III
LXXXV:XI	II
LXXXV:XII	III
LXXXV:XIII	II
LXXXV:XIV	II
LXXXVI:I	I. The intersecting verse is not spelled out but simply applied to the base verse.
LXXXVI:II	II
LXXXVI:III	II
LXXXVI:IV	II
LXXXVI:V	II
LXXXVI:VI	II
LXXXVII:I	I. As above.
LXXXVII:II	I. As above, the exegesis of the intersecting verse is principally in relationship to the base verse.
LXXXVII:III	I
LXXXVII:IV	II
LXXXVII:V	II
LXXXVII:VI	II. There are other verses adduced in explanation of the base verse. But the context is entirely exegetical, unlike those items classified with form I.
LXXXVII:VII	II
LXXXVII:VIII	II
LXXXVII:IX	II
LXXXVII:X	II
LXXXVIII:I	I
LXXXVIII:II	II
LXXXVIII:III	II
LXXXVIII:IV	II
LXXXVIII:V	II
LXXXVIII:VI	III
LXXXVIII:VII	II
LXXXIX:I	I
LXXXIX:II	I
LXXXIX:III	I
LXXXIX:IV	II
LXXXIX:V	II
LXXXIX: VI	II
LXXXIX:VII	II
LXXXIX:VIII	A. After the citation of the base verse, all we have is a formal miscellany on the theme of the base verse.
LXXXIX:IX	II
XC:I	I
XC:II	II
XC:III	II
XC:IV	II
XC:V	II
XC:VI	II
XCI:I.1-3	I
XCI:I.4	II
XCI:II	II
XCI:III	A. The passage is totally unrelated to the exegesis of a verse in Scripture.
XCI:IV	II. Note that the order in Theodor Albeck is different from the order presented here.
XCI:V	II
XCI:VI	II
XCI:VII	I
XCI:VIII	II
XCI:IX.1	No formal pattern I can discern.
XCI:IX.2-6	II
XCI:X	II
XCI:XI	II
XCII:I	I
XCII:II	I. But this composition does not conform to the requirements of the established pattern.
XCII:III	II
XCII:IV	II
XCII:V	II

XCII:VI	A. After the citation of the base verse, we have a story.	C:II	II. Then there is appended a sizable complement of materials of a non-exegetical character.
XCII:VII	III		
XCII:VIII	II	C:III	III
XCII:IX	II	C:IV	II
		C:V	II
XCIII:I	I	C:VI	II
XCIII:II	I	C:VII	A
XCIII:III	I. But the classification is at best conjectural.	C:VIII	II
		C:IX	II
XCIII:IV	I	C:X	III
XCIII:V	I	C:XI	II
XCIII:VI	II		
XCIII:IX	II		
XCIII:X	II		
XCIII:VII	II		
XCIII:VIII	II		
XCIII:XI	II		
XCIII:XII	II		
XCIV:I	I		
XCIV:II	II		
XCIV:III	II		
XCIV:V	II. But I see no conformity to the simplest requirements of form II.		
XCIV:VI	II		
XCIV:VII	II		
XCIV:VIII	II		
XCIV:IX	II		
XCV:I	I		
XCV:II	II		
XCV:III	II		
XCV:IV	II		
XCVI:I	III		
XCVI:II	I		
XCVI:III	I		
XCVI:IV	II		
XCVI:V	II		
XCVII:I	I		
XCVII:II	II		
XCVII:III	III		
XCVII:IV	II		
XCVII:V	II		
XCVIII:I	I		
XCVIII:II	II		
XCVIII:III	II		
XCVIII:IV	II		
XCVIII:V	II		
XCVIII:VI	II		
XCVIII:VII	II		
XCIX:I	I		
XCIX:II	III		
XCIX:III	II		
XCIX:IV	II		
C:I	I		

iii. The Order of Types of Units of Discourse in Genesis Rabbah

My translation of Genesis Rabbah systematically pursues the question of the place of the arrangers or redactors of the document in the formulation of the materials in hand. The single and uniform answer emerged: the work of formulating completed units of thought came prior to, and was separate from, the work of arranging those compositions into the larger document we now have in hand. That is why, at the present stage of our work, we turn forthwith to the classification of the units of discourse of the document and asked about whether, and how, they may be identified in terms of their recurrent literary and syntactic traits. We were able to investigate the extent to which patterns external to the meaning of what the authors wished to convey dictated the formulation of the authors' ideas. We have now to ask the correlative question about the ordering of the several forms of units of discourse. Let me now spell out the question in hand.

When the organizers or compositors of Genesis Rabbah turned their attention to the lay-out of their materials, they confronted at least three types of patterned compositions. We now wish to know whether, in arranging their materials, they made reference to these formal classifications of units of discourse. We want to know whether the classification-scheme of formulating ideas into compositions, which they evidently followed, also dictated to them the rule by which in the work of aggregation and large-scale organization one unit would take precedence over some other. Will a given form appear in a particular position in a cogent or substantively coherent sequence of units of discourse, e.g., always first, always last, or always in the middle? Or do the compositors ignore the types of units of discourse in arranging their verse-by-verse exegesis of the book of Genesis? So we want to know what difference, if any, the distinction between one formal and patterned syntactic construction and another actually made. Once more, in Smith's question, what difference does a difference make?

Each of the specified theses requires investigation in its own terms. The one involves considerations not only of the order of verses of the book of Scripture subjected to exegesis but also of the formal traits of the available units of thought. The other, the simpler, takes account only of the relevance of a given composition to a verse of Scripture. All things then are ordered solely (or mainly) by the criterion of the substantive requirements of the exegesis of verses of Scripture, in their given order.

The second of the two theories of redaction is the simpler. So we take it up first. In accord with the latter -- organization not in terms of the three formal types of units of discourse but without reference to the literary traits of the units of discourse to be ordered -- aesthetic or literary considerations take second place behind narrowly exegetical ones. How so? Editors interested principally in laying out their ideas on the meaning of the text by stating in regard to a given verse the main point they wish to make about that verse will ignore such traits of the materials in hand as pronounced formal characteristics. The dominant consideration will be the requirements of the exegesis of the verse at hand. The editors then will select a passage for insertion in a particular position, as defined by the sequence of verses, without regard to the literary traits of that passage. All that will interest them is conformity to the order of the verses of Scripture.

The first of the two theories, if followed, will impose a complex requirement on the ultimate arrangers of the units of discourse. They propose to create an exegesis of a book of the Hebrew Scriptures. But, in doing so, they also wish to call into play the aesthetic criteria which have governed the formulation of a given composition (or, at least, the definitive traits of formulation, e.g., at the beginning of the exercise in hand). In accord with the present theory of redaction -- organization not solely in terms of the order of verses of Scripture but also in terms of the three formal types of units of discourse, with reference to the literary traits of the units of hand -- considerations of form play a role. Editors with an interest in literary-formal as well as exegetical redaction of available materials then will choose a composition falling into one formal classification in preference to a composition belonging in some other. What will tell them to choose one over the other? It will be a theory of what is appropriate form for a given position in a large-scale composite. Thus they will choose a composition that falls into classification I for the beginning, middle, or end of their large-scale aggregations of completed units of thought, so too (in accord with the present theory) one of classification II or III.

Before we proceed to our exercise, I have to define one category just now introduced, namely, the notion of a beginning, middle, and end of a cogent or substantively coherent composition. Since that conception forms the foundation of the inquiry into the ordering of the forms of units of discourse, I have now to explain it. The book of Genesis validates the thesis that a sequence of compositions has a beginning, middle, and end. Why? Because the book of Genesis itself is made up of stories with beginnings, middles, and ends. The narrative of the book is not continuous; rather it is accomplished by the joining together of completed narratives. The marks of joining proved self-evident not only to scholars in modern times but also to the exegetes of the book of Genesis in Genesis Rabbah. We noticed how they repeatedly asked what one story has to do with some other, or why one story is told before some other. The premise of such a question is that one story is internally harmonious but distinct from the others, fore and aft, that define its setting. We hardly claim a great deal, therefore, in alleging that all materials relevant to a given passage -- a tale, a discussion of genealogy, a set of blessings, and the like -- form a continuous discourse, with a clearly defined beginning, middle, and end. How shall we, for our part, then designate beginnings and endings? For the purpose of this initial, therefore necessarily primitive, exercise in analysis and differentiation, I have chosen to follow the lines of division imposed by those copyists and printers who have given us the major divisions of our document into one hundred *parashiyyot*. Hence, for the present purpose, the beginning of a *parashah* will also indicate the beginning of a cogent discussion of a verse or a set of verses of the book of Genesis. Naturally, the end of a cogent set of verses -- hence, of an exegetical unit -- will be defined as well. So, to conclude, when I speak of a position at the beginning, middle, or ending of a cogent discussion, I believe the internal evidence of the documents under discussion -- both the book of Genesis and Genesis Rabbah as well -- validate my doing so.

Inductive evidence, already laid out in section ii of this chapter, allows us to settle the question of which of the two theories of ultimate redaction -- ordering of forms of units of discourse -- governed the work of the framers of Genesis Rabbah. The issue is very simple. Is it common for form I to stand at the beginning, middle, or end of a sequence of units of thought on a given verse or set of verses? Is it common for form II or for form III to stand in one or another of these same fixed positions? And, finally, does the document as a whole yield evidence of a uniform policy, or do we find indifference to the matter of the ordering of forms of the classifications we have identified? The matter will be settled very simply. If units of discourse of form I ordinarily come at the beginning, then as a matter of policy the framers invoked the first of the two criteria of ordering and redaction I have spelled out -- at least so far as form I is concerned. And if units of discourse of form I make their appearance promiscuously, at the beginning, middle, or end, of a sequence of coherent units of thought, then the second of the two criteria has governed the work. The same considerations of course affect forms II and III. The following charts settle the question.

Coherent sequences of units of discourse in which form I stands at the head

A. *Only a single example of form I heads these units of discourse*

II
IV
V
VII
XI
XIV
XVI
XIX
XX
XXII
XXIII
XXVIII
XXXVI
XLI
XLV
XLVII
XLVIII
XLIX
L
LI
LIV
LV
LVIII
LX
LXII
LXIII [?]
LXVII
LXX
LXXII
LXXIII
LXXIV
LXXVI
LXXVII
LXXVIII
LXXIX
LXXXI
LXXXV
LXXXVI
LXXXVIII
XC
XCI
XCIV
XCV
XCVII
XCVIII
XCIX
C

B. *Two or more examples of form I head these units of discourse*

I
III
VI
VIII
IX
X
XII

XXI
XXIV
XXVI
XXVII
XXIX
XXX
XXXI
XXXII
XXXIII
XXXIV
XXXVIII
XXXIX
XL
XLII
XLIII
XLVI
LII
LIII
LVII
LIX
LXI
LXIV
LXV
LXVI
LXVIII
LXIX
LXXI
LXXV
LXXXII
LXXXIII
LXXXIV
LXXXVII
LXXXIX
XCII
XCIII

Coherent sequences of units of discourse in which form II stands at the head

XIII
XV
XXV
XXXV
XXXVII
LVI

Coherent sequences of units of discourse in which form III stands at the head

XCVI

Coherent sequences of units of discourse in which a formally-miscellaneous composite (form A) stands at the head

XVII
XVIII
LXXX

The upshot may be simply stated:

Coherent sequences of units of discourse in which form
   I stands at the head 89%

   A. *Only a single example of form I heads these units of*
      discourse 47%

   B. *Two or more examples of form I head these units of*
      discourse 42%

Coherent sequences of units of discourse in which form
   II stands at the head 6%

Coherent sequences of units of discourse in which form
   III stands at the head 1%

Coherent sequences of units of discourse in which a
   formally-miscellaneous composite (form A) stands
   at the head 3%

The policy of the ultimate redactors dictated the choice of a form I unit of discourse for the beginning of a sustained discussion of a single cogent passage. What struck the compositors as important was not formal traits internal to the passage. How do we know it? Because a composition in which an intersecting verse was systematically worked out and only at the end brought into juxtaposition with the base verse -- which, standing outside, we should regard as a more compelling and subtle mode of discourse -- enjoyed no priority. The compositors could readily choose a simpler version of the intersecting verse-base verse form, in which the intersecting verse served, all by itself, as an exposition of the base verse. The nearly equal representation of both subdivisions of the classification at hand tells us that what mattered was the simple fact of the presence of an intersecting verse. Whether or not the language "opened" was used does not seem to have mattered very much.

Since the identification of "the middle" raises imprecise considerations, we shall skip that matter entirely and turn directly to the third of the three positions in a large scale composition. We ordinarily can identify the point at which one sequence of verses, or one cogent exposition of a theme, reaches its conclusion and another commences. So we ask whether a given formal form of unit of discourse ordinary will enjoy the preference of the ultimate organizers of the document as a whole, classification I, II, III, or the miscellaneous composites grouped as form A.

Coherent sequences of units of discourse in which form I stands at the end

LVII
LVIII
LXVI

Coherent sequences of units of discourse in which form II stands at the end

IV
VI
VI
XI
XII
XIII
XIV
XV
XVI
XX
XXII
XXIV
XXVI
XXVII
XXVIII
XXX
XXXI
XXXII
XXXVI
XXXVII
XXXIX
XLII
XLIII
XLIII [second set]
XLIV
XLV
XLVI
XLIX
L
LI
LII
LIII
LIV
LV
LVI
LIX
LX
LXII
LXIII
LXIV
LXXIV
LXXV
LXXVI
LXXVII
LXXVIII
LXXIX
LXXX
LXXXI
LXXXIV
LXXXV
LXXXVI
LXXXVII

LXXXVII
LXXXVIII
LXXXIX
XC
XCI
XCII
XCIII
XCIV
XCXV
XCXVI
XCVII
XCVIII
XCIX

Coherent sequences of units of discourse in which form III stands at the end

I
II
III
V
VIII
XVIII
XIX
XXI
XXIII
XXV
XXIX
XXXIV
XXXVIII
XL
XLI
XLVII
XLVIII
LXV
LXVII
LXVIII
LXIX
LXX
LXXI
LXXII
LXXIII
C

Coherent sequences of units of discourse in which classification A-materials stand at the end

IX
XVII
XXXIII
XXXV
LXI
LXXXII
LXXXIII

Once more we may readily summarize the result:

Coherent sequences of units of discourse in which form
   I stands at the end 3%

Coherent sequences of units of discourse in which form
   II stands at the end 65%

Coherent sequences of units of discourse in which form
   III stands at the end 26%

Coherent sequences of units of discourse in which
   classification A-materials stand at the end 7%

The compositors favored concluding their sustained discourses materials that fall into the formal classification of form II. These materials underlined the redactional purpose of the whole, which was exegetical. We may state, therefore, that the framers of Genesis Rabbah wished to do two things.

First, they proposed to read the book of Genesis in light of other books of the Hebrew Scriptures, so underlining the unity of the Scriptures.

Second,. they planned to read the book of Genesis phrase by phrase, so emphasizing the historical progression of the tale at hand, from verse to verse, from event to event.

So the book of Genesis now presents more than a single dimension. It tells the story of things that happened. The exegetes explain the meaning of these events, adding details and making explicit the implicit, unfolding message. So, read from beginning to end, time in the beginning moved in an orderly progression. The book of Genesis also tells the laws that govern Israel"s history. These laws apply at all times and under all circumstances. Facts of history, emerging at diverse times and under various circumstances, attest to uniform and simple laws of society and of history. That is why verses of Scripture originating here, there, everywhere, all serve equally well to demonstrate the underlying rules that govern. So, read out of all historical sequence but rather as a set of exemplifications of recurrent laws, the stories of Genesis do not follow a given order, a single sequence of timely events. Time now moves in deep, not shallow, courses; time is cyclical, or, more really, time matters not at all. The long stretches of timeless rules take over. Sequential exegeses, citing and commenting on verses, classified as form II, express the former of the two dimensions, and exercises in the clarification of a verse of Genesis through the message of a verse in another book of the Scriptures altogether, on the one side, and propositional or syllogistic compositions, on the other, forms I and III, express the latter. The book of Genesis is made greater than its first reading would suggest. Hence, Genesis Rabbah, meaning (from a later angle of vision only) a greater conception of the book of Genesis, vastly expands the dimensions of the story of the creation of the world, humanity, and Israel.

iv. Conclusion: Literary Patterns of Genesis Rabbah

In the aggregate Genesis Rabbah conforms to two important literary patterns.

First of all, *forms*: we are able to classify the bulk of its completed units of thought among three forms or patterns, as specified.

Second, *the ordering of forms*: we can demonstrate that the formal types of units of discourse will be arranged in accord with a single set of preferences. The redactors preferred overall to commence discourse with forms of type I and to conclude with forms of type II.

It follows that Genesis Rabbah, viewed overall, presents an orderly, not a random and unsystematic, picture of its literary traits, both formal and redactional. Materials are formulated in accord with a limited set of patterns. They then are laid out in accord with a clearly defined set of rules of ordering types of units of discourse. We discover a dual taxonomy, one formal, the other redactional. Formally and redactionally, therefore, Genesis Rabbah conforms to patterns to be discerned through simple inductive inquiry.

True, that judgment applies overall and in general. We found a fair amount of difficulty in classifying some of the units of discourse. More important, the traits that proved indicative turned out not to characterize the whole of the compositions in which they appear. Quite to the contrary, these traits make their appearance mainly at the beginning of a sequence of substantively cogent materials. Form I, for example, with its reference to an intersecting verse followed by its treatment of the base verse, not uncommonly carried in its wake materials of a formally quite miscellaneous character. Form II still more commonly permitted characterization only in the simplest way: first comes the citation of a verse of the book of Genesis, then comes some sort of comment on that verse. Within the requirements of so simple a pattern, a variety of arrangements and formulations found ample place. Form III, to be sure, offered more striking formal traits, with its emphasis upon the construction of a list of facts to prove a given proposition. But when we came to classify our units of discourse, we asked form III to make room for materials that do not in every detail conform to the formal rules of the pattern at hand. The upshot is simple. In the cases of form II and form III, the patterns we discern find a place not in the center but at the edges of the compositions in which they occur. These forms make only a superficial, external impact on the compositions in which they occur.

Form I in this regard requires the framer of a passage to pay attention, in the expression of his ideas, to the formal requirements of the pattern with which he is working. Accordingly, form I makes a deep and internal, not only a superficial, impact on the compositions in which it occurs. Yet once we differentiate among the two versions of form I -- the one in which the intersecting verse is extensively spelled out, and only at the end brought into juxtaposition with the base verse, the other in which the intersecting versed is forthwith spelled out in its intersection with the base verse -- the picture changes. The former of the two patterns does retain the appearance of substantial impact on the formulation of the passage that exemplifies the pattern. The latter does not. Why not? Because the second of the two versions of form I turns out to be nothing other than a variation -- and only one among a great many -- of form II -- citation of a verse, comment on that verse.

Accordingly, characterizing Genesis Rabbah as formally and redactionally disciplined requires considerable qualification. First, the taxonomy of forms leaves out sizable composites, though to be sure a small proportion of the whole document. Second, the definition of the traits of well-patterned forms leaves us with the impression that only rather superficial (if therefore all the more probative) aspects of a composition came under processes of formalization. Formal patterning affected superficial, not internal, formulation of units of discourse. Third, as we have seen throughout, overall the framers of Genesis Rabbah inherited a vast amount of material which they inserted whole and without substantial revision. They tended not to intervene into the already-formulated units of discourse in hand.

This we saw, in our detailed examination in the translation, in two probative aspects. First, if irrelevant materials were joined to relevant ones, they were not removed. How do we know it? Because we have irrelevant paragraphs before us. Second, we came across vast stretches of relevant materials conforming to a broad variety of formal patterns. This is to say, materials that inductive inquiry hardly suggests conformed to recurrent patterns found an ample place in the document. Our resort to category A hardly encompasses the bulk of evidence for that proposition.

But these judgments, standing by themselves, prove only suggestive. They will prove useful only when subjected to the scrutiny of comparative inquiry. For when we describe Genesis Rabbah as only superficially formalized in the formulation of its units of discourse, only partially formalized in its types of units of discoursed, and only casually organized, in its arrangement of its units of discourse in order, these judgments presuppose a fixed standard -- hence comparison. For as framed, the statements at hand open a set of fresh questions. What would a *truly* formal document look like? That would be a document in which the units of discourse ordinarily are formalized in their *deep* structures, not only in their more superficial literary traits, in which a simple taxonomic system encompassed the entirety of the units of discourse, and in which the types of units of discourse conformed to two or three simple rules of ordering. For comparative purposes we turn to Leviticus Rabbah, the associate and neighbor of Genesis Rabbah, and the joint heir of sizable blocks of already-formulated materials.

Part Two

RECURRENT LITERARY STRUCTURES OF LEVITICUS RABBAH

Chapter Four

Recurrent Literary Structures of Leviticus Rabbah
Forms of Units of Discourse and their Order
Leviticus Rabbah as a Whole

i. Sorting Out the Major Units of Discourse: Taxonomy of Units of Discourse of Leviticus Rabbah

As I explained with regard to Genesis Rabbah, a literary structure is a composition that adheres to conventions of expression, organization, or proportion, extrinsic to the message of the author. Leviticus Rabbah comprises large-scale literary structures. How do we know that fact? It is because, when we divide up the undifferentiated columns of words and sentences and point to the boundaries that separate one completed unit of thought or discourse from the next such completed composition, we produce rather sizable statements conforming to a single set of patterns. When we divide a given *parashah*, or chapter, of Leviticus Rabbah into its sub-divisions, we find these sub-divisions sustained and on occasion protracted, but also stylistically cogent and well-composed. So we look for large-scale patterns and point to such unusually sizable compositions as characteristic because they recur and define discourse, *parashah* by *parashah*. Indeed, as we shall now see, a given *parashah* is made up of a large-scale literary structure, which I shall define in a moment, followed by further, somewhat smaller, fairly formalized constructions.

Let us now turn to the literary structure and organization of Leviticus Rabbah. Leviticus Rabbah is made up of thirty-seven *parashiyyot*, and each *parashah* is comprised of from as few as five to as many as fifteen subdivisions, just we saw in the case of Genesis Rabbah. In my translation and explanation of the text, I was able to show that these subdivisions in the main formed cogent statements. So we now take up the taxonomy of units of discourse of Leviticus Rabbah. The first form (form I) is familiar: (1) a verse of the book of Leviticus will be followed by (2) a verse from some other book of the Hebrew Scriptures. The latter (2) will then be subjected to extensive discussion. But in the end the exposition of the intersecting-verse will shed some light, in some way, upon (1) the base-verse, cited at the outset. The second form (form II) is the exegetical one, in which a verse of Leviticus is cited and then explained. The sustained analysis and amplification makes no reference to an intersecting-verse but to numerous proof-texts, or to no proof-texts at all The third form (form III) is simply the citation of a verse of the book of Leviticus followed by an exegetical comment, corresponding to form II in Genesis Rabbah. (I regret the confusion that subdividing form I into two forms for Leviticus Rabbah necessarily causes.) Form **IV** represents a miscellany, no formal traits at all being discernible by me. Clearly this constitutes a close parallel to classification **A** of Genesis Rabbah.

1. Base-verse/intersecting-verse constructions

I:I	Lev. 1:1 and Ps. 103:20
I:V	Lev 1:1 and Prov. 25:7
I:VI	Lev 1:1 and Prov. 20:15
II:I-II	Lev. 1:2 and Jer. 31:20
III:I	Lev. 2:1-2 and Qoh. 4:6
IV:I	Lev. 4:1-2 and Qoh. 3:16
V:I-III	Lev. 4:3 and Job 34:29-30
VI:I	Lev. 5:1 and Prov. 24:28
VI:II	Lev. 5:1 and Prov. 29:24
VII:I	Lev. 6:2 and Prov. 10:12
VIII:I	Lev. 6:13 and Ps. 75:6
IX:I-III	Lev. 7:11-12 and Ps. 50:23
X:I-III	Lev. 8:1-3 and Ps. 45:7
XI:I-IV	Lev. 9:1 and Prov. 9:1-6
XII:I	Lev. 10:9 and Prov. 23:31-2
XIV:I	Lev. 12:1-2 and Ps. 139:5
XV:I-II	Lev. 13:1-3 and Job 28:25-27
XVI:I	Lev. 14:2 and Prov. 6:16-19
XVII:I	Lev. 14:33-34 and Prov. 73:1-5
XVIII:I	Lev. 15:1-2 and Qoh. 12:1-7
XIX:I-III	Lev. 15:25 and Song 5:11
XX:I	Lev. 16:1 and Qoh. 9:2
XXI:I-IV	Lev. 16:3 and Ps. 27:1
XXII:I-IV	Lev. 17:3-5 and Qoh. 5:8
XXIII:I-VII	Lev. 18:1-3 and Song 2:2
XXIV:I	Lev. 19:2 and Is. 5:16
XXV:I-II	Lev. 19:23-25 and Prov. 3:18
XXVI:I-III	Lev. 21:1 and Ps. 12:7
XXVII:I	Lev. 22:27 and Ps. 36:6
XXVIII:I-III	Lev. 23:10 and Qoh. 1:3 [not an ideal example of the form]
XXIX:I	Lev. 23:24 and Ps. 119:89
XXX:I	Lev. 23:39-40 and Prov. 8:10
XXXI:I	Lev. 24:1-2 and Ps. 71:19
XXXII:III	Lev. 24:10 and 1 Sam. 17:4
XXXV:IV	Lev. 26:3 and Jer. 33:25
XXXVII:I	Qoh. 5:5 and Lev. 27:2
XXXVII:II	Job 34:11 and Lev. 27:1-5

2. Intersecting-verse/base-verse constructions

These run parallel to the forms distinguished above, in which we find an intersecting verse joined to a base verse but *not* extensively analyzed or expounded. That is to say, we have an intersecting verse, then the base verse, then interpretation of the latter in terms of the form. So the base verse is read in light of the intersecting verse, which itself is not unpacked. In my form-analysis of Genesis Rabbah I did not distinguish the two somewhat different forms from one another but treated them as exempla of a single form, intersecting-verse/base verse. But in my taxonomy, I did, distinguish the one from the other. Here we treat them as separate forms entirely.

III:II	Ps. 22:23-4 and Lev. 2:1
III:III	Is. 55:7 and Lev. 2:1
[III:VI.3	Lev. 2:3 and Ps. 17:15]
IV:II	Qoh. 6:7 and Lev. 4:2
IV:III	Prov. 19:2 and Lev. 4:2
VII:II	Ps. 51:19-21 and Lev. 6:9
VIII:II	Jud. 14:14 and Lev. 6:13
IX:V	Prov. 14:9 and Lev. 7:12
X:IV	Prov. 24:11 and Lev. 8:2
XI:V-V	Ps. 18:26-27 and Lev. 9:1
XII:III	Ps. 19:7-9 and Lev. 10:8-9
XIII:I	Prov. 15:31-2 and Lev. 10:16-17
XIII:II	Hab. 3:6 and Lev. 11:1-2
XIII:III	Prov. 30:5 and Lev. 11:1-2
XIV:II	Job 36:3 and Lev. 12:2
XIV:III	Job 10:12 and Lev. 12:2
XIV:IV	Job 38:8-11 and Lev. 12:2
XIV:V	Ps. 51:5 and Lev. 12:2
XIV:VI	Ps. 130:3 and Lev. 12:2
XIV:VI	Qoh. 11:2 and Lev. 12:3
XV:III	Job 38:25 and Lev. 13:2
XVI:II	Prov. 34:12-13 and Lev. 14:2
XVI:III	Job 20:6-7 and Lev. 14:2
XVII:II	Job 20:28-29 and Lev. 14:34
XVIII:II	Hab. 1:7 and Lev. 15:2
XVIII:III	Is. 17:11 and Lev. 15:2
XIX:IV	Qoh. 10:18 and Lev. 15:25
XX:II	Ps. 75:4 and Lev. 16:2
XX:III	Qoh. 2:2 [and Lev. 16:2]
XX:IV	Job 38:27-29 and Lev. 16:2
XX:V	Job 37:1 and Lev. 16:2
XX:VI	Prov. 17:26 and Lev. 16:2
XXI:V-VI	Prov. 24:6 and Lev. 16:3
XXII:VI.2-3	Prov. 30:7-9 and Lev. 17:3
[XXIII.VII.2	Ez. 23:2 and Lev. 18:1-3]
XXIV:II	Ps. 92:8 and Lev. 19:2
XXIV:III-IV	Ps. 20:2 and Lev. 19:2
XXV:IV	Qoh. 2:24 and Lev. 19:23
XXV:V	Job 38:30 and Lev. 19:23
XXVI:IV-V	Ps. 19:3 and Lev. 21:1
XXVI:VI	Ps. 19:9 and Lev. 21:1
XXVII:II	Job 41:11 and Lev. 22:26
XXVII:III	Ez. 29:16 and Lev. 22:26

XXVII:IV-V   Qoh. 3:15 and Lev. 22:26-27
XXVII:VI   Mic. 6:3 and Lev. 22:26-27
XXVII:VII   Is. 41:24 and Lev. 22:26-27
XXVIII:IV   Job 5:5 and Lev. 23:10
XXIX:II   Jer. 30:10 and Lev. 23:24
XXIX:III   Ps. 47:5 and Lev. 23:24
XXIX:IV   Ps. 89:16 and Lev. 23:24
XXIX:V   Prov. 15:24, 6:23 and Lev. 23:24
XXIX:VI   Ps. 81:4 and Lev. 23:24
XXIX:VII   Is. 48:17 and Lev. 23:24
XXIX:VIII   Ps. 62:9 and Lev. 23:24
XXX:II   Ps. 16:11 and Lev. 23:40
XXX:III   Ps. 102:17-18 and Lev. 23:40
XXX:IV   Ps. 96:12-14 and Lev. 23:40
XXX:V   Ps. 26:6-7 and Lev. 23:40
XXXI:II   Ps. 119:140 and Lev. 24:2
XXXI:III   Job 14:15 and Lev. 24:2
XXXI:IV   Ps. 18:29 and Lev. 24:2
XXXI:V   Prov. 21:22 and Lev. 24:2
XXXI:VI   Job 25:3 and Lev. 24:2
XXXII:I   Ps. 12:8 and Lev. 24:10-13
XXXII:II   Qoh. 10:20 and Lev. 24:14
XXXII:V   Song 4:12 and Lev. 24:11
XXXIII:I   Prov. 18:21 and Lev. 25:14
XXXIII:III   Amos 9:1 and Lev. 25:14
XXXIV:I   Ps. 41:1-2 and Lev. 25:25
XXXIV:II   Prov. 19:17 and Lev. 25:25
XXXIV:III   Prov. 11:17 and Lev. 25:25
XXXIV:IV   Prov. 29:13 (and 22:2) and Lev. 25:25
XXXIV:V   Prov. 7:14 and Lev. 25:25
XXXV:I   Ps. 119:59 and Lev. 26:3
XXXV:II   Prov. 8:32 and Lev. 26:3
XXXVI:I.1,4 Ps. 102:25 and Lev. 26:42 [Reversal of order in Lev. 26:42 is what is noted. But the composi - tion as a whole in no way forms a suitable example of this pattern.]
XXXVI:II   Ps. 80:8-10 and Lev. 26:42
XXXVI:III   Prov. 11:21 and Lev. 26:42
[XXXVI:IV   Is. 43:1 and Lev. 26:42. Base-verse not cited.]

3. Form II: Verse-by-verse exege - tical   constructions

This form is familiar: the base verse is cited and then subjected to systematic amplification in some way or other. The form is characterized by the preliminary citation of the base verse (not much of a formalization of syntax or composition, to be sure).

I:VII-VIII.1	Lev. 1:1. Re God's calling Moses.
I:VIII.2-3	Lev. 1:1. Meaning of word "call."
I:IX	As above. Call to Moses in particular.
I:X-XI	Lev. 1:1. Tent of meeting.
II:IV	Lev. 1:2. Speak to Israel in particular.
II:V	Continues II:IV.
II:VI	Lev. 1:2. Why formulated this way.
II:VII	Lev. 1:2. Bringing offer - ings.
III:IV	Lev. 1:16
III:V	Lev. 1:16-17
III:VI	Lev. 2:1-2
IV:IV-V	Lev. 4:1
V:V-VI	Lev. 4:3
V:VII	Lev. 4:13-15
VI:IV	Lev. 5:1
VI:V	Lev. 5:1
VII:III	Lev. 6:1
VII:IV	Lev. 6:2
VII:V	Lev. 6:2
VIII:IV	Lev. 6:13
IX:IV	Lev. 7:12
X:VIII	Lev. 8:1-2
X:IX.1-2	Lev. 8:2-3
XI:VIII	Lev. 9:1
XIII:IV	Lev. 11:2
XV:V	Lev. 13:2 as juxtaposed to Lev. 12:2.
XV:VI	Lev. 13:2
XV:VIII	Lev. 13:3
XV:IX	Lev. 13:2
XVI:V	From this point the base verse is not specified.
XVI:VI	
XVI:VII	
XVI:IX	
XVII:III	
XVII:V	
XVII:III	
XVIII:IV	
XVIII:V	
XIX:VI	
XX:VIII	
XX:IX	
XX:X	
XX:XI	
XX:XII	
XXI:VII	
XXI:IX	
XXI:XI	
XXI:XII	
XXII:V	
XXII:VII	

XXII:VIII
XXIII:IX
XXIV:V
XXIV:VI
XXIV:VIII
XXIV:IX
XXV:VI
XXVI:VII.1
XXVI:VIII
XXVII:VIII
XXVII:IX
XXVII:X
XXVII:XI
XXVII:XII
XXVIII:V
XXVIII:VI
XXIX:VIII B
XXIX:IX
XXX:VI
XXX:VII
XXX:VIII
XXX:IX
XXX:X
XXX:XI
XXX:XII
XXX:XIV
XXX:XV
XXX:XVI
XXXI:X
XXXII:IV
XXXII:VI.1
XXXV:VI
XXXV:VII
XXXV:VIII
XXXV:IX
XXXV:X
XXXV:XI
XXXV:XII
XXXVI:V

4. Miscellanies

I:II
I:III
I:IV
I:XII
I:XIII
I:XIV
III:VI.5-8
[IV:IV   Joined to IV:V.]
IV:VI
IV:VII
IV:VIII
V:IV
V:VIII
VI:III
VI:VI
VII:II
VII:VI
VIII:III
IX:VI
IX:VII
IX:VIII
IX:IX
X:V

X:VI-VII
X:IX.3-8
X:VI-VII
X:IX
XI:VI
XI:IX
XII:II
XIII:V
XIV:VIII
XIV:IX
XV:IV
XV:VII
XVI:IV
XVI:VIII
XVI:IV
XIX:V
XX:VII
XXI:VIII
XXI:X
XXII:VI.1
XXII:IX
XXII:X
XXIII:VIII
XXIII:X
XXIII:XI
XXIII:XII
XXIII:XIII
XXIV:VII
XXV:III
XXV:VII
XXV:VIII
XXVI:VII.2-6
XXIX:X
XXIX:XI
XXIX:XII
XXX:XIII
XXI:VII
XXXI:VIII
XXXI:IX
XXXII:VI
XXXII:VII
XXXII:VIII
XXXIII:II
XXXIII:IV
XXXIII:V
XXXIII:VI.2
XXXIV:VI
XXXIV:VII
XXXIV:VIII
XXXIV:IX
XXXIV:X
XXXIV:XI
XXXIV:XII
XXXIV:XIII
XXXIV:XIV
XXXIV:XV
XXXIV:XVI
XXXV:III
XXXV:V
XXXVI:I
XXXVI:VI
XXXVII:III
XXXVII:IV

Let us now survey the results as a whole. We have counted, in all, 304 entries on the four catalogues:

I.	38	12.5%
II.	84	27.6%
III.	94	30.9%
IV.	88	28.9%

The three defined taxa thus cover 71% of the whole. The two truly distinctive patterns, forms I and II, cover a sizable part of the whole -- 40%.

Obviously, in due course, both for Leviticus Rabbah and for Genesis Rabbah we shall have to pay more attention to the materials catalogued as merely miscellaneous, since they are far from lacking all taxonomic traits. But the criteria for differentiation and classification will not derive from an inductive sorting out of materials in Leviticus Rabbah in particular. The definitive trait of the classification of miscellaneous remains the simple fact that all items at hand ignore the literary structure and organization definitive of Leviticus Rabbah. But most of those items can be shown in one way or another to serve the topical or even logical program of those who structured and organized the document.

ii. The Order of Types of Units of Discourse in Leviticus Rabbah

Having classified the units of discourse of which our thirty-seven *parashiyyot* are composed, we now go back to ask whether the forms of units of discourse follow a single pattern, or whether a given form will appear in any sequence promiscuously, at the beginning, middle, or end of a given *parashah*. So from the taxonomy of the units of discourse, we proceed to the structure of the thirty-seven *parashiyyot* as a whole. We ask whether the editors exhibited preferences for a given form of unit of discourse when they faced the task in particular of beginning a *parashah* or of ending one.

I:I   I
[I:II   IV.   The relevance to Moses is via the theme of the righteous proselyte, Pharaoh's daughter.]
[I:III   IV.   As above. Names of Moses.]
[I:IV   IV.   Ps. 89:20 applies to Abraham, David, Moses.]
I:V   I
I:VI   I
I:VII   III
I:VIII   III
I:IX   III
I:X   III
I:XI   III
[I:XII   IV.   Supplement on tent of meeting, the theme of I:X-XI.]
[I:XIII   IV.   Continues I:XII.]
I:XIV   IV.   As above.
II:I-III   I
II:IV-V   III
II:VI   III
II:VII   III
III:I   I
III:II   II
III:III   II
III:IV   III
III:V   III
III:VI   III
III:VI.5-8   IV
IV:I   I
IV:II   II
IV:III   II
IV:IV-V   III
[IV:VI   IV.   Collective responsibility. Relevant to Lev. 4:13.]
IV:VII   IV.   Soul-sayings.
IV:VIII   IV.   As above.
V:I   I
V:II   I
V:III   I
[V:IV   IV.   As explained.]
V:V-VI   III
V:VII   III
[V:VIII   IV.   As explained.]
VI:I   I
VI:II   I
[VI:III   IV.   Theme of VI:I-II, false oath.]
VI:IV   III
VI:V   III
VI:VI   IV.   Is. 8:18-20
VII:I   I
VII:II   II
VII:III   III
VII:IV   III
VII:V   III
VII:VI   IV.   Relevant in theme, not in detail.
VIII:I   I
VIII:II   II
[VIII:III   IV.   Thematically relevant.]

VIII:IV   III
IX:I   I
IX:II   I
IX:III   I
IX:IV   III
IX:V   II
[IX:VI   IV.   Thematically relevant.]
[IX:VII   IV.   Thematically relevant.]
[IX:VIII   IV.   Thematically relevant.]
[IX:IX   IV.   Continues theme of peace tangentially introduced in IX:VIII.]
X:I   I
X:II   I
X:III   I
X:IV   II
[X:V   IV.   Theme of repentance through prayer. Relevant in a general way.]
[X:VI-VII   IV.   Relevant to theme of atonement of sin.]
X:VIII   III
X:IX.1-2   III
X:IX.3-8   IV
XI:I   I
XI:II   I
XI:III   I
XI:IV   I
XI:V-VI   II
[XI:VI   IV.   Intersects with the base-verse only incidentally.]
XI:VIII   III
XI:IX   IV
XII:I   I
[XII:II   IV.   Theme relevant.]
XII:III   II
[XII:IV   IV.   As above.]
[XII:V   IV.   As above.]
XIII:I   II
XIII:II   II
XIII:III   II
XIII:IV   III
[XIII:V   IV.   Intersects in reference to the theme.]
XIV:I   I
XIV:II   II
XIV:III   II
XIV:IV   II
XIV:V   II
XIV:VI   II
XIV:VII   II
XIV:VIII   IV.   Thematically relevant.
XIV:IX   IV
XV:I   I
XV:II   I
XV:III   II
[XV:IV   IV.   Intersects with theme.]
XV:V   III
XV:VI   III

[XV:VII	IV. Same exegetical mode as foregoing.]
XV:VIII	III
XV:IX	III
XVI:I	I
XVI:II	II
XVI:III	II
[XVI:IV	IV. Intersects with theme.]
XVI:V	III
XVI:VI	III
XVI:VII	III
[XVI:VIII	IV. Intersects with theme.]
XVI:IX	III
XVII:I	I
XVII:II	II
XVII:III	III
[XVII:IV	IV. Intersects with theme.]
XVII:V	III
XVII:VI	III
XVII:VII	III
XVIII:	II
XVIII:II	II
XVIII:III	II
XVIII:IV	III
XVIII:V	III
XIX:I	I
XIX:II	I
XIX:III	I
XIX:IV	II
[XIX:V	IV. Shared language: many days.]
XIX:VI	III
XIX:VII	III
XX:I	I
XX:II	II
XX:III	II
XX:IV	II
XX:V	II
XX:VI	II
[XX:VII	IV. Introduces basic theme of XX:VIII.]
XX:VIII	III
XX:IX	III
XX:X	III
XX:XI	III
XX:XII	III
XXI:I	I
XXI:II	I
XXI:III	I
XXI:IV	I
XXI:V	II
XXI:VI	II
XXI:VII	III
[XXI:VIII	IV. Takes up theme of foregoing.]
XXI:IX	III
[XXI:X	IV. Continues fore - going.]
XXI:XI	III
XXI:XII	III
XXII:I	I
XXII:II	I
XXII:III	I

XXII:IV	I
XXII:V	III
XXII:VI.1	IV
XXII:VI.2-3	II
XXII:VII	III
XXII:VIII	III
[XXII:IX	IV. Intersects in theme.]
XXII:X	IV
XXIII:I	I
XXIII:II	I
XXIII:III	I
XXIII:IV	I
XXIII:V	I
XXIII:VI	I
XXIII:VII.1	I
[XXIII:VIII	IV. Defective text.]
XXIII:IX	III
[XXIII:X	IV. Continues foregoing theme.]
[XXIII:XI	IV. Continues foregoing theme.]
[XXIII:XII	IV. Continues foregoing theme.]
[XXIII:XIII	IV. Continues foregoing theme.]
XXIV:I	I
XXIV:II	II
XXIV:III	II
XXIV:IV	II
XXIV:V	III
XXIV:VI	III
[XXIV:VII	IV. Intersects in theme.]
XXIV:VIII	III
XXIV:IX	III
XXV:I	I
XXV:II	I
[XXV:III	IV. Thematic inter - section.]
XXV:IV	II
XXV:V	II
XXV:VI	III
[XXV:VII	IV. Continues theme of foregoing.]
[XXV:VIII	IV. Continues theme of foregoing.]
XXVI:I	I
XXVI:II	I
XXVI:III	I
XXVI:IV	II
XXVI:V	II
XXVI:VI	II
XXVI:VII.1	III
[XXVI:VII.2-6	IV. Intersects at the end.]
XXVI:VIII	III
XXVII:I	I
XXVII:II	II
XXVII:III	II
XXVII:IV	II
XXVII:V	II
XXVII:VI	II
XXVII:VII	II
XXVII:VIII	III
XXVII:IX	III
XXVII:X	III
XXVII:XI	III
XXVII:XII	III

XXVIII:I	I
XXVIII:II	I
XXVIII:III	I
XXVIII:IV	II
XXVIII:V	III
XXVIII:VI	III
XXIX:I	I
XXIX:II	II
XXIX:III	II
XXIX:IV	II
XXIX:V	II
XXIX:VI	II
XXIX:VII	II
XXIX:VIII	II
XXIX:VIII B	III
XXIX:IX	III
[XXIX:X	IV. Continues theme of foregoing.]
[XXIX:XI	IV. While Lev. 23:24 is cited, the point is distinctive to the unit of discourse.]
[XXIX:XII	IV. Intersects in theme.]
XXX:I	I
XXX:II	II
XXX:III	II
XXX:IV	II
XXX:V	II
XXX:VI	III
XXX:VII	III
XXX:VIII	III
XXX:IX	III
XXX:X	III
XXX:XI	III
XXX:XII	III
[XXX:XIII	IV. Intersects with base-verse.]
XXX:XIX	III
XXX:XV	III
XXX:XVI	III
XXXI:I	I
XXXI:II	II
XXXI:III	II
XXXI:IV	II
XXXI:V	II
XXXI:VI	II
[XXXI:VII	IV. Thematically relevant.]
[XXXI:VIII	IV. Thematically relevant.]
[XXXI:IX	IV. Thematically relevant.]
XXXI:X	III
XXXI:XI	III
XXXII:I	II
XXXII:II	II
XXXII:III	I
XXXII:IV	III
XXXII:V	II
[XXXII:VI	IV. Intersects in one detail.]
[XXXII:VII	IV. Continues foregoing.]
[XXXII:VIII	IV. Continues foregoing.]
XXXIII:I	II

[XXXIII:II	IV. Interest in exegesis of a word in the base-verse.]
XXXIII:III	II
[XXXIII:IV	IV. As above.]
[XXXIII:V	IV. As above.]
XXXIII:VI.1	III
[XXXIII.VI.2-7	[IV. Tacked on because of thematic intersection.]
XXXIV:I	II
XXXIV:II	II
XXXIV:III	II
XXXIV:IV	II
XXXIV:V	II
[XXXIV:VI	IV. Exegesis of word in the base-verse.]
[XXXIV:VII	IV. Thematic intersection.]
[XXXIV:VIII	IV. Thematic intersection.]
[XXXIV:IX	IV. Thematic intersection.]
[XXXIV:X	IV. Thematic intersection.]
[XXXIV:XI	IV. Thematic intersection.]
[XXXIV:XII	IV. Thematic intersection.]
[XXXIV:XIII-XVI	IV. Is. 58:7 -- thematic intersection.]
XXXV:I	II
XXXV:II	II
[XXXV:III	IV. May exemplify theme of base-verse.]
XXXV:IV	I
[XXXV:V	IV. Explains word in base-verse.]
XXXV:VI	III
XXXV:VII	III
XXXV:VIII	III
XXXV:IX	III
XXXV:X	III
XXXV:XI	III
XXXV:XII	III
XXXVI:I	[II] IV
XXXVI:II	II
XXXVI:III	II
XXXVI:IV	II
XXXVI:V	III
[XXXVI:VI	IV. Thematic intersection.]
XXXVII:I	II
XXXVII:II	II
[XXXVII:III	IV. Thematic intersection.]
[XXXVII:IV	IV. Thematic intersection.]

The results may now be stated through the summary that follows:

Form I comes in first position in the following *parashiyyot*:

I, II, III, IV, V, VI, VII, VIII, IX, X, XI, XII, XIV, XV, XVI, XVII, XVIII, XIX, XX, XXI, XXII, XXIII, XXIV, XXV, XXVI, XXVII, XXVIII.

Form II comes in first position in the following *parashiyyot*:
XII, XXXII, XXXIII, XXXIV, XXXV

Form III comes in first position in the following *parashiyyot*: --

Form IV comes in first position in the following *parashiyyot*:
XXXVI

Form I comes in second position in the following *parashiyyot*:

V, VI, IX, X, XI, XV, XVII, XXII, XXIII, XXVI, XXVII, XXVIII, XXXVII

Form II comes in second position in the following *parashiyyot*:

III, IV, VII, VIII, XIII, XIV, XVI, XVII, XVIII, XIX, XX, XXI, XXIV, XXV, XXIX, XXX, XXXI, XXXII, XXXIV, XXXV, XXXVI

Form III comes in second position in the following *parashiyyot*:
II

Form IV comes in second position in the following *parashiyyot*:
XII, XXXIII

Form I comes last in the following *parashiyyot*: --

Form II comes last in the following *parashiyyot*: --

Form III comes last in the following *parashiyyot*:

II, VIII, XV, XVI, XVII, XVIII, XIX, XX, XXI, XXIV, XXVI, XXVII, XXVIII, XXX, XXXI, XXXV

Form IV comes last in the following *parashiyyot*:

I, III, IV, V, VI, VII, IX, X, XI, XII, XIII, XIV, XXII, XXIII, XXV, XXIX, XXXII, XXXIII, XXXIV, XXXVI, XXXVII

We may compare the proportions as follows:

Form I comes in first position in	31/37	83.7%
Form II comes in first position in	5/37	13.5%
Form III comes in first position in	0/37	0.0%
Form IV comes in first position in	1/37	2.7%
Form I comes in second position in	13/37	35.1%
Form II comes in second position in	21/37	56.7%
Form III comes in second position in	1/37	2.7%
Form IV comes in second position in	21/37	5.4%
Form I comes in last position in	0/37	0.0%
Form II comes in last position in	0/37	0.0%
Form III comes in last position in	16/37	43.2%
Form IV comes in last position in	21/37	56.7%

I have probably overstated the instances in which form I comes in second position. Many of the entries of form I involve sustained and unitary compositions, in which a single intersecting-verse is worked out over a series of two or three subdivisions of a *parashah*. Otherwise the proportions conform to the impressions yielded by the catalogues just now presented.

To state the result very simply: the framer of a passage intended for use in Leviticus Rabbah ordinarily began with a base-verse/intersecting-verse construction. He very commonly proceeded with an intersecting-verse/base-verse construction. These would correspond to both sorts of form I in Genesis Rabbah. The upshot is that Leviticus Rabbah much more strictly follows a clear program in laying out types of forms of units of discourse, nearly always preferring to place form I prior to form II, and so on down. The organizers of Genesis Rabbah, by contrast, did not so conscientiously follow a similar program. What would the authorities who ordered Leviticus Rabbah choose for the secondary amplification of their composition? First, as is clear, the framer would take a composition in form I. Then he would provide such exegeses of pertinent verses of Leviticus as he had in hand. He would conclude either with form III (parallel in Genesis Rabbah: form II) or form IV constructions, somewhat more commonly the latter than the former.

So the program of the authors is quite simple. They began with forms I and II -- 100% of the first and second position entries, proceeded with form III, and concluded with form III or IV. When we observe that Genesis Rabbah does not appear so carefully arranged in the order of types of forms of units of discourse, that judgment now appears to rest upon the comparison of two documents, Leviticus Rabbah and Genesis Rabbah. It no longer sets upon foundations of impression and rough and ready guess-work.

Thus Leviticus Rabbah consists of two main forms of units of discourse, first in position, expositions of how verses of the book of Leviticus relate to verses of other books of the Hebrew bible, second in position, exposition of verses of the book of Leviticus viewed on their own, and, varying in position but in any event very often concluding a construction, miscellaneous materials.

May we now compare Leviticus Rabbah, therefore also Genesis Rabbah, to another document of the same age? Indeed we may do so, since the Talmud of the Land of Israel is assigned by the consensus of learning to exactly the same period as the two great Rabbah-collections, the ones serving Genesis and Leviticus. Most scholars concur that all three documents derive from the later fourth and earlier fifth centuries, in the rough order, Talmud of the Land of Israel, then Genesis Rabbah, then Leviticus Rabbah, all within a span of not a century. So we turn for a further comparative judgment to the first of the two Talmuds. The basis for our comparison is now the possibility of effecting a taxonomy of all units of discourse in all three documents. Let me explain.

As I showed in *The Talmud of the Land of Israel. 35. Introduction. Taxonomy* (Chicago, 1983), the compositors of the Yerushalmi began their discourse with a close reading of a Mishnah-paragraph, very often in reference to its Scriptural basis; they then proceeded to examine the principles of the Mishnah-paragraph and to expound them in their own terms, and finally, they went on to whatever else struck them as relevant in a given context. The exposition of one verse of the Hebrew Scriptures, one in Leviticus, in the light of some other, one in Job or Proverbs or Psalms, for example, served a purpose for Genesis Rabbah and Leviticus Rabbah not terribly different from that served in the Yerushalmi by the provision of scriptural proof-texts for Mishnah's sentences. The articulation and expansion of the explanation of a given verse in Genesis or Leviticus finds its counterpart in the Yerushalmi in exactly the same procedure for the Mishnah. And the rest would find its place in sequence afterward.

It would be bizarre to claim that Genesis Rabbah's or Leviticus Rabbah's authorship intended to supply a kind of Talmud to the book of Genesis or Leviticus. But it is not entirely farfetched to recognize points of correspondence. In the Yerushalmi the evocation of a scriptural proof-text for a Mishnaic sentence served to demonstrate the unity of the Mishnah's rules with the Scripture's principles. In Genesis Rabbah and Leviticus Rabbah the citation of a verse of Job or Proverbs or Psalms in amplification of a verse (and thus a theme) of Leviticus underlined the deep unity of the several parts of the Torah: Pentateuch and Writings. So the upshot in both documents was to show the cogency and harmony of what later would be called "the one whole Torah of Moses, our rabbi."

iii. Literary Patterns of Leviticus Rabbah

I have now established several facts. First, Leviticus Rabbah, viewed whole, does not comprise a mere random selection of diverse forms of literary expression. The fact that 70% of the whole falls into three taxonomic categories, of which two may be distinguished only on narrowly formal grounds, proves otherwise. The authors of the document adhered to extremely limited choices of literary conventions, saying whatever they wished to say about the book of Leviticus in essentially two ways only.

Second, it follows that, seeing the composition at the end of its formation as we do, the document had not only compilers, but authors. These authors (whether original writers or editors) took an active role in the formal expression of the points to be made. They produced not a collection but a composition. What in fact did the authors accomplish?

The authors of Leviticus Rabbah undertook a twofold program. They wished to provide both an exegesis and an expansion, into a larger context, of the book of Leviticus. This was along two lines. The one is representative by forms I, II of Leviticus Rabbah and form I of Genesis Rabbah. The other is carried forward by form III of Leviticus Rabbah and form II of Genesis Rabbah.

First, as I just said, the authorities at hand wished to establish links between statements in the book of Genesis or Leviticus and statements in other biblical books, among which Proverbs, Psalms, and Job figured prominently. They did this so as to set forth principles or beliefs or ideals or values transcending any one biblical book and (in their mind) expressed in many books. So they in some measure accomplished the demonstration that the Torah speaks everywhere about the same things, a single, cogent and everywhere harmonious revelation. The forms the authors took for making this large, substantive point prove congruent to their theological purpose. A verse from Leviticus juxtaposed with a verse from some other biblical book, standing fore or aft, established a tension to be resolved through the demonstration that the two diverse verses really meant the same thing.

Second, the compositors wished to amplify or explain points in individual verses of the book of Genesis or Leviticus, ordinarily those same verses that, earlier in a composition, stood in tension with verses of some other biblical book. This exercise came second in order. It served the purpose of clarifying details once the main point had been made.

The redactors in the case of Leviticus Rabbah also made ample provision for illustrative materials to hammer home their basic points. These illustrative materials, of a broad and diverse character, in no way conformed in literary patterns to the exegetical program that defined what was primary to the document as a whole. Materials I catalogued as miscellaneous exhibited noteworthy diversity in form, pattern, or structure. But in respect to the main point made by a given saying, story, or composite, each item simply restated the point dominant in a *parashah* as a whole.

I indicated the connections between miscellanies and classified units of discourse in the preceding catalogue. Ordinarily, where the editors proposed to insert such miscellanies, they would choose one of two positions for them. Either they would place a miscellaneous item either as a supplement to an item bearing the distinctive literary traits of the document as a whole, e.g., in immediate juxtaposition to a Form I or a Form II unit of discourse. Or they would locate such an item at the end of a given parashah, that is, after the repertoire of forms I, II, and III had been fully exposed. The parallel pattern for Genesis Rabbah would explain the juxtaposition of form III to form I, which we note in not a few instances.

We now therefore know that units of discourse that fall into the classifications of forms I, II, or III in their fixed order define that literary structure that imparts to Leviticus Rabbah the formal and stylistic unity exhibited by its principal components. So we may indeed speak of literary patterns -- structures of completed discourse -- that recur in Leviticus Rabbah. The recurrent traits prove to be both in formal character (for forms I and II) and in conventional sequence (for all four forms). Leviticus Rabbah, viewed whole and in its constitutive components, finds definition in a dominant literary structure and a recurrent mode of literary organization. It remains to draw together the results of our analyses of both documents.

Part Three

COMPARATIVE MIDRASH

The Plan and Program of Genesis Rabbah
and Leviticus Rabbah

Chapter Five

The Plan of Genesis Rabbah and Leviticus Rabbah

i. Comparing Two *Parashiyyot*

The general comparisons just now carried out in Parts One and Two will take on concreteness when, more or less at random, we analyze a *parashah* from each of the two compilations and compare formal taxonomy and redactional preferences revealed by each. Then we shall see the foundations for a point-by-point literary comparison and contrast between the two documents. Once we perceive in a concrete way that the two documents share a single taxonomy of form and redaction, we will ask how the theological programs compare. So we move from comparing the documents' formal plans to the comparative and contrastive analysis -- on a more subjective basis to be sure -- of their respective of programs (in Chapter Six).

Our interest in the plan of the two documents is once again to effect a taxonomy of the units of discourse, then to ask whether the types of units of discourse follow an order based on a redactor's preference for placing one type of unit of discourse at the start of his larger composite, another type at the end. We carry out the analysis separately, in sections ii and iii, and in section iv we compare the results for each compilation.

ii. Genesis Rabbah Parashah Ten
X:I.
1. A. "Thus the heavens [and the earth were finished (YKL) and all the host of them]" (Gen. 2:1):

    B. "For every purpose (TKLH) I have seen an end" (Ps. 119:96).

    C. For everything there is a measure, heaven and earth have a measure, except for one thing, which has no measure.

    D. And what is that? It is the Torah: "The measure thereof is longer than the earth" (Job 11:9).

2. A. Another interpretation: "For every purpose I have seen an end" (Ps. 119:96) refers to the work of making heaven, as it is written, "And the heaven...was finished..." (Gen. 2:1).

The intersecting verse returns to the base verse in No. 2; the paragraph must be regarded as a unity, once again linking the Torah to the creation of the natural world and placing the Torah above that world of creation.

X:II.

1. A. R. Hama bar Hanina opened [discourse by citing the following verse}: "Take away the dross from the silver" (Prov. 25:4).

B. Said R. Eliezer, "The matter may be compared to a bath that was full of water, and there were two lovely bas-reliefs in it. But so long as the bath was full of water, the artful work of the bas-reliefs could not be seen. Once the stopper was removed and the water emptied out from the bath, the beautiful work of the bas-reliefs became visible.

C. "So in the case of the world, so long as there was unformed chaos in the world, the artful work of heaven and earth was not visible. Once the unformed chaos was removed from the world, the artful work could become visible."

D. [Continuing A:] "'And there comes forth a vessel (KLY) for the refiner'(Prov. 28:4) thus means that [heaven and earth were turned into vessels: 'And the heaven and earth were turned into vessels (YKL)' (Gen. 2:1)."

I am inclined to see the entire message of Hama at A, D. The insertion of Eliezer's statement, B, C, does not appear to carry forward the base verse. But the theme of Eliezer's saying is the same, for taking away the dross is comparable to removing the water. The conclusion, D, in no way continues B, C. And the concluding statement, D, reverts explicitly to refining metal and making a utensil, the point at which Hama started. So the literary traits of the composition prove somewhat jarring.

X:III.

1. A. ["And the heaven and the earth were finished" (Gen. 2:1):] How did the Holy One, blessed be he, create his world?

B. Said R. Yohanan, "The Holy One, blessed be he, took two balls, one of fire, the other of snow, and he worked them together and from the mixture of the two the world was created."

C. R. Hanina said, "There were four, for the four directions."

D. [R. Hama said, "There were six, four for the four directions,] one for above, one for below."

2. A. Hadrian -- may his bones be smashed -- asked R. Joshua b. R. Hanina, saying to him, "How did the Holy One, blessed be he, create his world?"

B. He replied to him in accord with the statement of R. Hama.

C. He said to him, "Is such a thing possible?"

D. He brought him into a small room and said to him, "Stretch out your hand east and west, north and south."

E. He said to him, "That is the act of creation seemed to the Holy One, blessed be he."

The pericope moves on to the cosmological question, leaving the philological one. No. 1 explains how the various elements were joined into a cogent mixture, No. 2 proceeds to compare God's stretching out the heavens to man's stretching out his hands.

X:IV.

1. A. Said R. Hoshaia, "R. Ephes gave an interpretation in Antioch: 'The word, "...and were finished (YKL)...," bears the sense only of injury and destruction (KLYH).

B. "'The matter may be compared to the case of a king who came into a province, and the provincials praised him. Since the celebration pleased him very much, he gave them an abundance of foot-races and chariot races. [Jastrow: He increased for them the speed of the mail bearers and the number of mail stations (Freedman, p. 72, n. 6).]

C. "'After a time the people angered him, so he diminished the number of foot-races and chariot races.

D. "'So too there is a planet which completes its circuit in twelve months, such as the sun, and there is a planet which completes its circuit in twelve years, such as Jupiter, and there is a planet that completes its circuit in thirty days, such as the moon, and there is a planet that completes its circuit in thirty years, such as Saturn.

E. "'The exceptions are the planets Mercury, Venus, and Mars, for these complete their circuit in four hundred eighty years.'"

2. A. R. Phineas in the name of R. Hanan of Sepphoris: "We have learned in the Mishnah: **White figs are subject to the Sabbatical Year in the second year, since they produce a crop only once in three years** [M. Sheb. 8:1].

B. "But on that day they produced fruit on the same day [on which they are planted]. In the age to come, however, the Holy One, blessed be he, will heal that ailment, as it is said, 'And he will heal the stroke of their wound' (Is. 30:26). The meaning is, he will heal the wound of the world."

The fact that the planets complete their circuits at diverse times forms a mark of imperfection, so. No. 1. The fact that some species produce not annually but at more irregular or distant intervals likewise marks the imperfection of creation. No. 1 records the former injury, No. 2. the latter.

X:V.

1. A. Said R. Joshua b. Levi, "[When the cited verse refers to the completion of heaven and earth, the sense is that] the heaven was finished along with the sun, moon, and stars, and the earth along with trees, grasses, and the Garden of Eden." [The word-play treats YKL as related to KLL, wreath or crown, thus, "The heaven was crowned by the sun," so Freedman, p. 73, n. 5.]

B. R. Simon in the name of R. Joshua b. Levi: "They had earlier been completed but had gone on expanding [until the conclusion of the sixth day, and that is the sense of the word at hand]."

2. A. "And all their host" (Gen. 2:1):

B. Said R. Eleazar, "There are three 'hosts' [terms of enlistment] [Freedman: fixed periods. Thus heaven and earth were created for a definitely fixed time; a definite period is set for disciples when they shall attain the rank of teachers; and there is a fixed time beyond which a man's trials cease. The word 'host' then means here, 'period of service,' such as a soldier's.]

C. There is a 'host' [a term of enlistment for service] for heaven an earth, a 'host' for disciples, and a 'host' for one's troubles [which, in all three cases, means that there is a fixed limit to the matter at hand, as will now be explained].

D. "The 'host' for heaven and earth,' as it is written, 'And the heaven and the earth were finished, and all their host [fixed periods]' (Gen. 2:1).

E. "A 'host' for disciples: 'All the days of my appointed time would I wait, until my relief should come' (Job 41:14), until the one who takes my place will arise.

F. "A 'host' for trials: 'Is there not a fixed period for man upon earth' (Job 7:1)."

G. All of a man's fixed period is spent "upon earth." And what benefit does he derive? "Are not all his days like the days of a hired servant?" (Job 7:1).

3. A. Nahman, son of Samuel bar Nahman: "If a man has merit, the host is for him, and if not, the host is against him.

B. "If he built a building and it worked out, the host is for him, but if he fell off the house and died, the host is against him.

C. "If he ate his bread and it gave him benefit, the host is for him, but if it got stuck in his throat and choked him, the host is against him.

D. "Many hosts did the Holy One, blessed be he, designate to deal with man, to exact just penalty from him, many bears, lions, snakes, fiery serpents, and scorpions, and not only so, but 'His days are like the days of a hireling' (Job 7:1)."

No. 1 completes the analysis of YKL. Nos. 2, 3 take up the reference to "host," with No. 2 taking "host" to mean "fixed period," and No. 3 to mean "a host of agents," available to do God's will.

X:VI.

1. A. Bar Sira said, "The divinity produced medicine from the earth, with which the physician heals a wound and the pharmacist mixes his medicines."

B. Said R. Simon, "There is not a single herb which is not subject to the influence of a planet in heaven, which smites it and says to it, 'Grow!' as it is written, 'Do you know the ordinances of heaven? Can you establish the dominion thereof in the earth?' (Job 38:33). 'Can you bind the chains of Pleiades or loose the bands of Orion?' (Job 38:31)."

C. R. Hinena bar Pappa and R. Simon say, "Pleiades binds produce and Orion draws it out between knot and knot [Freedman], in line with the following verse of Scripture: 'Can you lead forth the constellations in their season?' (Job 38:32)."

D. R. Tanhum b. R. Hiyya and R. Simon: "For it is the constellation which makes the fruit ripen."

X:VII.

1. A. Rabbis say, "Even things that you regard as completely superfluous to the creation of the world, for instance, fleas, gnats, and flies, also fall into the classification of things that were part of the creation of the world.

B. "And the Holy One, blessed be he, carries out his purposes even with a snake, scorpion, gnat, or frog. [Stories follow to illustrate this point.]"

2. A. R. Aha reported the following story: "There was a man who was standing on the bank of a canal. He saw a frog carrying a scorpion and bringing it across the river. Once it had carried out its task, it brought it back to its place."

3. A. R. Phineas in the name of R. Hanan reported this story: "There was a man who was going to harvest a field. He saw a piece of grass and cut it and made it into a crown for his head. A snake came along, and the man hit it and killed it. Someone came along and was standing and looking at the snake, wondering who had killed it. The man said, 'I am the one who killed it.' The man saw the grass made into a wreath on the man's head.

B. "He said, 'Did you really kill it?'

C. "The man further said, 'Can you remove that grass from your head?'

D. "The other said, 'Yes.' When he had taken the grass off, he said to him, 'Can you touch the snake with your staff?'

E. "He said to him, 'Yes.' When he touched it, his limbs fell off. [The crown had earlier protected him from the poison of the snake.]"

4. A. R. Yannai was in session and expounding [a lesson] at the gate of his town. He saw a snake rushing along, moving from side to side. He said, "This creature is going to carry out his duty."

B. Almost immediately the report circulated in town, "So and so has been bitten by a snake and died."

5. A. R. Yannai was in session and expounding [a lesson] at the gate of his town. He saw a snake rushing along, moving from side to side. He said, "This creature is going to carry out his duty."

B. Almost immediately a certain citizen came by. The snake bit him and he died.

6. A. R. Eleazar was sitting and defecating in the privy. A Roman came along and made him get up and sat down himself. He said, "This is not for nothing." Forthwith a snake came out and bit the Roman and killed him.

B. Eleazar recited in his own regard the verse, "Therefore I will give an Edomite [Roman] [RSV: a man] for you" (Is. 43:4), [reading the word for man, Adam, as Edom, Rome].

7. A. R. Isaac bar Eleazar was walking on the sea cliffs at Caesarea. He saw a thigh bone and buried it, but it rolled about. He buried it and it rolled about. He said, "This bone has been designated for some purpose."

B. A runner jogged by and stumbled on the bone and fell and died. They went and rummaged through [the messenger's bag] and found that he was carrying harsh decrees against the Jews of Caesarea.

8. A. The vile Titus, when he went into the house of the Holy of Holies, pulled down the veil, blasphemed, and cursed. When he came out, a mosquito flew up his nose and chewed at his brain.

B. When he died, they split open his brain and found in it something like a bird, weighing two *litras*. [So the mosquito served God's purpose in punishing Titus.]

The entire sequence of course makes the point announced at the beginning. The polemic stresses the perfection of creation, and obviously the same point accounts for the inclusion of VII as well. Obviously we deal with set-piece stories, which have been collected because all of them make the point that seemingly needless, or even offensive, aspects of creation also serve a purpose known to God. But no story has been worked out for the particular purposes of the composition before us, for none even knows what interests us, namely, the exegesis of Gen. 2:1-2. So the issue of exegesis, so far as the present composition indicates, in the end proves to be syllogistic. That is to say, once we propose to demonstrate the proposition that everything that God created serves God's purpose, we shall draw together into a list of examples a variety of materials, some of them exegetical, some narrative, some propositional. But from a formal viewpoint the composition is a miscellany.

X:VIII.

1. A. "And on the seventh day God finished" (Gen. 2:2):

B. Said R. Hanina, "R. Ishmael b. R. Yose brought me to a certain innkeeper['s establishment]. He said, 'Here on the eve of the Sabbath [Friday] father said the Prayer for the Eve of the Sabbath."

C. R. Jeremiah and R. Ammi, R. Yohanan asked, "Here on the eve of the Sabbath father said the Prayer for the Eve of the Sabbath?! [How could he have said the Prayer for the Sabbath while it was still day, and he was not at home but near the inn?]"

D. But there was no need to see a difficulty in the matter, for lo, ass-drivers came up from Arab to Sepphoris and said, "R. Hanina b. Dosa already has welcomed the Sabbath in his town.' [So it was customary to receive the Sabbath before sunset, at which point others would have marked the advent of the holy day. Doing so early was not surprising.]

E. If you wish to present a problem, however, raise the question in connection with the following statement that R. Hanina made: "R. Ishmael b. R. Yose drew me to the establishment of a certain innkeeper, saying 'Here on the Sabbath day itself father said the Prayer for the end of the Sabbath. [How could Yose have ended the Sabbath prior to sunset?!]"

F. Said R. Assi, "Even in this matter there was no need to raise a difficulty, for lo, Rabbi was once in session and giving an exposition, and he said to Abedan, his loud-speaker, 'Inform the community to say the Prayer for the week day, even while it is still day [and the Sabbath has not ended].'

G. "And furthermore, R. Hiyya bar Ba was in session and giving an exposition, and he said to his loud-speaker, 'Inform the community to say the Prayer for the week day, even while it is still day [and the Sabbath has not ended].'"

We take up the question of how could God could have done work, finishing the world, on the seventh, that is, the Sabbath day. He should have completed it on the sixth day. But only at X:IX will that issue come to the fore. The relevance of this entire passage to the base verse is not yet clear. At X:IX the two points of intersection emerge, first, the presence of the names of Rabbi and Ishmael b. R. Yose, and also the issue of the point at which the Sabbath day begins, with the moment of sunset on Friday. The point of contact with the base verse, however, proves not merely thematic but exegetical.

X:IX.

1. A. Rabbi asked R. Ishmael b. R. Yose, saying to him, "Have you heard from your father the meaning of the verse, 'And on the seventh day God finished...' (Gen. 2:1)? [How on the seventh day could God have done any sort of work of completion?]"

   B. He said to him, "[The completion of the work of creation was simultaneous with sunset, so God did not actually work on the seventh day but only finished his work just at the split second at which the sunset,] as in the case of one who strikes the hammer on the anvil. He raises the hammer while it is yet day and brings it down just after night has come [so the act is begun by day and completed by night]. [Such an act, not performed entirely on the Sabbath day, is not regarded as a violation of the Sabbath.]"

   C. Said R. Simeon b. Yohai, "A mere mortal, who does not know how to calculate split seconds, let alone minutes or hours, is the one who has to add time from the week day to the holy day [just as we saw at X:VIII.1, saying the Prayer on Friday afternoon]. But the Holy One, blessed be he, who knows how to calculate split seconds, let alone minutes and hours, can stay within the rule even by a hair's breadth."

2. A. Geniba and rabbis [on what the work of completion of creation required]:

   B. Geniba said, "The matter may be compared to the case of a king who made a marriage canopy for himself. He plastered it, painted it, and decorated it. And what was the marriage canopy lacking? Only a bride to come into it. So too what did the world lack? It was the Sabbath."

   C. Rabbis say, "The matter may be compared to the case of a king who made a ring for himself. What did it lack? Only the seal. So too, what did the world lack? It was the Sabbath. [which is the seal of creation]"

3. A. This is one of the statements that the translators revised in presenting Scripture in Greek to King Ptolemy, phrasing matters in this way: "And he completed the work on the sixth day and observed the Sabbath on the seventh."

   B. King Ptolemy asked sages in Rome, "On how many days did the Holy One, blessed be he, create his world?"

   C. They said to him, "On six."

   D. He said to them, "And from that time Gehenna has been fired up for the wicked! Woe to the world [Freedman:] for the judgments it must render."

4. A. "His work" (Gen. 2:1) [Did God actually have to labor to create the world?]

   B. But did not R. Berekhiah in the name of R. Judah bar Simon say, "It was not with labor or hard work that the Holy One, blessed be he, made the world"?

   C. And yet do you say, "From all his work"!

   D. Rather, matters are phrased as they are to make it possible to exact punishment from the wicked, who destroy the world that was created with so much labor, and to provide the occasion to give a good reward to the righteous, who sustain the world that was created with so much labor.

5. A. [Since the text refers to work on the Sabbath, we ask,] What was created on that day?

   B. Tranquility, pleasure, well-being, and peace.

6. A. [Answering the same question, namely, in what did the completion of creation consist,] R. Levi in the name of R. Yose bar Nehorai: "So long as the hands of their creator were working with them, [heaven and earth] continued to stretch forth.

   B. "When his hands left off working with them, rest was given to them: 'He gave rest to his world on the seventh day' (Ex. 20:11)."

7. A. Said R. Abba, "In the case of a mortal, when he calls a halt, he does not give the troops a donation [of additional funds],

   B. "and when he gives out a donation, he does not call a halt.

   C. "But the Holy One, blessed be he, called a halt and also gave out largesse: 'And he observed the Sabbath and he blessed' (Gen. 2:3)."

The issue addresses the statement of Gen. 2:1-2 that God finished his work on the seventh day, not on the sixth. So how do we understand the fact that God continued his work on the Sabbath day? No. 1 presents Ishmael b. R. Yose's father's explanation of the matter, which is that, while the work had begun prior to the seventh day, it was precisely at the advent of the Sabbath day that the work was brought to a conclusion. We now understand, further, that X:VIII was joined to X:IX prior to the insertion of the whole into the present context. But the joining is not senseless, since the issue of X:VIII concerns the timing of the Sabbath prayer, that is to say, the timing of the advent of the Sabbath. As an exegetical exercise, however, only X:IX finds an appropriate place in connection with Gen. 2:1-2. The same issue -- the explanation of God's finishing the work on the seventh day, when no work should be done -- occupies Nos. 2-6, which present a variety of answers to the same question. No. 7 surely relates to XI:I, "And God blessed...," providing a transition from consideration of Gen. 2:1-2 to what is to follow. That sort of redactional joining of *parashah* to *parashah* proves quite common in our document.

iii. Leviticus Rabbah Parashah One
I:I

1. A. "The Lord called Moses [and spoke to him from the tent of meeting, saying, 'Speak to the children of Israel and say to them, "When any man of you brings an offering to the Lord, you shall bring your offering of cattle from the herd or from the flock"']."

   B. R. Tanhum bar Hanilai opened [discourse by citing the following verse:] "'Bless the Lord, you his messengers, you mighty in strength, carrying out his word, obeying his word' [Ps. 103:20].

   C. "Concerning whom does Scripture speak?

D. "If [you maintain that] Scripture speaks about the upper world's creatures, [that position is unlikely, for] has not [Scripture in the very same passage already referred to them, in stating], 'Bless the Lord, all his hosts [his ministers, who do his word]' [Ps. 103:21]?

E. "If [you maintain that] Scripture speaks about the lower world's creatures, [that position too is unlikely,] for has not [Scripture in the very same passage already referred to them, in stating], 'Bless the Lord, [you] his messengers' [Ps. 103:20]? [Accordingly, concerning whom does Scripture speak?]

F. "[We shall now see that the passage indeed speaks of the lower ones.] But, since the upper world's creatures are perfectly able to fulfill the commands assigned to them by the Holy One, blessed be he, therefore it is said, 'Bless the Lord, all of his hosts.' But as to the earthly creatures of the lower world [here on earth], because they cannot endure the commands of the Holy One, blessed be he, [the word all is omitted, therefore the verse of Scripture states,] 'Bless the Lord, [you] his messengers' -- but not all of his messengers."

2. A. Another matter: Prophets are called messengers [creatures of the lower world], in line with the following passage, "And he sent a messenger and he took us forth from Egypt" (Num. 20:16).

B. Now was this a [heavenly] messenger, [an angel]? Was it not [merely] Moses [a creature of the lower world]?

C. Why then does Scripture [referring to what Moses did,] call him a "messenger?"

D. But: It is on the basis of that usage that [we may conclude] prophets are called "messengers" [in the sense of creatures of the lower world].

E. "Along these same lines, 'And the messenger of the Lord came up from Gilgal to Bochim' [Judges 2:1]. Now was this a [heavenly] messenger, [an angel]? Was it not [merely] Phineas?

F. "Why then does Scripture [referring to Phineas], call him a 'messenger?'"

G. Said R. Simon, "When the holy spirit rested upon Phineas, his face burned like a torch."

H. But rabbis say, "What did Manoah's wife say to him [concerning Phineas]? 'Lo, a man of God came to me, and his face was like the face of a messenger of God'" (Judges 13:6).

I. [Rabbis continue,] "She was thinking that he is a prophet, but he is in fact a [heavenly] messenger [so the two looked alike to her]."

3. A. Said R. Yohanan, "From their very essence, we derive evidence that the prophets are called 'messengers,' in line with the following passage: 'Then said Haggai, the messenger of the Lord, in the Lord's agency, to the people, "I am with you, says the Lord"' [Hag. 1:13].

B. "Accordingly, you must reach the conclusion that [from] their very character, we prove that the prophets are called 'messengers.'"

4. A. [Reverting to the passage cited at the very outset,] "You mighty in strength, carrying out his word [obeying his word]" (Ps. 103:20).

B. Concerning what [sort of mighty man or hero] does Scripture speak?

C. Said R. Isaac, "Concerning those who observe the restrictions of the Seventh Year [not planting and sowing their crops in the Sabbatical Year] does Scripture speak.

D.   "Under ordinary conditions a person does a religious duty for a day, a week, a month.   But does one really do so for all the rest of the days of an entire year?

E.   "Now [in Aramaic:]   this man sees his field lying fallow, his vineyard lying fallow, yet he pays his anona tax [a share of the crop] and does not complain.

F.   "[In Hebrew:]   Do you know of a greater hero than that!"

G.   Now if you maintain that Scripture does not speak about those who observe the Seventh Year, [I shall bring evidence that it does].

H.   "Here it is stated, 'Carrying out his word' [Ps. 103:20] and with reference to the Seventh Year, it is stated, 'This is the word concerning the year of release' [Deut. 15:2].

I.   "Just as the reference to 'word' stated at that passage applies to those who observe the Seventh Year, so reference to 'word' in the present passage applies to those who observe the Seventh Year."

5.   A.   [Continuing discussion of the passage cited at the outset:]   "Carrying out his word, harkening to his word" (Ps. 103:20):

B.   R. Huna in the name of R. Aha: "It is concerning the Israelites who stood before Mount Sinai that Scripture speaks, for they first referred to doing [what God would tell them to do], and only afterward referred to hearing [what it might be], accordingly stating 'Whatever the Lord has said we shall carry out and we shall harken'" (Ex. 24:7).

6.   A.   [Continuing the same exercise:]   "Harkening to his word" (Ps. 103:20):

B.   Said R. Tanhum bar Hanilai, "Under ordinary circumstances a burden which is too heavy for one person is light for two, or too heavy for two is light for four.

C.   "But is it possible to suppose that a burden that is too weighty for six hundred thousand can be light for a single individual?

D.   "Now the entire people of Israel were standing before Mount Sinai and saying, 'If we hear the voice of the Lord our God any more, then we shall die' [Deut. 5:22].   But, [for his part], Moses heard the sound of the [Divine] word himself and lived.

E.   "You may find evidence that that is the case, for, among all [the Israelites], the [act of] speech [of the Lord] called only to Moses, on which account it is stated, 'The Lord called Moses'" (Lev. 1:1).

Lev. 1:1 intersects with Ps. 103:20 to make the point that Moses was God's messenger par excellence, the one who blesses the Lord, is mighty in strength, carries out God's word, obeys God's word. This point is made first implicitly at No. 1 by proving that the verse speaks of earthly, not heavenly, creatures. Then it is made explicit at No. 6. Nos.1-2 present two sets of proofs. The second may stand by itself. It is only the larger context that suggests otherwise. No. 3 is continuous with 2. No. 4 and No. 5 refer back to the cited verse, Ps. 103:20 but not to the context of Lev. 1:1. So we have these units:

1.A-F................Ps. 103:20 refers to some earthly creatures.

1.G-M, 2, 3.......Prophets are called messengers.

4......................Ps. 103:20 refers to a mighty man who observes the Sabbatical Year.

5......................Ps. 103:20 refers to the Israelites before Mount Sinai

6......................Ps. 103:20 refers to Moses.

If then we ask what is primary to the redaction resting on Lev. 1:1, it can be only 1.A-F and 6. But since 1.A-F does not refer to Moses at all, but only sets up the point made at No. 6. No. 6 does not require No. 1. It makes its point without No. 1's contribution. Furthermore, No. 1, for its part, is comprehensible by itself as a comment on Ps. 103:20 and hardly requires linkage to Lev. 1:1. If, therefore, I may offer a thesis on the history of the passage, it would begin with Lev. 1:1 + No. 6. Reference to Ps. 103:20 then carried in its wake Nos. 1.A-F, G-M, 2, 3, 4, and 5 -- all of them to begin with autonomous sayings formed into a kind of handbook on Ps. 103:20. So first came the intersection of Lev. 1:1 and Ps. 103:20 presented by No. 6, and everything else followed in the process of accretion and aggregation, mostly of passages in Ps. 103:20.

I:II

1.   A. R. Abbahu opened [discourse by citing the following verse]: "'They shall return and dwell beneath his shadow, they shall grow grain, they shall blossom as a vine, their fragrance shall be like the wine of Lebanon' [Hos. 14:7].

   B.   "'They shall return and dwell beneath his shadow' -- these are proselytes who come and take refuge in the shadow of the Holy One, blessed be he.

   C.   "'They shall grow grain' -- they are turned into [part of] the root, just as [any other] Israelite.

   D.   "That is in line with the following verse: 'Grain will make the young men flourish, and wine the women' [Zech. 9:17].

   E.   "'They shall blossom as a vine' -- like [any other] Israelite.

   F.   "That is in line with the following verse: 'A vine did you pluck up out of Egypt, you did drive out the nations and plant it'" (Ps. 80:9).

2.   A. Another interpretation [= Genesis Rabbah 66:3]: "They shall grow grain" -- in Talmud.

   B.   "They shall blossom as a vine" -- in lore.

3.   A. "Their fragrance shall be like the wine of Lebanon [and Lebanon signifies the altar]" --

   B.   Said the Holy One, blessed be he, "The names of proselytes are as dear to me as the wine offering that is poured out on the altar before me."

4.   A. And why [is it that mountain or that altar] called "Lebanon?"

   B.   In line with [the following verse]: "That goodly mountain and the Lebanon" (Deut. 3:25).

   C.   R. Simeon b. Yohai taught [= Sifre Deut. 6, 28], "Why is it called Lebanon (LBNN)? Because it whitens (MLBYN) the sins of Israel like snow.

D. "That is in line with the following verse: 'If your sins are red as scarlet, they shall be made white (LBN) as snow'" (Is. 1:18).

E. R. Tabyomi said, "It is [called Lebanon (LBNN)] because all hearts (LBB) rejoice in it.

F. "That is in line with the following verse of Scripture: 'Fair in situation, the joy of the whole world, even Mount Zion, at the far north'" (Ps. 48:3).

G. And rabbis say, "It is [called Lebanon] because of the following verse: 'And my eyes and heart (LB) shall be there all the days'" (1 Kgs. 9:3).

So far as we have a sustained discourse, we find it at Nos. 1 and 3. No. 2 is inserted whole because of its interest in the key verse, Hos. 14:7. Reference at that verse to "Lebanon" explains the set-piece treatment of the word at No. 4. These units may travel together, but the present location seems an unlikely destination. But someone clearly drew together this anthology of materials on, first, Hos. 14:7, and, by the way, second, the word "Lebanon." Why the two sets were assembled is much clearer than how they seemed to the compositor of the collection as a whole to belong to the exposition of Lev. 1:1. Margulies's thesis that the theme of the righteous proselyte intersects with the personal biography of Moses through Pharaoh's daughter (a proselyte!) for the moment seems farfetched. So, in all, the construction of the passage surely is prior to any consideration of its relevance to Lev. 1:1, and the point of the construction certainly is the exegesis of Hos. 14:7 -- that alone. Whether the materials shared with other collections fit more comfortably in those compositions than they do here is not a pressing issue, since, as is self-evident, there is no link to Lev. 1:1 anyhow.

I:III

1. A. R. Simon in the name of R. Joshua b. Levi, and R. Hama, father of R. Hoshaiah, in the name of Rab: "The Book of Chronicles was revealed only for the purposes of exegetical exposition."

2. A. "And his wife Hajehudijah bore Jered, the father of Gedor, and Heber, the father of Soco, and Jekuthiel the father of Zanoah -- and these are the sons of Bithiah, the daughter of Pharaoh, whom Mered took" (1 Chron. 4:17).

B. "And his wife, Hajehudijah [= the Judah-ite]" -- that is Jochebed.

C. Now was she from the tribe of Judah, and not from the tribe of Levi? Why then was she called Hajehudijah [the Judah-ite]?

D. Because she kept Jews (Jehudim) alive in the world [as one of the midwives who kept the Jews alive when Pharaoh said to drown them].

3. A. "She bore Jered" -- that is Moses.

B. R. Hanana bar Papa and R. Simon:

C. R. Hanana said, "He was called Jered (YRD) because he brought the Torah down (HWRYD) from on high to earth."

D. "Another possibility: 'Jered' -- for he brought down the Presence of God from above to earth."

E.   Said R. Simon, "The name Jered connotes only royalty, in line with the following verse: 'May he have dominion (YRD) from sea to sea, and from the river to the end of the earth' [Ps. 72:8].

F.   "And it is written, 'For he rules (RWDH) over the entire region on this side of the River'" (1 Kgs. 5:4).

4.   A.   "Father of Gedor" --

B.   R. Huna in the name of R. Aha said, "Many fence-makers (GWDRYM) stood up for Israel, but this one [Moses] was the father of all of them."

5.   A.   "And Heber" --

B.   For he joined (HBR) the children to their father in heaven.

C.   Another possibility: "Heber" -- for he turned away (HBYR) punishment from coming to the world.

6.   A.   "The father of Soco" --

B.   This one was the father of all the prophets, who perceive (SWKYN) by means of the holy spirit.

C.   R. Levi said, "It is an Arabic word. In Arabia they call a prophet 'sakya.'"

7.   A.   "Jekuthiel" (YQWTYL) --

B.   R. Levi and R. Simon:

C.   R. Levi said, "For he made the children hope [MQWYN] in their Father in heaven."

D.   Said R. Simon, "When the children sinned against God in the incident of the Golden Calf ... "

E.   "The father of Zanoah' --

F.   "Moses came along and forced them to give up (HZNYHN) that transgression.

G.   "That is in line with the following verse of Scripture: '[And he took the calf which they had made and burned it with fire and ground it to powder] and strewed it upon the water'" (Ex. 32:20).

8.   A.   "And these are the sons of Bithiah (BT\YH), the daughter of Pharaoh" --

B.   R. Joshua of Sikhnin in the name of R. Levi: "The Holy One, blessed be he, said to Bithiah, the daughter of Pharaoh, 'Moses was not your child, but you called him your child. So you are not my daughter, but I shall call you my daughter' [thus BT\YH, daughter of the Lord]."

9.   A.   "These are the sons of Bithiah ... whom Mered took" --

B.   [Mered] is Caleb.

C.   R. Abba bar Kahana and R. Judah bar Simon:

D.   R. Abba bar Kahana said, "This one [Caleb] rebelled [MRD] against the counsel of the spies, and that one [Bathiah] rebelled [MRDH] against the counsel of her father [Pharaoh]. Let a rebel come and take as wife another rebellious spirit."

E.   [Explaining the link of Caleb to Pharaoh's daughter in a different way], R. Judah b. R. Simon said, "This one [Caleb] saved the flock, while that one [Pharaoh's daughter] saved the shepherd [Moses]. Let the one who saved the flock come and take as wife the one who saved the shepherd."

10. A. Moses [thus] had ten names (at 1 Chron. 4:17): Jered, Father of Gedor, Heber, Father of Soco, Jekuthiel, and Father of Zanoah [with the other four enumerated in what follows].

B. R. Judah bar Ilai said, "He also was called [7] Tobiah, in line with the following verse: 'And she saw him, that he was good (TWB)' [Ex. 2:2]. He is Tobiah."

C. R. Ishmael bar Ami said, "He also was called [8] Shemaiah."

11. A. R. Joshua bar Nehemiah came and explained the following verse: "'And Shemaiah, the son of Nethanel the scribe, who was of the Levites, wrote them in the presence of the king and the princes and Zadok the priest and Ahimelech the son of Abiathar' [1 Chron. 24:6].

B. "[Moses was called] Shemaiah because God heard (SM\YH) his prayer.

C. "[Moses was called] the son of Nethanel because he was the son to whom the Torah was given from Hand to hand (NTN L).

D. "'The scribe,' because he was the scribe of Israel.

E. "'Who was of the Levites,' because he was of the tribe of Levi.

F. "'Before the king and the princes' -- this refers to the King of kings of kings, the Holy One, blessed be he, and his court.

G. "'And Sadoq the priest' -- this refers to Aaron the priest.

H. "'Ahimelech' -- because [Aaron] was brother (H) of the king.

I. "'The son of Abiathar' (BYTR) -- the son through whom the Holy One, blessed be he, forgave (WYTR) the deed of the Golden Calf."

12. A. R. Tanhuma in the name of R. Joshua b. Qorhah, and R. Menehemiah in the name of R. Joshua b. Levi: "He also was called [9] Levi after his eponymous ancestor: 'And is not Aaron, your brother, the Levite'" (Ex. 4:14).

B. And [he of course was called] [10] Moses -- hence [you have] ten names.

C. Said the Holy One, blessed be he, to Moses, "By your life! Among all the names by which you are called, the only one by which I shall ever refer to you is the one which Bithiah, the daughter of Pharaoh, called you: 'And she called his name Moses'" (Ex. 2:10), so God called Moses.

D. So: "He called Moses" (Lev. 1:1).

Now we see the basis for Margulies's view of the relevance of I:II, that the daughter of Pharaoh named Moses, and she was a proselyte. But the passage at hand (I:III) stands fully by itself, leading to the climax at the very end, at which the opening words of the opening verse of the book of Leviticus are cited. The point of the entire, vast construction is the inquiry into the various names of Moses. From that standpoint we have a strikingly tight composition. But still, the unit is a composite, since it draws together autonomous and diverse materials. The first passage, No. 1, is surely independent, yet it makes for a fine superscription to the whole. Then the pertinent verse, at No. 2.A, 1 Chron. 4:17, is cited and systematically spelled out in Nos. 2, 3, 4, 5, 6, 7, 8, 9. Not only so, but at No. 10, we review the matter and amplify it with an additional, but completely appropriate, set of further names of Moses, Nos. 10 + 12, to be viewed, in line with No. 12, as a unified construction. No. 11 is inserted and breaks the thought. Then 12.C tells us the point of it all, and that brings us back to Lev. 1:1, on the one side, and to No. 8. But, as we have seen, we cannot refer to No. 8 without drawing along the whole set, Nos. 2-9. So the entire passage forms a single, sustained discussion, in which diverse materials are determinedly drawn together into a cogent statement. We notice that No. 7 presents a text problem, since Levi's statement is not matched by Simon's. Levi speaks of Jekuthiel and Simon of "the father of Zanoah." But the only problem is at 7.B. If we omit that misleading superscription -- which served perfectly well at 3.B + C-F -- and have 7.D and E change places, we get a perfectly fine autonomous statement.

I:IV

1. A. R. Abin in the name of R. Berekhiah the Elder opened [discourse by citing the following verse]: "'Of old you spoke in a vision to your faithful ones, saying, "I have set the crown upon one who is mighty, I have exalted one chosen from the people'" [Ps. 89:20].

B. "[The Psalmist] speaks of Abraham, with whom [God] spoke both in word and in vision.

C. "That is in line with the following verse of Scripture: 'After these words the word of God came to Abram in a vision, saying ... ' [Gen. 15:1].

D. "' ... to your faithful one' -- 'You will show truth to Jacob, faithfulness to Abraham' [Mic. 7:20].

E. "' ... saying, "I have set the crown upon one who is mighty" -- for [Abraham] slew four kings in a single night.'

F. "That is in line with the following verse of Scripture: 'And he divided himself against them by night ... and smote them'" (Gen. 14:15).

2. A. Said R. Phineas, "And is there a case of someone who pursues people already slain?

B. "For it is written, 'He smote them and he [then] pursued them' [Gen. 14:15]!

C. "But [the usage at hand] teaches that the Holy One, blessed be he, did the pursuing, and Abraham did the slaying.

3. A. [Abin continues,] "'I have exalted one chosen from the people' [Ps. 89:20].

B. "'It is you, Lord, God, who chose Abram and took him out of Ur in Chaldea'" (Neh. 9:7).

4. A. ["I have exalted one chosen from the people" (Ps. 89:20)] speaks of David, with whom God spoke both in speech and in vision.

B. That is in line with the following verse of Scripture: "In accord with all these words and in accord with this entire vision, so did Nathan speak to David" (2 Sam. 7:17).

C. "To your faithful one" (Ps. 89:20) [refers] to David, [in line with the following verse:] "Keep my soul, for I am faithful" (Ps. 86:2).

D. " ... saying, 'I have set the crown upon one who is mighty," (Ps. 89:20) --

E.   R. Abba bar Kahana and rabbis:

F.   R. Abba bar Kahana said, "David made thirteen wars."

G.   And rabbis say, "Eighteen."

H.   But they do not really differ. The party who said thirteen wars [refers only to those that were fought] in behalf of the need of Israel [overall], while the one who held that [he fought] eighteen includes five [more, that David fought] for his own need, along with the thirteen [that he fought] for the need of Israel [at large].

I.   "I have exalted one chosen from the people" (Ps. 89:20) -- "And he chose David, his servant, and he took him ... " (Ps. 78:70).

5.   A.   ["Of old you spoke in a vision to your faithful one ... "] speaks of Moses, with whom [God] spoke in both speech and vision, in line with the following verse of Scripture: "With him do I speak mouth to mouth [in a vision and not in dark speeches]" (Num. 12:8).

B.   "To your faithful one" -- for [Moses] came from the tribe of Levi, the one concerning which it is written, "Let your Thummim and Urim be with your faithful one" (Deut. 33:8).

C.   " ... saying, 'I have set the crown upon one who is mighty'" --

D.   The cited passage is to be read in accord with that which R. Tanhum b. Hanilai said, "Under ordinary circumstances a burden which is too heavy for one person is light for two, or too heavy for two is light for four. But is it possible to suppose that a burden that is too weighty for six hundred thousand can be light for a single individual? Now the entire people of Israel were standing before Mount Sinai and saying, 'If we hear the voice of the Lord our God any more, then we shall die' [Deut. 5:22]. But, for his part, Moses heard the voice of God himself and lived" [= I:I.6.B-D].

E.   You may know that that is indeed the case, for among them all, the word [of the Lord] called only to Moses, in line with that verse which states, "And [God] called to Moses" (Lev. 1:1).

F.   "I have exalted one chosen from the people" (Ps. 89:20) -- "Had not Moses, whom he chose, stood in the breach before him to turn his wrath from destroying them" [he would have destroyed Israel] (Ps. 106:23).

The whole constitutes a single, beautifully worked out composition, applying Ps. 89:20 to Abraham, David, then Moses, at Nos. 1 and 3 (Abraham), 4 (David), and 5 (Moses). No. 2 is a minor interpolation, hardly spoiling the total effect. No. 5.D is jarring and obviously inserted needlessly. That the purpose of the entire construction was to lead to the climactic citation of Lev. 1:1 hardly can be doubted, since the natural chronological (and eschatological) order would have dictated Abraham, Moses, David. That the basic construction, moreover, forms a unity is shown by the careful matching of the stichs of the cited verse in the expositions of how the verse applies to the three heroes. If we had to postulate an "ideal form," it would be simply the juxtaposition of verses, A illustrated by X, B by Y, etc., with little or no extraneous language. But where, in the basic constituents of the construction, we do find explanatory language or secondary development, in the main it is necessary for sense.

Accordingly, we see as perfect a construction as we are likely to find: whole, nearly entirely essential, with a minimum of intruded material. To be sure, what really looks to be essential is the notion of God's communicating by two media to the three great heroes. That is the clear point of the most closely corresponding passages of the whole. In that case, the reorganization and vast amplification come as an afterthought, provoked by the construction of a passage serving Lev. 1:1. Since 5.E contradicts the message of the rest, that must be regarded as a certainty. Then the whole, except 5.E (hence, 5.D too), served Ps. 89:20, and 5.F is the original conclusion, with 5.D-E inserted by the redactor.

I: V

1. A. R. Joshua of Sikhnin in the name of R. Levi opened [discourse by citing the following] verse: "'For it is better to be told, "Come up here," than to be put lower in the presence of the prince'" (Prov. 25:7).

B. R. Aqiba repeated [the following tradition] in the name of R. Simeon b. Azzai, "Take a place two or three lower and sit down, so that people may tell you, 'Come up,' but do not go up [beyond your station] lest people say to you, 'Go down.' It is better for people to say to you, 'Come up, come up,' than that they say to you, 'Go down, go down.'"

C. And so did Hillel say, "When I am degraded, I am exalted, but when I am exalted, I am degraded."

D. What is the pertinent biblical verse? "He who raises himself is to be made to sit down, he who lowers himself is to be [raised so that he is] seen" (Ps. 113:5).

E. So too you find that, when the Holy One, blessed be he, revealed himself to Moses from the midst of the bush, Moses hid his face from him.

F. That is in line with the following verse of Scripture: "Moses hid his face" (Ex. 3:6).

2. A. Said to him the Holy One, blessed be he, "And now, go (LKH), I am sending you to Pharaoh" (Ex. 3:10).

B. Said R. Eleazar, "[Taking the word 'Go,' LK, not as the imperative, but to mean, 'to you,' and spelled LKH, with an H at the end, I may observe that] it would have been sufficient to write, 'You (LK),' [without adding] an H at the end of the word. [Why then did Scripture add the H?] To indicate to you, 'If you are not the one who will redeem them, no one else is going to redeem them.'

C. "At the Red Sea, Moses stood aside. Said to him the Holy One, blessed be he, 'Now you, raise your rod and stretch out your hand [over the sea and divide it]' [Ex. 14:16].

D. "This is to say, 'If you do not split the sea, no one else is going to split it.'

E. "At Sinai Moses stood aside. Said to him the Holy One, blessed be he, 'Come up to the Lord, you and Aaron' [Ex. 24:1].

F. "This is to say, 'If you do not come up, no one else is going to come up.'

G. "At the [revelation of the instructions governing sacrifices at] the tent of meeting, [Moses] stood to the side. Said to him the Holy One, blessed be he, 'How long are you going to humble yourself? For the times demand only you.'

H. "You must recognize that that is the case, for among them all, the Word [of God] called only to Moses, as it is written, 'And [God] called to Moses'" (Lev. 1:1).

We have once more to work backward from the end to find out what, at the outset, is necessary to make the point of the unit as a whole. It obviously is the emphasis upon how the humble man is called to take exalted position and leadership, that is, No. 2. Then what components of No. 1 are thematically irrelevant? None, so far as I can see. We may regard 1.A as standing by itself, a suitable introduction to a statement on the theme at hand, namely, it is better to be called upon, as at Lev. 1:1. Then Nos. 1.B, C-D, E-F illustrate the same theme, leading to the introduction of the figure of Moses. E-F are so formulated ("so too you find") as to continue the foregoing, but, of course, they form a bridge to what follows, No. 2. Accordingly, a rather deft editorial hand has drawn together thematically pertinent materials. I find it difficult to imagine that the composition was not worked out essentially within a unitary framework, with the exegetical program of the whole, expressed at No. 2, fully in hand before the anthology of No. 1 was gathered. But the fact is that Nos. 1.B, C-D, do come from already framed materials.

I:VI

1. A. R. Tanhuma opened [discourse by citing the following verse:] "There are gold and a multitude of rubies, but lips [that speak] knowledge are the [most] valuable ornament' [Prov. 20:15].

B. "Under ordinary circumstances [if] a person has gold, silver, precious stones, pearls, and all sorts of luxuries, but has no knowledge -- what profit does he have?

C. "In a proverb it says, 'If you have gotten knowledge, what do you lack? But if you lack knowledge, what have you gotten?'"

2. A. "There is gold" -- all brought their free will offering of gold to the tabernacle.

B. That is in line with the following verse of Scripture: "And this is the offering [which you shall take from them, gold] ... " (Ex. 25:3).

C. "And a multitude of rubies" -- this refers to the free will offering of the princes.

D. That is in line with the following verse of Scripture: "And the rulers brought [onyx stones and the stones to be set]" (Ex. 35:27).

E. "But lips [that speak] knowledge are the [most] valuable ornament" (Prov. 20:15).

F. Now Moses was sad, for he said, "Everyone has brought his free will offering for the tabernacle, but I have not brought a thing!"

G. Said to him the Holy One, blessed be he, "By your life! Your words [of address to the workers in teaching them how to build the tabernacle] are more precious to me than all of these other things."

H. You may find proof for that proposition, for among all of them, the Word [of God] called only to Moses, as it is written, "And [God] called to Moses" (Lev. 1:1).

Once more we see a complete construction, with a seemingly irrelevant introduction, No. 1, serving to cite a verse in no way evoked by the passage at hand. The exposition of the verse, further, does not appear to bring us closer to the present matter. But at No. 2, both the cited verse and the exposition of the verse are joined to the verse before us. If we may venture a guess at the aesthetic jeu d'esprit involved, it is this: how do we move from what appears to be utterly irrelevant to what is in fact the very heart of the matter? The aesthetic accomplishment is then to keep the hearer or reader in suspense until the climax, at which the issue is worked out, the tension resolved. It must follow, of course, that we deal with unitary composition.

I:VII

1 . A. What subject matter is discussed just prior to the passage at hand? It is the passage that deals with the building of the tabernacle [in which each pericope concludes with the words,] "As the Lord commanded Moses" (see Ex. 38:22; 39:1, 5, 7, 21, 26, 29, 31, 32, 42, 43; 40:16, 19, 21, 23, 25, 27, 29, 32).

B. To what may this matter be compared? To a king who commanded his servant, saying to him, "Build a palace for me."

C. On everything that [the employee] built, he wrote the name of the king. When he built the walls, he inscribed the name of the king, when he set up the buttresses, he wrote the name of the king on them, when he roofed it over, he wrote the name of the king on [the roof]. After some days, the king came into the palace, and everywhere he looked, he saw his name inscribed. He said, "Now my employee has paid me so much respect, and yet I am inside [the building he built], while he is outside!" He called him to enter.

D. So when the Holy One, blessed be he, called to Moses, "Make a tabernacle for me," on [every] thing that Moses made, he inscribed, " ... as the Lord commanded Moses."

E. Said the Holy One, blessed be he, "Now Moses has paid me so much respect, and yet I am inside, while he is outside!"

F. He called him to come in, on which account it is said, "And [God] called Moses" (Lev. 1:1).

The exegetical resource is the repeated reference, as indicated, to Moses doing as God had commanded him. But this is now read as Moses inscribing God's name everywhere on the tabernacle as he built it, and the rest follows.

I:VIII

1 . A. R. Samuel bar Nahman said in the name of R. Nathan, "Eighteen times are statements of [God's] commanding written in the passage on the building of the tabernacle, corresponding to the eighteen vertebrae in the backbone.

B. "Correspondingly, sages instituted eighteen statements of blessing in the Blessings of the Prayer, eighteen mentions of the divine name in the recitation of the Shema, eighteen mentions of the divine name in the Psalm, 'Ascribe to the Lord, you sons of might'" (Ps. 29).

C. Said R. Hiyya bar Ada, "[The counting of the eighteen statements of God's commandment to Moses] excludes [from the count the entry prior to the one in the verse], 'And with him was Oholiab, son of Ahisamach of the tribe of Dan' [Ex. 38:23], [thus omitting reference to Ex. 38:22, 'And Bezalel, son or Uri son of Hur of the tribe of Judah, made all that the Lord commanded Moses']. [But the counting then includes all further such references to the end of the book [of Exodus]."

2. A. To what is the matter comparable? To a king who made a tour of a province, bringing with him generals, governors, and lesser officers, and, [in watching the procession], we do not know which one among them is most favored. But [when we see] to whom the king turns and speaks, we know that he is the favorite.

B. So everyone surrounded the tabernacle, Moses, Aaron, Nadab and Abihu, and the seventy elders, so we do not know which one of them is the favorite. But now, since the Holy One, blessed be he, called to Moses and spoke to him, we know that he was the favorite of them all.

C. On that account it is said, "And [God] called Moses" (Lev. 1:1).

3. A. To what may the matter be compared? To a king who made a tour of a province. With whom will he speak first? Is it not with the market inspector, who oversees the province? Why? Because he bears responsibility for the very life of the province.

B. So Moses bears responsibility for Israel's every burden,

C. saying to them, "This you may eat" (Lev. 11:2), "and this you may not eat" (Lev. 11:4); "This you may eat of whatever is in the water" (Lev. 11:9), and this you may not eat; "This you shall treat as an abomination among fowl" (Lev. 11:13), and so these you shall treat as an abomination, and others you need not abominate, "And these are the things that are unclean for you" (Lev. 11:29), so these are unclean, and those are not unclean.

D. Therefore it is said, "And [God] called Moses" (Lev. 1:1).

No. 1 bears no relationship to what follows. It continues I:VII, with its interest in the repetitions of the statement about Moses having done as God had commanded him. 1.A-B however stand completely outside the present frame of reference, Lev. 1:1. 1.C harmonizes the number of times the cited phrase actually occurs with the number of vertebrae in the backbone. No. 1 further occurs at B. Ber. 28b, Y. Ber. 4:3, so we may be certain the passage was tacked on because of the interest in the verse at the center of the preceding item. No. 2 and No. 3 match one another, making essentially the same point and leading up to the citation of the verse by establishing the same connotation, "called" in the sense of "recognized, gave preference to." 3.C is wildly out of place, since, as it is now composed, the emphasis is on the fact that, if Scripture says you may not eat a certain thing, whatever is not covered in the negative statement then may be eaten. That is why the language of the verse is repeated, " ... not this ...

but then that is permitted." In fact, we should move from 3.A-B to D. The passage as a whole then is a composite of three distinct items.

I:IX

1. A. "And [the Lord] called to Moses" (Lev. 1:1) [bearing the implication, to Moses in particular].

B. Now did he not call Adam? [But surely he did:] "And the Lord God called Adam" (Gen. 3:9).

C. [He may have called him, but he did not speak with him, while at Lev. 1:1, the Lord "called Moses and spoke to him"], for is it not undignified for a king to speak with his tenant farmer [which Adam, in the Garden of Eden, was]?

D. " ... and the Lord spoke to him" (Lev. 1:1) [to him in particular].

E. Did he not speak also with Noah? [But surely he did:] "And God speak to Noah" (Gen. 8:15).

F. [He may have spoken to him, but he did not call him,] for is it not undignified for a king to speak with [better: call] his ship's captain [herding the beasts into the ark]?

G. "And [the Lord] called to Moses" (Lev. 1:1) [in particular].

H. Now did he not call Abraham? [But surely he did:] "And the angel of the Lord called Abraham a second time from heaven" (Gen. 22:15).

I. [He may have called him, but he did not speak with him,] for is it not undignified for a king to speak with his host (Gen. 18:1)?

J. "And the Lord spoke with him" (Lev. 1:1) [in particular].

K. And did he not speak with Abraham? [Surely he did:] "And Abram fell on his face, and [God] spoke with him" (Gen. 17:3).

L. But is it not undignified for a king to speak with his host?

2. A. "And the Lord called Moses" (Lev. 1:1), but not as in the case of Abraham.

B. [How so?] In the case of Abraham, it is written, "And an angel of the Lord called Abraham a second time from heaven" (Gen. 22:15). The angel did the calling, the Word [of God] then did the speaking.

C. "Here, [by contrast,]" said R. Abin, "the Holy One, blessed be he, said, 'I am the one who does the calling, and I am the one who does the speaking.'

D. "'I, even I, have spoken, yes, I have called him, I have brought him and he shall prosper in his way'" (Is. 48:15).

The point of No. 1 is clear, but the text is not. What is demanded is three instances in which God called someone but did not speak with him, or spoke with him but did not call him, in contrast with the use of both verbs, "call" and "speak," in regard to Moses at Lev. 1:1. If that is what is intended, then the pattern does not work perfectly for all three: Adam, Noah, and Abraham. 1.A-D and E-G are smooth. With Abraham, however, the exposition breaks down, since the point should be that he called Abraham but did not actually speak with him, and it is only No. 2 that makes that point. The repetition of J at M therefore is only part of the problem of the version. We can readily reconstruct what is needed, of course, in the model of the passages for Adam and Noah. No. 2 of course is independent of No. 1, and handsomely worked out. But No. 2 cannot have served the form selected by the framer of the triplet at No. 1. My guess is that No. 1 fails as it does because of yet another problem. E does have God speaking with Noah, while F says that that is undignified, and the same problem recurs with Abraham. In all, No. 2 is a success, and No. 1 is not. Here it is difficult to claim that someone deliberately worked up the entire unit, leading to the climax at the very end. Two existing sets have been combined, and the first of the two turns out to be flawed.

I:X

1. A.   "[And the Lord called Moses and spoke to him] from the tent of meeting" (Lev. 1:1).

B.   Said R. Eleazar, "Even though the Torah [earlier] had been given to Israel at Sinai as a fence [restricting their actions], they were liable to punishment on account of [violating] it only after it has been repeated for [taught to] them in the tent of meeting.

C.   "This may be compared to a royal decree, that had been written and sealed and brought to the province. The inhabitants of the province became liable to be punished on account of violating the decree only after it had been proclaimed to them in a public meeting in the province.

D.   "Along these same lines, even though the Torah had been given to Israel at Sinai, they bore liability for punishment on account of violating it[s commandments] only after it had been repeated for them in the tent of meeting.

E.   "That is in line with the following verse of Scripture: 'Until I had brought him into my mother's house and into the chamber of my teaching [lit.: parent]' [Song 3:4].

F.   "' ... into my mother's house' refers to Sinai.

G.   "' ... and into the chamber of my teaching' refers to the tent of meeting, from which the Israelites were commanded through instruction [in the Torah]."

The passage is formally perfect, running from the beginning, a general proposition, 1.B, through a parable, C, explicitly linked to the original proposition, D, and then joined to the exposition of a seemingly unrelated verse of Scripture, which turns out to say exactly what the general proposition has said. So the original statement, B, is worked out in two separate and complementary ways, first, parabolic, second, exegetical. I cannot see any problem but one: What has the stated proposition to do with the present context? In fact, the theme is the tent of meeting, that alone. We may expect an anthology of materials on the tent of meeting, none of which bears any distinctive relationship to what happens there, so far as Lev. 1:1ff. will tell us. In other words, the redaction of materials following the order of verses of Scripture in the present instance imposes no thesis upon what will be said about those materials, what is important in them. Rather we have nothing more than a list of topics, each to be treated through the formation of an anthology of materials relevant to a topic, not through the unpacking of a problematic indicated by the substance and the context at hand.

I:XI

1.   A.   Said R. Joshua b. Levi, "If the nations of the world had known how valuable the tent of meeting was to them, they would have sheltered it with tents and ballustrades.

      B.   "[How so?] You note that before the tabernacle was erected, the nations of the world used to hear the sound of [God's] word and [fearing an earthquake(?)] they rushed out of their dwellings.

      C.   "That is in line with the following verse of Scripture: 'For who is there of all flesh, who has heard the voice of the living God [speaking out of the midst of the first as we have, and lived]?'" (Deut. 5:23).

2.   A.   Said R. Simon, "The word [of God] went forth in two modes, for Israel as life, for the nations of the world as poison.

      B.   "That is in line with the following verse of Scripture: '\... as you have, and lived' [Deut. 4:33].

      C.   "You hear [the voice of God] and live, while the nations of the world hear and die."

      D.   That is in line with what R. Hiyya taught [= Sifra Dibura dinedabah 2:10], "' ... from the tent of meeting' [Lev. 1:1] teaches that the sound was cut off and did not go beyond the tent of meeting."

Nos. 1 and 2 go over the same ground but are unrelated. For the sense of 1.B, I follow Margulies. But then the relevance of the verse cited at 1.C is not clear. I should have thought that the nations of the world would benefit from the possibility of hearing God's speech, which would then have warned them about an impending earthquake, for example, getting them out of their houses in time. But 1.C and No. 2 make the point that the tent of meeting prevented the gentiles from hearing God's voice, and this was good for them, since the Torah was life for Israel and death for the gentiles. Accordingly, the sense of 1.B as Margulies reads it seems incongruous to the meaning required by its context. Israelstam (p. 14) gives: " ... rushed in fright out of their camps." I cannot suggest anything better. As noted above, the larger context of Lev. 1:1 makes no impact upon the exegesis of the passage, which is focused upon the theme, the tent of meeting, and not on the meaning of the place or tent in this setting.

I:XII

1.   A.   Said R. Isaac, "Before the tent of meeting was set up, prophecy was common among the nations of the world. Once the tent of meeting was set up, prophecy disappeared from among them. That is in line with the following verse of Scripture: 'I held it' [the holy spirit, producing], 'and would not let it go [until I had brought it ... into the chamber of her that conceived me]'" (Song 3:4).

      B.   They said to him, "Lo, Balaam [later on] practiced prophecy!"

C.   He said to them, "He did so for the good of Israel: 'Who has counted the dust of Jacob' [Num. 23:10]. 'No one has seen iniquity in Jacob' [Num. 23:21]. 'For there is no enchantment with Jacob' [Num. 23:23]. 'How goodly are your tents, O Jacob' [Num. 24:5]. 'There shall go forth a star out of Jacob' [Num. 24:17]. 'And out of Jacob shall one have dominion'" (Num. 24:19).

"The chamber" of 1.A is the tent of meeting, as before. In fact the passage at hand is continuous with the foregoing. As we shall see, the established theme then moves forward in what follows. The construction is of course unitary. "They said to him" of B simply sets up discourse; it is not meant to signify an actual conversation, rather serves as a convention of rhetoric. B then allows C to string out the relevant verses. We now continue the same matter of Balaam, prophet of the gentiles, and Israel.

I:XIII

1.   A.   What is the difference between the prophets of Israel and those of the nations [= Gen. R. 52:5]?

B.   R. Hama b. R. Haninah and R. Issachar of Kepar Mandi:

C.   R. Hama b. R. Hanina said, "The Holy One, blessed be he, is revealed to the prophets of the nations of the world only in partial speech, in line with the following verse of Scripture: 'And God called [WYQR, rather than WYQR, as at Lev. 1:1] Balaam' [Num. 23:16]. On the other hand, [he reveals himself] to the prophets of Israel in full and complete speech, as it is said, 'And [the Lord] called (WYQR) to Moses'" (Lev. 1:1).

D.   Said R. Issachar of Kepar Mandi, "Should that [prophecy, even in partial form] be [paid to them as their] wage? [Surely not, in fact there is no form of speech to gentile prophets, who are frauds]. [The connotation of] the language, 'And [God] called (WYQR) to Balaam' [Num. 23:16] is solely uncleanness. That is in line with the usage in the following verse of Scripture: 'That is not clean, by that which happens (MQRH) by night' [Deut. 23:11]. [So the root is the same, with the result that YQR at Num. 23:16 does not bear the meaning of God's calling to Balaam. God rather declares Balaam unclean.]

E.   "But the prophets of Israel [are addressed] in language of holiness, purity, clarity, in language used by the ministering angels to praise God. That is in line with the following verse of Scripture: 'And they called (QR) one to another and said'" (Is. 6:3).

2.   A.   Said R. Eleazar b. Menahem, "It is written, 'The Lord is far from the evil, but the prayer of the righteous does he hear' [Prov. 5:29].

B.   "'The Lord is far from the wicked' refers to the prophets of the nations of the world.

C.   "'But the prayer of the righteous does he hear' refers to the prophets of Israel.

D.   "You [furthermore] find that the Holy One, blessed be he, appears to the prophets of the nations of the world only like a man who comes from some distant place.

E.   "That is in line with the following verse of Scripture: 'From a distant land they have come to me, from Babylonia' [Is. 39:3].

F.   "But in the case of the prophets of Israel [he is always] near at hand: 'And he [forthwith] appeared [not having come from a great distance]' (Gen. 18:1), 'and [the Lord] called'" (Lev. 1:1).

3.   A.   Said R. Yose b. Biba, "The Holy One, blessed be he, is revealed to the prophets of the nations of the world only by night, when people leave one another: 'When men branch off, from the visions of the night, when deep sleep falls on men' [Job 4:13], 'Then a word came secretly to me' [Job 4:12]. [Job is counted among the prophets of the gentiles.]"

4.   A.   R. Hanana b. R. Pappa and rabbis [= Gen. R. 74:7]:

B.   R. Hanana b. R. Pappa said, "The matter may be compared to a king who, with his friend, was in a hall, with a curtain hanging down between them. When [the king] speaks to his friend, he turns back the curtain and speaks with his friend."

C.   And rabbis say, "[The matter may be compared] to a king who had a wife and a concubine. When he walks about with his wife, he does so in full public view. When he walks about with his concubine, he does so in secret. So, too, the Holy One, blessed be he, is revealed to the prophets of the nations of the world only at night, in line with that which is written: 'And God came to Abimelech in a dream by night' [Gen. 29:3]. 'And God came to Laban, the Aramean, in a dream by night' [Gen. 22:24]. 'And God came to Balaam at night' [Num. 22:20].

D.   "To the prophets of Israel, however, [he comes] by day: '[And the Lord appeared to Abraham ...] as he sat at the door of his tent in the heat of the day' [Gen. 18:1]. 'And it came to pass by day that the Lord spoke to Moses in the land of Egypt' [Ex. 6:28]. 'On the day on which he commanded the children of Israel' [Lev. 6:38]. 'These are the generations of Aaron and Moses. God spoke to Moses by day on Mount Sinai'" (Num. 3:1).

Once the topic of comparing Israel's receiving of revelation to that of the nations of the world has arisen, at I:XII, we pursue it further, and, as we shall see, I:XIV adds still more pertinent material. We have a fine superscription in X:XIII, 1.A, with three independent items strung together, 1.B-D, 2, 3, and 4. Nos. 1.B-D and 4, follow an obvious, simple pattern, and Nos. 2 and 3 simply assign a protracted saying to a given name. We have no reason to suppose the entire set has come from a single hand. Since the same points are made by two or more authorities, it is likely that a redactor has chosen pertinent materials out of what he had available.

I:XIV

1.   A.   What is the difference between Moses and all the other [Israelite] prophets?

B.   R. Judah b. R. Ilai and rabbis:

C.   R. Judah said, "All the other prophets saw [their visions] through nine lenses [darkly], in line with the following verse of Scripture: 'And the appearance of the vision which I saw was like the vision that I saw when I came to destroy the city; and the visions were like the vision that I saw by the River

Chebar, and I fell on my face' [Ex. 43:3] [with the root RH occurring once in the plural, hence two, and seven other times in the singular, nine in all].

D. "But Moses saw [his vision] through a single lens: 'in [one vision] and not in dark speeches'" (Num. 12:8).

E. Rabbis said, "All other [Israelite] prophets saw [their visions] through a dirty lens. That is in line with the following verse of Scripture: 'And I have multiplied visions, and by the ministry of the angels I have used similitudes' [Hos. 12:11].

F. "But Moses saw [his vision] through a polished lens: 'And the image of God does he behold'" (Num. 12:8).

2. A. R. Phineas in the name of R. Hoshaia: "[The matter may be compared] to a king who makes his appearance to his courtier in his informal garb [as an intimate] [Lieberman in Margulies, p. 870 to p. 32].

B. "For in this world the Indwelling Presence makes its appearance only to individuals [one by one], while concerning the age to come, what does Scripture say? 'The glory of the Lord shall be revealed, and all flesh shall see [it together, for the mouth of the Lord has spoken]'" (Is. 40:5).

The continuous discourse continues its merry way, ignoring not only the passage at hand -- Lev. 1:1 -- but the several topics provoked by exposition of the theme under discussion in connection with the tent of meeting. Having compared Balaam to Israelite prophets, we proceed to compare Israelite prophets to Moses, with the predictable result. No. 1 preserves the matter. But No. 2 on the surface is wildly out of place, since Moses now is forgotten, and the contrast is between prophecy in this age and in the time to come -- a subject no one has hitherto brought up. But the messianic finis is a redactional convention.

iv. Some Obvious Points of Comparison: Taxonomy of the Forms and the Order of Forms of the Units of Discourse of Genesis Rabbah *Parashah* Ten and Leviticus Rabbah *Parashah* One

1. Taxonomy of Units of Discourse

Form I is defined as an intersecting verse-base verse composition, form II as an exegetical composition in which the base verse is cited and then some sort of comment appended, and form III as a syllogistic composition, in which verses of Scripture are cited in a list of facts in behalf of a given proposition.

Genesis Rabbah *Parashah* Ten

    X:I................I

    X:II...............I

    X:III..............III. I do not see a clear intent to provide an exegesis of the base verse either in No. 1 or in No. 2

X:IV..............II. No. 2 is tacked on.

X:V..............II. No. 3 is tacked on.

X:VI-VII.........A. After the base-verse is cited, a set of stories are tacked on to illustrate the theme of the story.

X:IX..............A

Leviticus Rabbah *Parashah* One

I:I.................I

I:II................I

I:III...............III. This is clearly a syllogistic composition, citing a range of verse to make its point. It is tacked on because it is essential to the antecedent composition. There is nothing miscellaneous either in form, or exegetical program.

I:IV...............I

I:V...............I

I:VI..............I

I:VII..............II

I:VIII.............III. This is a good example of syllogistic composition.

I:IX...............II

I:X................II

I:XI...............III. No. 1 clearly is a syllogism, and so too No. 2.

I:XII..............III

I:XIV.............III

2. Order of the Forms of the   Units of Discourse

Genesis Rabbah *Parashah* Ten follows with some clearly exegetical forms. The remainder from a formal viewpoint seems to me completely miscellaneous. My impression is that Leviticus Rabbah *Parashah* One is so arranged as to place in the beginning materials in the model of form I, then exegetical ones, and, finally, syllogistic ones. We see nothing that we cannot classify in a formal way, although some instances adhere more closely than others to the defined form. In all, however, a comparison of the two *parashiyyot* yields a single impression. The repertoire of forms and the conventions of the ordering of formalized materials for Genesis Rabbah and Leviticus Rabbah proves nearly identical. While the form-analysis must yield a more refined and nuanced articulation, even this preliminary and primitive classification proves that the two compilations' framers found guidance in a single set of forms, used in the same way and for the same purpose. On formal grounds therefore a comparison of the two documents is justified, since, on taxonomic grounds, they fall into a single genus.

The same judgment applies, although not quite so firmly, to the redactional question of the way in which the materials of the several forms are ordered. Here Leviticus Rabbah certainly yields the impression of a firm decision to make use of form I materials first, form II materials second, and form III materials third. Genesis Rabbah by contrast seems in a general way to prefer to place form II materials at the end, with form III materials not so consistently located, occurring more or less at random in the middle or at the end of sustained compositions. Of greater consequence, Genesis Rabbah contains sizable stretches of materials that have not been subjected to the processes of formalization executed by the framers or redactors of the document, while Leviticus Rabbah overall gives the impression that the bulk of its materials have undergone redactional formalization.

The upshot of form-analysis and inquiry into the processes of laying out formalized material may be stated very simply. We have now demonstrated in acute detail and in a sustained way that Genesis Rabbah and Leviticus Rabbah fall within a single formal and redactional taxon. To state the result simply: the formal repertoire of the two documents is pretty much the same. A single taxonomic system of formal classification serves them both. The policy of arranging formalized materials in a consistent order is cogent, if not completely consistent. So, viewed as the outcome of a literary and formal policy dictating rules of how things would be formulated and ordered, the plan of Genesis Rabbah and that of Leviticus Rabbah are one. Formally and redactionally they fall into the same literary genus. On that basis it is surely reasonable to undertake comparison of the the two documents' theological programs as well.

Chapter Six

The Program of Genesis Rabbah
and Leviticus Rabbah

i. From Plan to Program

We more easily describe the plan of the two compilations, the formal and redactional policy governing their formulation and layout, than their respective programs. A measure of subjectivity inevitably affects judgment of the compilers' theological program, message, and principal point(s) of emphasis. My rough and ready characterization of the forms in which authors or editors framed ideas and the ordering of these forms by framers of the document therefore finds no immediate counterpart. For it is easier, in prolix and complex documents such as these, to say how things are formulated and arranged than why compilers made the hermeneutical choices that they made. It is still difficult to specify precisely the message they wished to convey -- difficult, but not impossible.

For if we focus upon the central issue, demonstrably critical to discourse in both compilations, we may come to a preliminary determination on the question, do the framers say the same thing or different things? Answering that question involves two judgments. First, does a given document really deliver a cogent message? Second, are the messages of the two documents coherent with one another, and, if so, how do they fit together? So we ask whether the theological programs of the two documents, the proposition critical to their respective large scale arguments, cogent or incoherent. To respond to that question we review what I believe to be the central concern of the framers of both Genesis Rabbah and Leviticus Rabbah, and how that paramount issue reaches expression. I shall describe each on its own. The reader may then assess the accuracy of my characterization of the two documents and of how they compare in program.

In my judgment, both Genesis Rabbah and Leviticus Rabbah emphasize the same theme and lay out the same thesis. The theme is the meaning of Israel's history. The message is that when Israel obeys the will of their father in heaven, no nation can rule over them, and, when they do not, then the least of nations governs them. The thesis is that because of God's rule Israel should take heart; Israel can overcome its sorry condition in this time, in this world.

The point of emphasis of Genesis Rabbah is that the entire meaning of Israel's history derives from the stories of the very beginnings of creation. The creation of the world and the lives of the founders, patriarchs and matriarchs, foretell what will happen later on and lay down the meaning of Israel's history. So the deeds of the founders present lessons to the descendants, and the future already is known out of the past of creation and of the creation of Israel.

The message of Leviticus Rabbah is that the laws of history may be known, and that these laws, so far as Israel is concerned, focus upon the holy life of the community. If Israel then obeys the laws of society aimed at Israel's sanctification, then the foreordained history, resting on the merit of the ancestors, will unfold as Israel hopes. So there is no secret to the meaning of the events of the day, and Israel, for its part, can affect its destiny and effect salvation.

Accordingly, both documents repeatedly turn attention to the meaning of Israel's history in the time of the patriarchs and Moses (Genesis, Leviticus, respectively), and, of greater consequence, the lessons and rules that govern Israel's history, as these are revealed in the story of Israel's beginning, on the side of Genesis, and Israel's holy life, on the side of Leviticus.

Rather than provide general argument, let alone merely anecdotal evidence, for that proposition, let me turn directly to the description of the two documents' programs. On that basis we may tell whether a single, critical concern proves predominant, and, if it does, what sages have to say about that concern. I describe the program of Genesis Rabbah through extended illustration of my main thesis,[1] and the program of Leviticus Rabbah through a sequence of outlines.[2] In the former case I show that a single paramount concern makes its appearance in a continuing sequence of thematic arenas. Whatever the topic, sages wished to make the same point. In the latter case at issue is the discovery of the laws of history and society. I therefore cover the topical plan of the document as a whole, rather than attending to details of what is said about one theme or another. Genesis Rabbah and Leviticus Rabbah do present contrasts, therefore, since the former prefers an anecdotal mode of illustrating its proposition, which, therefore, is easier to identify. The latter selects a syllogistic mode of argument, making long lists of facts that all together prove a given law of history., The plan of the whole, the prevailing mode of argument - - these testify to the intent of the compilers. In presenting matters as I do, I review results already presented in detail elsewhere. In the case of both compilations the sustained work of analytical description has been accomplished,

---

[1] Cf. *Genesis and Judaism. The Perspective of Genesis Rabbah. An Analytical Anthology* (Atlanta, 1986: Scholars Press for Brown Judaic Studies).

[2] Cf. *Judaism and Scripture. The Evidence of Leviticus Rabbah* (Chicago, 1986: University of Chicago Press).

each in its own context and for its own purpose.[3] That is the best way of avoiding an ad hoc description of the two, done all at once and aimed at making them say the same thing.

ii.   The Program of Genesis Rabbah

In Genesis Rabbah the entire narrative of Genesis is so formed as to point toward the sacred history of Israel, the Jewish people: its slavery and redemption; its coming Temple in Jerusalem; its exile and salvation at the end of time. The powerful message of Genesis in Genesis Rabbah proclaims that the world's creation commenced a single, straight line of events, leading in the end to the salvation of Israel and through Israel all humanity. Israel's history constitutes the counterpart of creation, and the laws of Israel's salvation form the foundation of creation. Therefore a given story out of Genesis, about creation, events from Adam to Noah and Noah to Abraham, the domestic affairs of the patriarchs, or Joseph, will bear a deeper message about what it means to be Israel, on the one side, and what in the end of days will happen to Israel, on the other. So the persistent theological program requires sages' to search in Scripture for meaning for their own circumstance and for the condition of their people. If, therefore, I had to point to the single most important proposition of Genesis Rabbah, it is that, in the story of the beginnings of creation, humanity, and Israel, we find the message of the meaning and end of the life of the Jewish people. The deeds of the founders supply signals for the children about what is going to come in the future. So the biography of Abraham, Isaac, and Jacob also constitutes a protracted account of the history of Israel later on. If the sages could announce a single syllogism and argue it systematically, that is the proposition upon which they would insist.

Before proceeding, let me give a single example of the tendency of the document as a whole. It derives from the single critical moment, in sages' view, in the narrative of Genesis. The binding of Isaac, critical in sages' reading of lessons taught by Abraham's deeds for the direction of their descendants, formed the centerpiece of their quest for the laws of history as well. At each point, in each detail, they discovered not only what we going to happen but also why. The single most important paradigm for history therefore emerged from the deed at Moriah.

---

[3]   In the one instance, I wanted to show the recurrence of one proposition in the exposition of a broad variety of themes, so that the discrete stories of Genesis are made to say the same thing. In the other instance, I wanted to investigate the mode of thought and argument characteristic of the document, so as to understand precisely the role and place of Scripture in the system of Judaism represented by Leviticus Rabbah. This required a quite different approach to the characterization of the program of the document as a whole.

LVI:I.

1. A. "On the third day Abraham lifted up his eyes and saw the place afar off" (Gen. 22:4):

B. "After two days he will revive us, on the third day he will raise us up, that we may live in his presence" (Hos.16:2).

C. On the third day of the tribes: "And Joseph said to them on the third day, 'This do and live'" (Gen. 42:18).

D. On the third day of the giving of the Torah: "And it came to pass on the third day when it was morning" (Ex. 19:16).

E. On the third day of the spies: "And hide yourselves there for three days" (Josh 2:16).

F. On the third day of Jonah: "And Jonah was in the belly of the fish three days and three nights" (Jonah 2:1).

G. On the third day of the return from the Exile: "And we abode there three days" (Ezra 8:32).

H. On the third day of the resurrection of the dead: "After two days he will revive us, on the third day he will raise us up, that we may live in his presence" (Hos. 16:2).

I. On the third day of Esther: "Now it came to pass on the third day that Esther put on her royal apparel" (Est. 5:1).

J. She put on the monarchy of the house of her fathers.

K. On account of what sort of merit?

L. Rabbis say, "On account of the third day of the giving of the Torah."

M. R. Levi said, "It is on account of the merit of the third day of Abraham: 'On the third day Abraham lifted up his eyes and saw the place afar off' (Gen. 22:4)."

2. A. "...lifted up his eyes and saw the place afar off" (Gen. 22:4):

B. What did he see? He saw a cloud attached to the mountain. He said, "It would appear that that is the place concerning which the Holy One, blessed be he, told me to offer up my son."

The third day marks the fulfillment of the promise, at the end of time of the resurrection of the dead, and, at appropriate moments, of Israel's redemption. The reference to the third day at Gen. 22:2 then invokes the entire panoply of Israel's history. The relevance of the composition emerges at the end. Prior to the concluding segment, the passage forms a kind of litany and falls into the category of a liturgy. Still, the recurrent hermeneutic which teaches that the stories of the patriarchs prefigure the history of Israel certainly makes its appearance.

The sages understood that stories about the progenitors, presented in the book of Genesis, define the human condition and proper conduct for their children, Israel in time to come. Accordingly, they systematically asked Scripture to tell them how they were supposed to conduct themselves at the critical turnings of life. The first thing to notice is how a variety of events is made to prove a syllogism. The stories of Genesis therefore join stories of other times and persons in Israel's history. All of them equally, and timelessly, point to prevailing rules. Syllogistic argument, resting on lists of facts of the same classification, wrests the narrative out of its one-time and time-bound setting and turns it into a statement of rules that prevail everywhere and all the time for Israel. Here is a good example of the mode of argument of the document:

XCVI:III.

1. A. "And when the time drew near that Israel must die, [he called his son Joseph and said to him, 'If now I have found favor in your sight, put your hand under my thigh and promise to deal loyally and truly with me. Do not bury me in Egypt, but let me lie with my fathers; carry me out of Egypt and bury me in their burying place.' He answered, I will do as you have said.' And he said, 'Swear to me.' And he swore to him. Then Israel bowed himself upon the head of his bed]" (Gen. 47:29-31):

B. "There is no man that has power of the spirit...neither is there dominion in the day of death" (Qoh. 8:8).

C. Said R. Joshua of Sikhnin in the name of R. Levi, "As to the trumpets that Moses made in the wilderness, when Moses lay on the point of death, the Holy One, blessed be he, hid them away, so that he would not blow on them and summon the people to him.

D. "This was meant to fulfill this verse: '...neither is there dominion in the day of death' (Qoh. 8:8).

E. "When Zimri did his deed, what is written? 'And Phineas went after the man of Israel into the chamber' (Num. 25:8). So where was Moses, that Phineas should speak before he did?

F. "'...neither is there dominion in the day of death' (Qoh. 8:8).

G. "But the formulation expresses humiliation. Salvation was handed over to Phineas, [and Moses] abased himself.

H. "So too with David: 'How king David was old' (1 Kgs. 1:1). What is stated about him when he lay dying? 'Now the days of David drew near, that he should die' (1 Kgs. 21:1).

I. "What is said is not '*king* David,' but merely 'David.'

J. "The same applies to Jacob, when he was on the point of death, he humbled himself to Joseph, saying to him, 'If now I have found favor in your sight.' [So he abased himself, since there is no dominion on the day of death.]

K. "When did this take place? As he drew near the end: 'And when the time drew near that Israel must die.'"

What strikes the exegete is the unprepossessing language used by Jacob in speaking to Joseph. The intersecting verse makes clear that, on the day of one's death, one no longer rules. Several examples of that fact are given, Moses, David, finally Jacob. So the syllogism about the loss of power on the occasion of death derives proof from a number of sources, and the passage has not been worked out to provide the exegesis of our base verse in particular. The exposition is all the more moving because the exegete focuses upon his proposition, rather than on the great personalities at hand. His message obviously is that even the greatest lose all dominion when they are going to die. In this way the deeds of the founders define the rule for the descendants.

As a corollary to the view that the biography of the fathers prefigures the history of the descendants, sages maintained that the deeds of the children -- the holy way of life of Israel -- follow the model established by the founders long ago. So they looked in Genesis for the basis for the things they held to be God's will for Israel. And they found ample proof. Sages invariably searched the stories of Genesis for evidence of the origins not only of creation and of Israel, but also of Israel's cosmic way of life, its understanding of how, in the passage of nature and the seasons, humanity worked out its relationship with God. The holy way of life that Israel lived through the seasons of nature therefore would make its mark upon the stories of the creation of the world and the beginning of Israel

Part of the reason sages pursued the interest at hand derived from polemic. From the first Christian century theologians of Christianity maintained that salvation did not depend upon keeping the laws of the Torah. Abraham, after all, had been justified and he did not keep the Torah, which, in his day, had not yet been given. So sages time and again would maintain that Abraham indeed kept the entire Torah even before it had been revealed. They further attributed to Abraham, Isaac, and Jacob rules of the Torah enunciated only later on, for example, the institution of prayer three times a day. But the passage before us bears a different charge. It is to Israel to see how deeply embedded in the rules of reality were the patterns governing God's relationship to Israel. That relationship, one of human sin and atonement, divine punishment and forgiveness, expresses the most fundamental laws of human existence. Here is yet another rule that tells sages what to find in Scripture.

XCVIII:I.

1. A. "Then Jacob called his sons [and said, 'Gather yourselves together, that I may tell you what shall befall you in days to come. Assemble and hear, O sons of Jacob, and hearken to Israel, your father. Reuben, you are my first-born, my might and the first fruits of my strength, pre-eminent in pride and pre-eminent in power. Unstable as water, you shall not have pre-eminence, because you went up to your father's bed, then you defiled it, you went up to my couch!']" (Gen. 49:1-4):

   B. "I will cry to God Most High, [unto God who completes it for me]" (Ps. 57:3):

   C. "I will cry to God Most High:" on the New Year.

   D. "...unto God who completes it for me:" on the Day of Atonement.

   E. To find out which [goat] is for the Lord and which one is for an evil decree.

2. A. Another matter: "I will cry to God Most High, [unto God who completes it for me]" (Ps. 57:3):

   B "I will cry to God Most High:" refers to our father, Jacob.

C. "...unto God who completes it for me:" for the Holy One, blessed be he, concurred with him to give each of the sons a blessing in accord with his character.

D. "Then Jacob called his sons [and said, 'Gather yourselves together, that I may tell you what shall befall you in days to come]."

The intersecting verse invites the comparison of the judgment of the Days of Awe to the blessing of Jacob, and that presents a dimension of meaning that the narrative would not otherwise reveal. Just as God decides which goat serves what purpose, so God concurs in Jacob's judgment of which son/tribe deserves what sort of blessing. So Jacob stands in the stead of God in this stunning comparison of Jacob's blessing to the day of judgment. The link between Jacob's biography and the holy life of Israel is fresh.

What, then, tells sages how to identify the important and avoid the trivial? The answer derives from the fundamental theological conviction that gives life to their search of Scripture. It is that the task of Israel is to hope, and the message of Genesis -- there for the sages to uncover and make explicit -- is always to hope. For a Jew it is a sin to despair. This I think defines the iron law of meaning, telling sages what matters and what does not, guiding their hands to take up those verses that permit expression of hope -- that above all. Given the definitive event of their day -- the conversion of the great empire of Rome to Christianity -- the task of hope proved not an easy assignment.

XCVIII:XIV.

4. A. "I hope for your salvation, O Lord" (Gen. 49:18):

B. Said R. Isaac, "All things depend on hope, suffering depends on hope, the sanctification of God's name depends on hope, the merit attained by the fathers depends on hope, the lust for the age to come depends on hope.

C. "That is in line with this verse: 'Yes, in the way of your judgments, O Lord, we have hoped for you, to your name, and to your memorial, is the desire of our soul' (Is. 26:8). The way of your judgments refers to suffering.

D. "'...to your name:' this refers to the sanctification of the divine name.

E. "'...and to your memorial:' this refers to the merit of the fathers.

F. "'...is the desire of our soul:' this refers to the lust for the age to come.

G. "Grace depends on hope: 'O Lord, be gracious to us, we have hoped for you' (Is. 33:2).

H. "Forgiveness depends on hope: 'For with you is forgiveness' (Ps. 133:4), then: 'I hope for the Lord' (Ps. 130:5)."

The interesting unit is No. 4, which is explicit on the critical importance of hope in the salvific process, and which further links the exclamation to the setting in which it occurs. This seems to me to typify the strength of the exegesis at hand, with its twin-powers to link all details to a tight narrative and to link the narrative to the history of Israel.

Sages read the narrative of creation and the fall of Adam to testify to the redemption and the salvation of Israel. Let me begin with a single example of the syllogism at hand and then offer a more general statement of it. The following passage provides a stunning example of the basic theory of sages on how the stories of creation are to be read:

XXIX:III.

1. A. "And Noah found grace" (Gen. 6:8):

B. Said R. Simon, "There were three acts of finding on the part of the Holy One, blessed be he:

C. "'And you found [Abraham's] heart faithful before you' (Neh. 9:8).

D. "'I have found David my servant' (Ps. 89:21).

E. "'I found Israel like grapes in the wilderness' (Hos. 9:10)."

F. His fellows said to R. Simon, "And is it not written, 'Noah found grace in the eyes of the Lord' (Gen. 6:8)?"

G. He said them, "He found it, but the Holy One, blessed be he, did not find it."

H. Said R. Simon, "'He found grace in the wilderness' (Jer. 31:1) on account of the merit of the generation of the Wilderness."

The proposition draws on the verse at hand, but makes its own point. It is that the grace shown to Noah derived from Israel. Noah on his own -- that is, humanity -- enjoyed salvation only because of Israel's merit. The proposition is striking and daring. God "found," that is, made an accidental discovery, of a treasure, consisting only of three: Abraham, David, and Israel. These stand for the beginning, the end, and the holy people that started with Abraham and found redemption through David. As if to underline this point, we refer, H, to the generation of the Wilderness and its faith, which merited gaining the Land.

A cogent and uniform world-view accompanied the sages at hand when they approached the text of Genesis. This world-view they systematically joined to that text, fusing the tale at hand with that larger context of imagination in which the tale was received and read. Accordingly, when we follow the sages' mode of interpreting the text, we find our way deep into their imaginative life. Scripture becomes the set of facts that demonstrate the truth of the syllogisms that encompassed and described the world, as sages saw it. The next stage in my demonstration of the systematic and deeply polemical reading at hand will take the simple form of successive illustration of the basic thesis. That thesis is that Israel's salvific history informs and infuses the creation of the world. That story takes on its true meaning from what happened to Israel, and it follows that Israel's future history accounts for the creation of the world.

XX:I.

1. A. "Then the Lord God said to the serpent, 'Because you have done this, cursed are you above all cattle and above all wild animals'" (Gen. 3:14):

B. "A slanderer shall not be established in the earth; the violent and wicked man shall be hunted with thrust upon thrust" (Ps. 140:12).

C. Said R. Levi, "In the world to come the Holy One, blessed be he, will take the nations of the world and bring them down to Gehenna. He will say to them, 'Why did you impose fines upon my children.' They will say to him, 'Some of them slandered others among them. The Holy One, blessed be he, will then take these [Israelite slanderers] and those and bring them down to Gehenna."

2. A. Another interpretation: "A slanderer" refers to the snake, who slandered his creator.

B. "Will not be established [standing upright] on earth:" "Upon your belly you shall go" (Gen. 3:14).

C. "The violent and wicked man shall be hunted:" What is written is not "with a thrust" but "with thrust after thrust," [since not only the serpent was cursed]. What is written is "thrust after thrust," for man was cursed, woman was cursed, and the snake was cursed.

D. "And the Lord God said to the serpent...."

We have an exegesis of a base verse and intersecting verse, that is in that "classic" form in which the intersecting verse is fully worked out and only then drawn to meet the base verse. No. 1 treats the intersecting verse as a statement on its own, and then No. 2 reads the verse in line with Gen. 3:14. But the intersecting verse is hardly chosen at random, since it speaks of slander in general, and then at No. 2 the act of slander of the snake is explicitly read into the intersecting verse. So the intersection is not only thematic, not by any means. The upshot of the exercise links Israel's history to the history of humanity in the garden of Eden. No. 1 focuses upon the sacred history of Israel, making the point that slanderers in Israel cause the nation's downfall, just as the snake caused the downfall of humanity.

XIX:VII.

1. A. "And they heard the sound of the Lord God walking in the garden in the cool of the day" (Gen. 3:8):

2. A. Said R. Abba bar Kahana, "The word is not written, 'move,' but rather, 'walk,' bearing the sense that [the Presence of God] leapt about and jumped upward.

B. "[The point is that God's presence leapt upward from the earth on account of the events in the garden, as will now be explained:] The principal location of the Presence of God was [meant to be] among the creatures down here. When the first man sinned, the Presence of God moved up to the first firmament. When Cain sinned, it went up to the second firmament. When the generation of Enosh sinned, it went up to the third firmament. When the generation of the Flood sinned, it went up to the fourth firmament. When the generation of the dispersion [at the tower of Babel] sinned, it went up to the fifth. On account of the Sodomites it went up to the sixth, and on account of the Egyptians in the time of Abraham it went up to the seventh.

C. "But, as a counterpart, there were seven righteous men who rose up: Abraham, Isaac, Jacob , Levi, Kahath, Amram, and Moses. They brought the Presence of God [by stages] down to earth.

D. "Abraham brought it from the seventh to the sixth, Isaac brought it from the sixth to the fifth, Jacob brought it from the fifth to the fourth, Levi brought it down from the forth to the third, Kahath brought it down from the third to the second, Amram brought it down from the second to the first. Moses brought it down to earth."

E. Said R. Isaac, "It is written, 'The righteous will inherit the land and dwell therein forever' (Ps. 37:29). Now what will the wicked do? Are they going to fly in the air? But that the wicked did not make it possible for the Presence of God to take up residence on earth [is what the verse wishes to say]."

What is striking is the claim that while the wicked (gentiles) drove God out of the world, the righteous (Israelites) brought God back into the world. This theme, linking the story of the fall of man to the history of Israel, with Israel serving as the counterpart and fulfillment of the fall at creation. The next composition still more strikingly shows that the creation and fall of man finds its counterpart in the formation and sanctification of Israel. So Israel serves, as did the first man, as the embodiment of humanity. But while Adam sinned and was driven from paradise, Israel through atonement will bring humanity salvation. In this way the book of Genesis serves a purpose quite pertinent to the theological program of the compilers of Genesis Rabbah.

XIX:IX.

1. A. "And the Lord God called to the man and said to him, 'Where are you?'" (Gen. 3:9):

B. [The word for "where are you" yields consonants that bear the meaning,] "How has this happened to you?"

C. [God speaks:] "Yesterday it was in accord with my plan, and now it is in accord with the plan of the snake. Yesterday it was from one end of the world to the other [that you filled the earth], and now: 'Among the trees of the garden' (Gen. 3:8) [you hide out]."

2. A. R. Abbahu in the name of R. Yose bar Haninah: "It is written, 'But they are like a man [Adam], they have transgressed the covenant' (Hos. 6:7).

B. "'They are like a man,' specifically, like the first man. [We shall now compare the story of the first man in Eden with the story of Israel in its land.]

C. "'In the case of the first man, I brought him into the garden of Eden, I commanded him, he violated my commandment, I judged him to be sent away and driven out, but I mourned for him, saying "How..."'[which begins the book of Lamentations, hence stands for a lament, but which, as we just saw, also is written with the consonants that also yield, 'Where are you'].

D. "'I brought him into the garden of Eden,' as it is written, 'And the Lord God took the man and put him into the garden of Eden' (Gen. 2:15).

E. "'I commanded him,' as it is written, 'And the Lord God commanded...' (Gen. 2:16).

F. "'And he violated my commandment,' as it is written, 'Did you eat from the tree concerning which I commanded you' (Gen. 3:11).

G. "'I judged him to be sent away,' as it is written, "And the Lord God sent him from the garden of Eden' (Gen. 3:23).

H. "'And I judged him to be driven out.' 'And he drove out the man' (Gen. 3:24).

I. "'But I mourned for him, saying, "How...".' 'And he said to him, "Where are you"' (Gen. 3:9), and the word for 'where are you' is written, 'How....'

J. "'So too in the case of his descendants, [God continues to speak,] I brought them into the Land of Israel, I commanded them, they violated my commandment, I judged them to be sent out and driven away but I mourned for them, saying, "How...."'

K. "'I brought them into the Land of Israel.' 'And I brought you into the land of Carmel' (Jer. 2:7).

L. "'I commanded them.' 'And you, command the children of Israel' (Ex. 27:20). 'Command the children of Israel' (Lev. 24:2).

M. "'They violated my commandment.' 'And all Israel have violated your Torah' (Dan. 9:11).

N. "'I judged them to be sent out.' 'Send them away, out of my sight and let them go forth' (Jer 15:1).

O. "'....and driven away.' 'From my house I shall drive them' (Hos. 9:15).

P. "'But I mourned for them, saying, "How...."'" 'How has the city sat solitary, that was full of people' (Lam. 1:1)."

No. 1 simply contrasts one day with the next, a stunning and stark statement, lacking all decoration. No. 1 certainly sets the stage for No. 2 and the whole must be regarded as a cogent, thoughtful composition. The other, No. 2, equally simply compares the story of man in the Garden of Eden with the tale of Israel in its Land. Every detail is in place, the articulation is perfect, and the result, completely convincing as an essay in interpretation. All of this rests on the simple fact that the word for "where are you" may be expressed as "How...," which, as is clear, invokes the opening words of the book of Lamentations. So Israel's history serves as a paradigm for human history, and vice versa. What then is the point? It is obedience, as the following indicates:

XIX:XI.

1. A. "The man said, 'The woman whom you gave to be with me gave me fruit of the tree, and I ate'" (Gen. 3:12):

B. There are four on whose pots the Holy One, blessed be he, knocked, only to find them filled with piss, and these are they: Adam, Cain, the wicked Balaam, and Hezekiah.

C. Adam: "The man said, 'The woman whom you gave to be with me gave me fruit of the tree and I ate" (Gen. 3:12).

D. Cain: "And the Lord said to Cain, 'Where is Abel, your brother?'" (Gen. 4:9).

E. The wicked Balaam: "And God came to Balaam and said, 'What men are these with you?'" (Num. 22:9)

F. Hezekiah: "Then came Isaiah the prophet to king Hezekiah and said to him, 'What did these men say?'" (2 Kgs. 20:14).

G. But Ezekiel turned out to be far more adept than any of these: "'Son of man, can these bones live?' And I said, 'O Lord God, you know'" (Ez. 37:3).

H. Said R., Hinena bar Pappa, "The matter may be compared to the case of a bird that was caught by a hunter. The hunter met someone who asked him, 'Is this bird alive or dead?'

I. "He said to him, 'If you want, it is alive, but if you prefer, it is dead.' So: "'Will these bones live?" And he said, "Lord God, you know."'"

The colloquy once more serves to find in Israel's history a counterpart to the incident at hand. Only Ezekiel knew how to deal with a question that bore with it the answer: God will do as he likes, God knows the answer. That is, the sole appropriate response is one of humility and acceptance of God's will. With what result? With the result of the salvation of humanity through Israel. History through Israel becomes the story of the salvation of humanity:

XXI:I.

1. A. "Then the Lord God said, 'Behold, the man has become like one of us, [knowing good and evil, and now, lest he put forth his hand and take also of the tree of life and eat and live forever]'" (Gen. 3:22):

B. "It is written, "Then I heard a holy one speaking, and another holy one said to that certain one who spoke" (Dan. 8:13).

C. "The one" refers to the Holy One, blessed be he: "The Lord, our God, the Lord is One" (Deut. 6:4).

D. "Holy," for everyone says before him, "Holy...."

E. "Speaking" means "issuing harsh decrees against his creatures."

F. [For example,] "Thorns and thistles it shall bring forth to you" (Gen. 3:18).

G. "And another holy one said to that certain one who spoke:"

H. R. Huna said, "It was to Mr. So-and-so."

I. Aqilas translated the passage, "It was to one who was within that he spoke, meaning the first man, whose presence lay within [and closer to God than] that of the serving angels [since he stood closer to God than they did]." [The remainder of the exegesis flows from Aqilas's view of the locus of discourse.]

J. "How long shall be the vision concerning the continual burnt offering?" (Dan. 8:13);

K. "Will the decree that has been issued against the first man go on forever?"

L. "And the transgression that causes desolation" (Deut. 8:13):

M. "So too will his transgression desolate him even in the grave?"

N. "To give both the sanctuary and the host to be trampled underfoot" (Dan. 8:13):

O. "Will he and his descendants be made into chaff before the angel of death?"

P. "And he said to me, 'Until evening, morning two thousand and three hundred, then shall the sanctuary be victorious'" (Dan. 8:14):

Q. R. Azariah, R. Jonathan b. Haggai in the name of R. Isaac: "In any case in which it is evening, it is not morning, and in any case in which it is morning, it surely is not evening. [So what is the sense of this passage?] But when it is morning for the nations of the world, it is evening for Israel, and as to 'morning,' at that time [at which it is morning for Israel],' then 'shall the sanctuary be victorious,' for at that time I shall declare him justified of that decree: 'Behold, let the man become like one of us' (Gen. 3:22)."

The fully exploited intersection of the intersecting and base verses turns the statement of Gen. 3:22 into a powerful promise. Man will indeed become like the One, at the time that the gentiles reach their evening, and Israel, morning. So once more the condition of Israel serves as a paradigm for the human situation, but this in a most concrete and specific way. The nations of the world embody the curse of God to man, and Israel, the promised future blessing. The framer of the passage carefully avoids speculation on the meaning of the numbers used in Daniel's passage, so the apocalyptic power of Daniel's vision serves the rather generalized messianic expectations of sages, without provoking dangerous speculation on the here and now.

XXI:VII.

3. A. Judah b. Padaiah interpreted, "Who will remove the dust from between your eyes, O first man! For you could not abide in the commandment that applied to you for even a single hour, and lo, your children can wait for three years to observe the prohibition of the use of the fruit of a tree for the first three years after it is planted: 'Three years shall it be as forbidden to you, it shall not be eaten' (Lev. 19:23)."

B. Said R. Huna, "When Bar Qappara heard this, he said, 'Well have you expounded matters, Judah, son of my sister!'"

No. 3 then compares the character of Israel to the character of the first man, calling Israel "descendants of the first man" and pointing out that they can observe a commandment for a long time. The example is apt, since Israel observes the prohibition involving the fruit of a newly planted tree, and does so for three years, while the first man could not keep his hands off a fruit tree for even an hour. This of course restates with enormous power the fact that Israel's history forms the counterpart to the history of humanity. But while the first man could not do what God demanded, Israel can and does do God's will. We come at the end to a simple and clear statement of the main point of it all:

LXXXIII:V.

1. A. Wheat, straw, and stubble had a fight.

   B. Wheat said, "It was on my account that the field was sown."

   C. Stubble said, "It was on my account that the field was sown."

   D. Wheat said, "The day will come and you will see."

   E. When the harvest time came, the householder began to take the stubble and burn it, and the straw and spread it, but the wheat he made into heaps.

   F. Everyone began to kiss the wheat. [I assume this is a reference to the messianic passage, "Kiss the son" which is also to be translated, "Kiss the wheat" (Ps. 2:12).]

   G. So too Israel and the nations of the world have a fight.

   H. These say, "It was on our account that the world was created," and those say, "It was on our account that the world was created."

   I. Israel says, "The day will come and you will see."

   J. In the age to come: "You shall fan them and the wind will carry them away" (Is. 41:16).

   K. As to Israel: "And you shall rejoice in the Lord, you shall glory in the Holy One of Israel" (Is. 41:16).

Here at the end sages make explicit their basic view. The world was created for Israel, and not for the nations of the world. At the end of days everyone will see what only Israel now knows. Since sages read Genesis as the history of the world with emphasis on Israel, the lives portrayed, the domestic quarrels and petty conflicts with the neighbors, as much as the story of creation itself, all serve to yield insight into what was to be. We now turn to a detailed examination of how sages spelled out the historical law at hand. The lives of the patriarchs signaled the history of Israel. Every detail of the narrative therefore served to prefigure what was to be, and Israel found itself, time and again, in the revealed facts of the history of the creation of the world, the decline of humanity down to the time of Noah, and, finally, its ascent to Abraham, Isaac, and Israel. In order to illustrate the single approach to diverse stories, whether concerning Creation, Adam, and Noah, or concerning Abraham, Isaac, and Jacob, we focus on two matters, Abraham, on the one side, and Rome, on the other. In the former we see that Abraham serves as well as Adam to prove the point of it all. In the latter we observe how, in reading Genesis, the sages who compiled Genesis Rabbah discovered the meaning of the events of their own day.

Let us begin with an exemplary case of how sages discovered social laws of history in the facts of Scripture. What Abraham did corresponds to what Balaam did, and the same law of social history derives proof from each of the two contrasting figures.

LV:VIII.

1 . A. "And Abraham rose early in the morning, [saddled his ass, and took two of his young men with him, and his son Isaac, and he cut the wood for the burnt offering and arose and went to the place which God had told him]" (Gen. 22:3):

B. Said R. Simeon b. Yohai, "Love disrupts the natural order of things, and hatred disrupts the natural order of things.

C. "Love disrupts the natural order of things we learn from the case of Abraham: '...he saddled his ass.' But did he not have any number of servants? But that proves love disrupts the natural order of things.

D. "Hatred disrupts the natural order of things we learn from the case of Balaam: 'And Balaam rose up early in the morning and saddled his ass' (Num. 22:21). But did he not have any number of servants? But that proves hatred disrupts the natural order of things.

E. "Love disrupts the natural order of things we learn from the case of Joseph: 'And Joseph made his chariot ready' (Gen. 46:29). But did he not have any number of servants? But that proves love disrupts the natural order of things.

F. "Hatred disrupts the natural order of things we learn from the case of Pharaoh: 'And he made his chariot ready' (Ex. 14:6). But did he not have any number of servants? But that proves hatred disrupts the natural order of things."

2 . A. Said R. Simeon b. Yohai, "Let one act of saddling an ass come and counteract another act of saddling the ass. May the act of saddling the ass done by our father Abraham, so as to go and carry out the will of him who speak and brought the world into being counteract the act of saddling that was carried out by Balaam when he went to curse Israel.

B. "Let one act of preparing counteract another act of preparing. Let Joseph's act of preparing his chariot so as to meet his father serve to counteract Pharaoh's act of preparing to go and pursue Israel."

C. R. Ishmael taught on Tannaite authority, "Let the sword held in the hand serve to counteract the sword held in the hand.

D. "Let the sword held in the hand of Abraham, as it is said, 'Then Abraham put forth his hand and took the knife to slay his son' (Gen. 22:10) serve to counteract the sword taken by Pharaoh in hand: 'I will draw my sword, my hand shall destroy them' (Ex. 15:9)."

We see that the narrative is carefully culled for probative facts, yielding laws. One fact is that there are laws of history. The other is that laws may be set aside, by either love or hatred. Yet another law of history applies in particular to Israel, as distinct from the foregoing, deriving from the life of both Israel and the nations, Abraham and Balaam. What follows presents the law that Israel never is orphaned of holy and heroic leaders.

LVIII:II.

1 . A. "The sun rises and the sun goes down" (Qoh. 1:5):

B. Said R. Abba, "Now do we not know that the sun rises and the sun sets? But the sense is this: before the Holy One, blessed be he, makes the sun of one righteous man set, he brings up into the sky the sun of another righteous man.

C. "On the day that R. Aqiba died, Our Rabbi [Judah the Patriarch] was born. In his regard, they recited the following verse: 'The sun rises and the sun goes down' (Qoh. 1:5).

D. "On the day on which Our Rabbi died, R. Adda bar Ahbah was born. In his regard, they recited the following verse: 'The sun rises and the sun goes down' (Qoh. 1:5).

E. "On the day on which R. Ada died, R. Abin was born. In his regard, they recited the following verse: 'The sun rises and the sun goes down' (Qoh. 1:5).

F. "On the day on which R. Abin died, R. Abin his son was born. In his regard, they recited the following verse: 'The sun rises and the sun goes down' (Qoh. 1:5).

G. "On the day on which R. Abin died, Abba Hoshaiah of Taraya was born. In his regard, they recited the following verse: 'The sun rises and the sun goes down' (Qoh. 1:5).

H. "On the day on which Abba Hoshaiah of Taraya died, R. Hoshaiah was born. In his regard, they recited the following verse: 'The sun rises and the sun goes down' (Qoh. 1:5).

I. "Before the Holy One, blessed be he, made the sun of Moses set, he brought up into the sky the sun of Joshua: 'And the Lord said to Moses, Take you Joshua, the son of Nun' (Num. 27:18).

J. "Before the Holy One, blessed be he, made the sun of Joshua set, he brought up into the sky the sun of Othniel, son of Kenaz: 'And Othniel the son of Kenaz took it' (Joshua 15:17).

K. "Before the Holy One, blessed be he, made the sun of Eli set, he brought up into the sky the sun of Samuel: 'And the lamp of God was not yet gone out, and Samuel was laid down to sleep in the Temple of the Lord' (1 Sam. 3:3)."

L. Said R. Yohanan, "He was like an unblemished calf."

M. [Reverting to K:] "Before the Holy One, blessed be he, made the sun of Sarah set, he brought up into the sky the sun of Rebecca: 'Behold Milcah also has borne children' (Gen. 22:20). 'Sarah lived a hundred and twenty-seven years. These were the years of the life of Sarah' (Gen. 23:1)."

One rule of Israel's history is yielded by the facts at hand. Israel is never left without an appropriate hero or heroine. The relevance the long discourse becomes clear at the end. Each story in Genesis may forecast the stages in Israel's history later on, beginning to end. A matter of deep concern focused sages' attention on the sequence of world-empires to which, among other nations, Israel was subjugated, Babylonia, Media, Greece, and Rome -- Rome above all. What will follow? Sages maintained that beyond the rule of Rome lay the salvation of Israel:

XLII:IV.

1. A. "And it came to pass in the days of Amraphel" (Gen. 14:1):

4. A. Another matter: "And it came to pass in the days of Amraphel, king of Shinar" (Gen. 14:1) refers to Babylonia.

B. "Arioch, king of Ellasar" (Gen. 14:1) refers to Greece.

C. "Chedorlaomer, king of Elam" (Gen. 14:1) refers to Media.

D. "And Tidal, king of Goiim [nations]" (Gen. 14:1) refers to the wicked government [Rome], which conscripts troops from all the nations of the world.

E. Said R. Eleazar bar Abina, "If you see that the nations contend with one another, look for the footsteps of the king-messiah. You may know that that is the case, for lo, in the time of Abraham, because the kings struggled with one another, a position of greatness came to Abraham."

Obviously, No. 4 presents the most important reading of Gen. 14:1, since it links the events of the life of Abraham to the history of Israel and even ties the whole to the messianic expectation. I suppose that any list of four kings will provoke inquiry into the relationship of the entries of that list to the four kingdoms among which history, in Israel's experience, is divided. The process of history flows in both directions. Just as what Abraham did prefigured the future history of Israel, so what the Israelites later on were to do imposed limitations on Abraham. Time and again events in the lives of the patriarchs prefigure the four monarchies, among which, of course, the fourth, last, and most intolerable was Rome. Here is another such exercise in the recurrent proof of a single proposition.

XLIV:XVII.

4. A. "[And it came to pass, as the sun was going down,] lo, a deep sleep fell on Abram, and lo, a dread and great darkness fell upon him" (Gen. 15:12):

B. "...lo, a dread" refers to Babylonia, as it is written, "Then was Nebuchadnezzar filled with fury" (Gen. 3:19).

C. " and darkness" refers to Media, which darkened the eyes of Israel by making it necessary for the Israelites to fast and conduct public mourning.

D. "...great..." refers to Greece.

E. R. Simon said, "The kingdom of Greece set up one hundred and twenty commanders, one hundred and twenty hyparchs, and one hundred and twenty generals."

F. Rabbis said, "It was sixty of each, as it is written, 'Serpents, fiery serpents, and scorpions' (Gen. 8:15). Just as the scorpion produces sixty eggs at a time, so the kingdom of Greece set up sixty at a time."

G. "...fell upon him" refers to Edom, as it is written, "The earth quakes at the noise of their fall" (Jer. 49:21).

H. Some reverse matters:

I. "...fell upon him" refers to Babylonia, since it is written, "Fallen, fallen is Babylonia" (Is. 21:9).

J. "...great..." refers to Media, in line with this verse: "King Ahasuerus did make great" (Est. 3:1).

K. " and darkness" refers to Greece, which darkened the eyes of Israel by its harsh decrees.

L. "...lo, a dread" refers to Edom, as it is written, "After this I saw...,a fourth beast, dreadful and terrible" (Dan. 7:7).

No. 4 successfully links the cited passage once more to the history of Israel. Israel's history falls under God's dominion. Whatever will happen carries out God's plan. The fourth kingdom is part of that plan, which we can discover by carefully studying Abraham's life and God's word to him. What of Rome in particular? Edom, Ishmael, and Esau all stand for Rome, perceived as a special problem, an enemy who also is a brother. In calling now-Christian Rome brother, sages conceded the Christian claim to share in the patrimony of Israel. For example, Ishmael, standing for Christian Rome, claims God's blessing, but Isaac gets it, as Jacob will take it from Esau.

XLVII:V.

1. A. "God said, 'No, but Sarah your wife [shall bear you a son, and you shall call his name Isaac. I will establish my covenant with him as an everlasting covenant for his descendants after him.] As for Ishmael, I have heard you. Behold, I will bless him and make him fruitful and multiply him exceedingly. He shall be the father of twelve princes, and I will make him a great nation]'" (Gen. 17:19-20).

B. R. Yohanan in the name of R. Joshua b. Hananiah, "In this case the son of the servant-woman might learn from what was said concerning the son of the mistress of the household:

C. "'Behold, I will bless him' refers to Isaac.

D. "'...and make him fruitful' refers to Isaac.

E. "'...and multiply him exceedingly' refers to Isaac.

F. "'...As for Ishmael, I have informed you' through the angel. [The point is, Freedman, p. 401, n. 4, explains, Ishmael could be sure that his blessing too would be fulfilled.]"

G. R. Abba bar Kahana in the name of R. Birai: "Here the son of the mistress of the household might learn from the son of the handmaiden:

H. "'Behold, I will bless him' refers to Ishmael.

I. "'...and make him fruitful' refers to Ishmael.

J. "'...and multiply him exceedingly' refers to Ishmael.

K. "And by an argument *a fortiori* : 'But I will establish my covenant with Isaac' (Gen. 17:21)."

2. A. Said R. Isaac, "It is written, 'All these are the twelve tribes of Israel' (Gen. 49:28). These were the descendants of the mistress [Sarah].

B. "But did Ishmael not establish twelve?

C. "The reference to those twelve is to princes, in line with the following verse: 'As princes and wind' (Prov. 25:14). [But the word for *prince* also stands for the word *vapor* , and hence the glory of the sons of Ishmael would be transient (Freedman, p. 402, n. 2).]

D. "But as to these tribes [descended from Isaac], they are in line with this verse: 'Sworn are the tribes of the word, selah' (Hab. 3:9). [Freedman, p. 402, n. 3: The word for *tribe* and for *staff* or *rod*, in the cited verse, are synonyms, both meaning tribes, both meaning rods, and so these tribes would endure like rods that are planted.]"

Nos. 1 and 2 take up the problem of the rather fulsome blessing assigned to Ishmael. One authority reads the blessing to refer to Isaac, the other maintains that the blessing refers indeed to Ishmael, and Isaac will gain that much more. No. 2 goes over the same issue, now with the insistence that the glory of Ishmael will pass like vapor, while the tribes of Isaac will endure as well planted rods. The polemic against Edom/Rome, with its transient glory, is familiar.

By this point readers must find themselves altogether at home in reading the book of Genesis as if it portrayed the history of Israel and Rome. For that is the single obsession binding sages of the document at hand to common discourse with the text before them. Why Rome in the form it takes in Genesis Rabbah? And how come the obsessive character of sages disposition of the theme of Rome? Were their picture merely of Rome as tyrant and destroyer of the Temple, we should have no reason to link the text to the problems of the age of redaction and closure. But now it is Rome as Israel's brother, counterpart, and nemesis, Rome as the one thing standing in the way of Israel's, and the world's, ultimate salvation. So the stakes are different, and much higher. It is not a political Rome but a Christian and messianic Rome that is at issue: Rome as surrogate for Israel, Rome as obstacle to Israel. Why? It is because Rome now confronts Israel with a crisis, and, I argue, the program of Genesis Rabbah constitutes a response to that crisis. Rome in the fourth century became Christian. Sages respond by facing that fact quite squarely and saying, "Indeed, it is as you say, a kind of Israel, an heir of Abraham as your texts explicitly claim. But we remain the sole legitimate Israel, the bearer of the birthright -- we and not you. So you are our brother: Esau, Ishmael, Edom." And the rest follows.

By rereading the story of the beginnings, sages discovered the answer and the secret of the end. Rome claimed to be Israel, and, indeed, sages conceded, Rome shared the patrimony of Israel. That claim took the form of the Christians' appropriate of the Torah as "the Old Testament," so sages acknowledged a simple fact in acceding to the notion that, in some way, Rome too formed part of Israel. But it was the rejected part, the Ishmael, the Esau, not the Isaac, not the Jacob. The advent of Christian Rome precipitated the sustained, polemical, and, I think, rigorous and well-argued rereading of beginnings in light of the end. Rome then marked the conclusion of human history as Israel had known it. Beyond? The coming of the true Messiah, the redemption of Israel, the salvation of the world, the end of time. So the issues were not inconsiderable, and when the sages spoke of Esau/Rome, as they did so often, they confronted the life-or-death decision of the day.

Let us begin with a simple example of how ubiquitous is the shadow of Ishmael/Esau/Edom/Rome. Whenever sages reflect on future history, their minds turn to their own day. They found the hour difficult, because Rome, now Christian, claimed that very birthright and blessing that they understood to be theirs alone. Christian Rome posed a threat without precedent. Now another dominion, besides Israel's, claimed the rights and blessings that sustained.Israel. Wherever in Scripture they turned, sages found comfort in the iteration that the birthright, the blessing, the Torah, and the hope -- all belonged to them and to none other. As the several antagonists of Israel stand for Rome in particular, so the traits of Rome, as sages perceived them, characterized the biblical heroes. Esau provided a favorite target. From the womb Israel and Rome contended.

LXIII:VI.

11. A. "And the children struggled together [within her, and she said, 'If it is thus, why do I live?' So she went to inquire of the Lord. And the Lord said to her, 'Two nations are in your womb, and two peoples, born of you, shall be divided; the one shall be stronger than the other, and the elder shall serve the younger'] " (Gen. 25:22-23):

B. R. Yohanan and R. Simeon b. Laqish:

C. R. Yohanan said, "[Because the word, 'struggle,' contains the letters for the word, 'run,'] this one was running to kill that one and that one was running to kill this one."

D. R. Simeon b. Laqish: "This one releases the laws given by that one, and that one releases the laws given by this one."

2. A. R. Berekhiah in the name of R. Levi said, "It is so that you should not say that it was only after he left his mother's womb that [Esau] contended against [Jacob].

B. "But even while he was yet in his mother's womb, his fist was stretched forth against him: 'The wicked stretch out their fists [so Freedman] from the womb' (Ps. 58:4)."

3. A. "And the children struggled together within her:"

B. [Once more referring to the letters of the word "struggled," with special attention to the ones that mean, "run,"] they wanted to run within her.

C. When she went by houses of idolatry, Esau would kick, trying to get out: "The wicked are estranged from the womb" (Ps. 58:4).

D. When she went by synagogues and study-houses, Jacob would kick, trying to get out: "Before I formed you in the womb, I knew you" (Jer. 1:5)."

Nos. 1-3 take for granted that Esau represents Rome, and Jacob, Israel. Consequently the verse underlines the point that there is natural enmity between Israel and Rome. Esau hated Israel even while he was still in the womb. Jacob, for his part, revealed from the womb those virtues that would characterize him later on, eager to serve God as Esau was eager to worship idols

LXIII:VII.

2. A. "Two nations are in your womb, [and two peoples, born of you, shall be divided; the one shall be stronger than the other, and the elder shall serve the younger]" (Gen. 25:23):

B. There are two proud nations in your womb, this one takes pride in his world, and that one takes pride in his world.

C. This one takes pride in his monarchy, and that one takes pride in his monarchy.

D. There are two proud nations in your womb.

E. Hadrian represents the nations, Solomon, Israel.

F. There are two who are hated by the nations in your womb. All the nations hate Esau, and all the nations hate Israel.

G. [Following Freedman's reading:] The one whom your creator hates is in your womb: "And Esau I hated" (Mal. 1:3).

The syllogism invokes the base-verse as part of its repertoire of cases. No. 2 augments the statement at hand, still more closely linking it to the history of Israel. What follows explicitly introduces the issue of the Messiah:

LXIII:VIII.

3 . A. "The first came forth red:"

B. R. Haggai in the name of R. Isaac: "On account of the merit attained by obeying the commandment, 'You will take for yourself on the first day...,' (Lev. 23:40),

C. "I shall reveal myself to you as the First, avenge you on the first, rebuild the first, and bring you the first.

D. "I shall reveal myself to you the First: 'I am the first and I am the last' (Is. 44:6).

E. "...avenge you on the first: 'Esau, 'The first came forth red.'

F. "...rebuild the first: that is the Temple, of which it is written, 'You throne of glory, on high from the first, you place of our sanctuary' (Jer. 17:12).

G. "...and bring you the first: that is, the messiah-king: 'A first unto Zion will I give, behold, behold them, and to Jerusalem' (Is. 41:27)."

LXIII:X.

1 . A. "[When the boys grew up,] Esau was a skillful hunter, [a man of the field, while Jacob was a quiet man, dwelling in tents]" (Gen. 25:27):

B. He hunted people through snaring them in words [as the Roman prosecutors do:] "Well enough, you did not steal. But who stole with you? You did not kill, but who killed with you?"

2 . A. R. Abbahu said, "He was a trapper and a fieldsman, trapping at home and in the field.

B. "He trapped at home: 'How do you tithe salt?' [which does not, in fact, have to be tithed at all!]

C. "He trapped in the field: 'How do people give tithe for straw?' [which does not, in fact, have to be tithed at all!]"

3 . A. R. Hiyya bar Abba said, "He treated himself as totally without responsibility for himself, like a field [on which anyone tramples].

B. "Said the Israelites before the Holy One, blessed be he, 'Lord of all ages, is it not enough for us that you have subjugated us to the seventy nations, but even to this one, who is subjected to sexual intercourse just like a woman?'

C. "Said to them the Holy One, blessed be he, 'I too will exact punishment from him with those same words: 'And the heart of the mighty men of Edom at that day shall be as the heart of a woman in her pangs' (Jer. 49:22).

4. A. "...while Jacob was a quiet man, dwelling in tents" (Gen. 25:27):

B. There is a reference to two tents, that is, the school house of Shem and the school house of Eber.

Nos. 1-3 deal with the description of Esau, explaining why he was warlike and aggressive. Nothing Esau did proved sincere. He was a hypocrite, even when he tried to please his parents.

LXV:I.

1. A. "When Esau was forty years old, he took to wife Judith, the daughter of Beeri, the Hittite, and Basemath the daughter of Elon the Hittite; and they made life bitter for Isaac and Rebecca" (Gen. 26:34-35):

B. "The swine out of the wood ravages it, that which moves in the field feeds on it" (Ps. 80:14).

C. R. Phineas and R. Hilqiah in the name of R. Simon: "Among all of the prophets, only two of them spelled out in public [the true character of Rome, represented by the swine], Asaf and Moses.

D. "Asaf: 'The swine out of the wood ravages it.'

E. "Moses: 'And the swine, because he parts the hoof' (Deut. 14:8).

F. "Why does Moses compare Rome to the swine? Just as the swine, when it crouches, puts forth its hoofs as if to say, 'I am clean,' so the wicked kingdom steals and grabs, while pretending to be setting up courts of justice.

G. "So Esau, for all forty years, hunted married women, ravished them, and when he reached the age of forty, he presented himself to his father, saying, 'Just as father got married at the age of forty, so I shall marry a wife at the age of forty.'

H. "'When Esau was forty years old, he took to wife Judith, the daughter of Beeri, the Hittite, and Basemath the daughter of Elon the Hittite.'"

The exegesis of course once more identifies Esau with Rome. The roundabout route linking the fact at hand, Esau's taking a wife, passes through the territory of Roman duplicity. Whatever the government does, it claims to do in the general interest. But it really has no public interest at all. Esau for his part spent forty years pillaging women and then, at the age of forty, pretended, to his father, to be upright. That, at any rate, is the parallel clearly intended by this obviously unitary composition. The issue of the selection of the intersecting verse does not present an obvious solution to me; it seems to me only the identification of Rome with the swine accounts for the choice. The contrast between Israel and Esau produced the following anguished observation. But here the Rome is not yet Christian, so far as the clear reference is concerned. The union of the two principal motifs of exegesis, the paradigmatic character of the lives of the patriarchs and matriarchs, the messianic message derived from those lives, is effected in the following:

LXXXIII:I.

1.   A.   "These are the kings who reigned in the land of Edom before any king reigned over the Israelites: Bela the son of Beor reigned in Edom, the name of his city being Dinhabah" (Gen. 36:31-32):

B.   R. Isaac commenced discourse by citing this verse: "Of the oaks of Bashan they have made your oars" (Ez. 27:6).

C.   Said R. Isaac, "The nations of the world are to be compared to a ship. Just as a ship has its mast made in one place and its anchor somewhere else, so their kings: 'Samlah of Masrekah' (Gen. 36:36), 'Shaul of Rehobot by the river' (Gen. 36:27), and: 'These are the kings who reigned in the land of Edom before any king reigned over the Israelites.'"

2.A.   ["An estate may be gotten hastily at the beginning, but the end thereof shall not be blessed" (Prov. 20:21)]: "An estate may be gotten hastily at the beginning:" "These are the kings who reigned in the land of Edom before any king reigned over the Israelites."

B.   "...but the end thereof shall not be blessed:" "And saviors shall come up on mount Zion to judge the mount of Esau" (Ob. 1:21).

No. 1 contrasts the diverse origin of Roman rulers with the uniform origin of Israel's king in the house of David. No. 2 makes the same point still more forcefully. How so? Though Esau was the first to have kings, his land will eventually be overthrown (Freedman, p. 766, n. 3). So the point is that Israel will have kings after Esau no longer does, and the verse at hand is made to point to the end of Rome, a striking revision to express the importance in Israel's history to events in the lives of the patriarchs.

The final passage once more stresses the correspondence between Israel's and Edom's governments, respectively. The reciprocal character of their histories is then stated in a powerful way, with the further implication that, when the one rules, the other waits. So now Israel waits, but it will rule. The same point is made in what follows, but the expectation proves acute and immediate.

LXXXIII:IV.

3.   A.   "Magdiel and Iram: these are the chiefs of Edom, that is Esau, the father of Edom, according to their dwelling places in the land of their possession" (Gen. 36:42):

B.   On the day on which Litrinus came to the throne, there appeared to R. Ammi in a dream this message: "Today Magdiel has come to the throne."

C.   He said, "One more king is required for Edom [and then Israel's turn will come]."

4.   A.   Said R. Hanina of Sepphoris, "Why was he called Iram? For he is destined to amass [a word using the same letters] riches for the king-messiah."

B. Said R. Levi, "There was the case of a ruler in Rome who wasted the treasuries of his father. Elijah of blessed memory appeared to him in a dream. He said to him, 'Your fathers collected treasures and you waste them.'

C. "He did not budge until he filled the treasuries again."

Nos. 3 presents once more the theme that Rome's rule will extend only for a foreordained and limited time, at which point the Messiah will come. No. 4 explains the meaning of the name Iram. The concluding statement also alleges that Israel's saints even now make possible whatever wise decisions Rome's rulers make. That forms an appropriate conclusion to the matter. How the compilers of Leviticus Rabbah deal with the situation we shall now see.

iii.   The Program of Leviticus Rabbah

The framers of Leviticus Rabbah treat topics, not particular verses. They make generalizations that are freestanding. They express cogent propositions through extended compositions, not episodic ideas. Earlier, in Genesis Rabbah, as we have seen, things people wished to say were attached to predefined statements based on an existing text, constructed in accord with an organizing logic independent of the systematic expression of a single, well-framed idea. That is to say, the sequence of verses of Genesis and their contents played a massive role in the larger-scale organization of Genesis Rabbah and expression of its propositions. Now the authors of Leviticus Rabbah so collected and arranged their materials that an abstract proposition emerges. That proposition is not expressed only or mainly through episodic restatements, assigned, as I said, to an order established by a base text (whether Genesis or Leviticus, or a Mishnah-tractate, for that matter). Rather it emerges through a logic of its own. What is new is the move from an essentially exegetical mode of logical discourse to a fundamentally philosophical one. It is the shift from discourse framed around an established (hence old) text to syllogistic argument organized around a proposed (hence new) theorem or proposition. What changes, therefore, is the way in which cogent thought takes place, as people moved from discourse contingent on some prior principle of organization to discourse autonomous of a ready-made program inherited from an earlier paradigm.

What happens in Leviticus Rabbah (and, self-evidently, in other documents of the same sort)? Reading one thing in terms of something else, the builders of the document systematically adopted for themselves the reality of the Scripture, its history and doctrines. They transformed that history from a sequence of one-time events, leading from one place to some other, into an ever-present mythic world. No longer was there one Moses, one David, one set of happenings of a distinctive and never-to-be-repeated character. Now whatever happens, of which the thinkers propose to take account, must enter and be absorbed into that established and ubiquitous pattern and structure founded in Scripture. It is not that biblical history repeats itself. Rather, biblical history no longer constitutes history as a story of things that happened once, long ago, and pointed to some one moment in the future. Rather it becomes an account of things that happen every day -- hence, an ever-present mythic world, as I said.

That is why, in Leviticus Rabbah, Scripture as a whole does not dictate the order of discourse, let alone its character. In this document they chose in Leviticus itself a verse here, a phrase there. These then presented the pretext for propositional discourse commonly quite out of phase with the cited passage. The verses that are quoted ordinarily shift from the meanings they convey to the implications they contain, speaking about something, anything, other than what they seem to be saying. So the as-if frame of mind brought to Scripture brings renewal to Scripture, seeing everything with fresh eyes. And the result of the new vision was a reimagining of the social world envisioned by the document at hand, I mean, the everyday world of Israel in its Land in that difficult time. For what the sages now proposed was a reconstruction of existence along the lines of the ancient design of Scripture as they read it. What that meant was that, from a sequence of one-time and linear events, everything that happened was turned into a repetition of known and already experienced paradigms, hence, once more, a mythic being. The source and core of the myth, of course, derive from Scripture -- Scripture reread, renewed, reconstructed along with the society that revered Scripture.

So the mode of thought that dictated the issues and the logic of the document, telling the thinkers to see one thing in terms of something else, addressed Scripture in particular and collectively. And thinking as they did, the framers of the document saw Scripture in a new way, just as they saw their own circumstance afresh, rejecting their world in favor of Scripture's, reliving Scripture's world in their own terms. That, incidentally, is why they did not write history, an account of what was happening and what it meant. It was not that they did not recognize or appreciate important changes and trends reshaping their nation's life. They could not deny that reality. In their apocalyptic reading of the dietary and leprosy laws, they made explicit their close encounter with the history of the world as they knew it. But they had another mode of responding to history. It was to treat history as if it were already known and readily understood. Whatever happened had already happened. Scripture dictated the contents of history, laying forth the structures of time, the rules that prevailed and were made known in events. Self-evidently, these same thinkers projected into Scripture's day the realities of their own, turning Moses and David into rabbis, for example. But that is how people think in that mythic, enchanted world in which, to begin with, reality blends with dream, and hope projects onto future and past alike how people want things to be.

Let us turn, now, from these somewhat abstract observations to a concrete account of what happened, in particular, when the thinkers at hand undertook to reimagine reality -- both their own and Scripture's. Exactly how did they think about one thing in terms of another, and what did they choose, in particular, to recognize in this rather complex process of juggling unpalatable present and unattainable myth? We turn to the specifics by reverting to the tried and true method of listing all the data and classifying them. Exactly what did the framers of Leviticus Rabbah learn when they opened the book of Leviticus? To state the answer in advance, when they read the rules of sanctification of the priesthood, they heard the message of the salvation of all Israel. Leviticus became the story of how Israel, purified from social sin and sanctified, would be saved.

Let us turn, then, to the classifications of rules that sages located in the social laws of Leviticus. The first, and single paramount, category takes shape within the themes associated with the national life of Israel. The principal lines of structure flow along the fringes: Israel's relationships with others. These are (so to speak) horizontal, with the nations, and vertical, with God. But, from the viewpoint of the framers of the document, the relationships form a single, seamless web, for Israel's vertical relationships dictate the horizontals as well; when God wishes to punish Israel, the nations come to do the work. The relationships that define Israel, moreover, prove dynamic, not static, in that they respond to the movement of the Torah through Israel's history. When the Torah governs, then the vertical relationship is stable and felicitous, the horizontal one secure, and, when not, God obeys the rules and the nations obey God. So the first and paramount, category takes shape within the themes associated with the national life of Israel. The principal lines of structure flow along the fringe, Israel's relationships with others. The relationships form a single, seamless web, for Israel's vertical relationships dictate the horizontals as well; when God wishes to punish Israel, the nations come to do the work. The relationships that define Israel, moreover, prove dynamic, not static, in that they respond to the movement of the Torah through Israel's history. When the Torah governs, then the vertical relationship is stable and felicitous, the horizontal one secure, and, when not, God obeys the rules and the nations obey God.

We now catalogue and classify all of the propositions emerging from the paragraphs of thought of Leviticus Rabbah. My effort is to state, as simply and accurately as I can, what the framer of a given paragraph wished to express, either directly or through rich illustrative materials.

The national life of Israel: Israel, God, and the Nations

I:XI. Torah is life to Israel, poison to nations.

I:XII. Gentiles have no prophets.

I:XIII. Gentile prophets are inferior.

II:I. Israel is precious to God.

II:IV-V. God gave Israel many laws so as to express his love and ongoing concern. This was because they enthroned God at the Red Sea.

II:VI. Scripture is so worded as to treat Israel with respect.

V:II. God punishes Israel's sins by placing gentile rulers over them, e.g., Sennacherib.

V:VII. Virtues of Israel are vices for nations [see I:XI, XIII].

VI:I. Israel are God's witnesses.

VI:V. Israel violated its oath at Sinai, but God forgave Israel. [Also: VII:I.]

VII:IV. God is concerned not to waste Israel's resources.

X:I-III. God favors prophets and priests who justify Israel.

XII:II. God meets Israel in the tent of meeting.

XIII:II. Israel alone was worthy to receive the Torah. By observing food taboos, Israel shows its special position. [Also: XIII:III.]

XIII:IV-V. Food taboos symbolize Israel's fate among the nations. The four kingdoms as exemplary of food laws.

XV:IX. Skin ailments symbolize Israel's fate among the nations. The four kingdoms.

[XVI:I. Leprosy as punishment for social sins, e.g., gossip.]

XVII:I. Israel is singled out to be punished for specific sins. Others suffer at last judgment.

XVII:V. If Israel sins in the Land, it will be punished as Canaan was.

XVII:VI. Canaanites hid their treasures, and by afflicting the houses, God revealed the hiding place.

XVII:VII. The Temple's affliction is symbolized by the leprosy disease affecting houses.

XVIII:II. Individuals and nations cause their own punishment. [Also: XVIII:III.]

XVIII:IV. Israel was unafflicted at Sinai. After they sinned, various afflictions appeared.

XVIII:V. God governs Israel the same way kings govern kingdoms. But God heals with that with which he punishes.

XIX:IV. Israel's sins provoke punishment.

XX:VIII-IX. Sins in the cult caused death of Nadab and Abihu.

XX:X. Social sins and the death of Nadab and Abihu. Snootiness, pride.

XXI:XI. Israel is sustained by merits of the patriarchs.

XXII:VIII. God permitted sacrifice as an antidote to sin.

XXIII:I-III. Israel is the rose, the nations, the thorns. Various circumstances in Israel's history at which that fact was shown.

XXIII:V. Israel among the nations is steadfast in loyalty to God and will be redeemed.

XXIII:VI. Israel was created only to do religious duties and good deeds.

XXIII:VII. Israel must be different from gentiles, particularly in sexual practices. [Also XXIII:IX, XXIII:XIII.]

XXIV:I-II. When God exalts a people, it is done justly and so his act endures.

XXV:I. The Torah is what protects Israel.

XXV:IV. God kept his promises to the patriarchs to favor their descendants.

XXVII:V. God favors the victim.

XXVII:VI. God shows Israel special favor, which disappoints the nations. He does not demand much from Israel. [Also: XXVII:VIII.]

XXVII:IX. The animals used in the cult stand for the meritorious ancestors.

XXVII:XI. God will ultimately save Israel even from its cruelest enemies.

XXVIII:III. God asks very little of Israel.

XXVIII:IV. Merely with prayer Israel is saved, not with weapons.

XXVIII:VI. The merit of the religious duty of the sheaf of first fruits causes Israel to inherit the land, peace is made, Israel is saved.

XXIX:II. Israel's suffering among the nations is due to Jacob's lack of faith.

XXIX:V. Israel is redeemed because of keeping commandments. [Also: XXIX:VIIIB.]

XXIX:VII. Israel is saved through the merit of the patriarchs. [Also: XXIX:VIII, XXIX:X.]

XXX:I. Israel serves Esau [Rome] because of insufficient devotion to Torah study.

XXX:II. Israel's victory is signified by palm branches.

XXX:IX-XII. The symbols of Sukkot stand for God, the patriarchs, Israel's leaders, Israel. [Also: XXX:XIV.]

XXXI:III. God wants from Israel something he surely does not need, e.g., lamp, and that is the mark of God's love. [Also: XXXI:IV, XXXII:VIII.]

XXXII:I. Israel is reviled among the nations but exalted by God.

XXXII:VIII. God goes into exile with Israel.

XXXIII:VI. Israel, sold to the nations, joins their Creator with them.

XXXIV:VI. God forgives Israel's sin and repeatedly redeems them.

XXXIV:XIII. If Israel is not liberal to the poor, their wealth will go to Esau [Rome].

XXXV:I. If Israel attains merit, curses are turned into blessings.

XXXVI:II. Israel compared to a vine.

XXXVI:III. Patriarchs left their merit to Israel.

XXXVI:IV. World was created through the merit of Jacob.

XXXVI:V. Israel saved through the merits of the patriarchs.

XXXVI:VI. That merit yet endures.

The recurrent messages may be stated in a single paragraph. God loves Israel, so gave them the Torah, which defines their life and governs their welfare. Israel is alone in its category (*sui generis*), so what is a virtue to Israel is a vice to the nation, life-giving to Israel, poison to the gentiles. True, Israel sins, but God forgives that sin, having punished the nation on account of it. Such a process has yet to come to an end, but it will culminate in Israel's complete regeneration. Meanwhile, Israel's assurance of God's love lies in the many expressions of special concern, for even the humblest and most ordinary aspects of the national life: the food the nation eats, the sexual practices by which it procreates. These life-sustaining, life-transmitting activities draw God's special interest, as a mark of his general love for Israel. Israel then is supposed to achieve its life in conformity with the marks of God's love. These indications moreover signify also the character of Israel's difficulty, namely, subordination to the nations in general, but to the fourth kingdom, Rome, in particular. Both food laws and skin diseases stand for the nations. There is yet another category of sin, also collective and generative of collective punishment, and that is social. The moral character of Israel's life, the treatment of people by one another, the practice of gossip and small-scale thuggery -- these too draw down divine penalty. The nation's fate therefore corresponds to its moral condition. The moral condition, however, emerges not only from the current generation. Israel's richest hope lies in the merit of the ancestors, thus in the Scriptural record of the merits attained by the founders of the nation, those who originally brought it into being and gave it life.

The world to come is so portrayed as to restate these same propositions. Merit overcomes sin, and doing religious duties or supererogatory acts of kindness will win merit for the nation that does them. Israel will be saved at the end of time, and the age, or world, to follow will be exactly the opposite of this one. Much that we find in the account of Israel's national life, worked out through the definition of the liminal relationships, recurs in slightly altered form in the picture of the world to come.

Israel and the world to come. Salvific doctrines and symbols

II:II. In this world and in the world to come, Israel, Levites, priesthood, heave offerings, firstlings, Land, Jerusalem, etc., will endure.

III:I. Israel will be redeemed on the Sabbath.

VII:III. Israel will be redeemed through the merit of Torah study.

IX:I. The thanksgiving offering will continue in the world to come. [Also: IX:VIII.]

X:IX. Jerusalem in the world to come.

XI:II. Rebuilding of Jerusalem in the world to come.

XVII:VII. Temple will be rebuilt.

XXI:I-IV. Israel is saved because of the merit of the people at various turnings in their history, e.g., at the Red Sea. Also through merit of atonement.

XXI:V-VI. Religious duties counteract sin.

XXIII:V. Israel will be saved through its steadfast faith.

XXIII:VI. Israel will be redeemed when Esau no longer rules.

XXX:XVI. Through merit of lulab, Temple will be rebuilt.

XXXI:XI. Merit of eternal light brings messiah.

The world to come will right all presently unbalanced relationships. What is good will go forward, what is bad will come to an end. The simple message is that the things people revere, the cult and its majestic course through the year, will go on; Jerusalem will come back, so too the Temple, in all their glory. Israel will be saved through the merit of the ancestors, atonement, study of Torah, practice of religious duties. The prevalence of the eschatological dimension at the formal structures, with its messianic and other expressions, here finds its counterpart in the repetition of the same few symbols in the expression of doctrine. The theme of the moral life of Israel produces propositions concerning not only the individual but, more important, the social virtues that the community as a whole must exhibit.

The Laws of Society for Israel's Holy Community

I:X. Israel became punishable for violating divine law only after the Torah was taught to them a second time in the tent of meeting.

II:VII. Offerings should not derive from stolen property. [Also: III:IV.]

III:I. Not expiating sin through an inexpensive offering is better than doing so through an expensive one. Better not sin at all. [Also: IX:I, IX:V, IX:VIII.]

III:II-III. God will not despise a meager offering of a poor person. [Also: III:V, VIII:IV.]

IV:I. God punishes with good reason and not blindly.

IV:II. The soul wants to do ever more religious duties.

IV:III. Unwitting sin is caused by haste.

IV:IV-V. Soul and body are jointly at fault for sin.

IV:VI. Israelites are responsible for one another.

IV:VIII. Soul compared to God.

V:IV. Philanthropy makes a place for the donor.

V:VIII. Israel knows how to please God.

VI:III. False oath brings terrible punishment.

VII:II. If one repents sin, it is as if he made an offering in the rebuilt Temple.

VII:II. God favors the contrite and penitent. [Also: VII:VI, VIII:I, IX:I, IV, VI, God favors the thanksgiving offering.]

IX:III. God favors those who bring peace even more than those who study Torah.

IX:IX. Peace is the highest value.

X:V. Repentance and prayer effect atonement for sin.

X:VI. Priests' acts effect atonement.

XI:V. God responds to human virtue by acting in the same way.

XII:I, IV. Wine leads to poverty, estrangement.

XIV:V. Even the most pious person has a sinful side to his nature.

XV:IV. Gossip causes a specific ailment. God punishes Israel because he cares about Israel's moral condition.

XV:V. Sin of mother effects embryo.

XV:VI. Correspondence of sin and punishment. People get what they deserve.

XVI:I. Leprosy punishes gossip, other sins. [Also: XVI:II, XVII:III, XVIII:IV.]

XVI:V. Sinning through speech -- general principle and particular examples.

XVI:VI. Skin disease and gossip. [Also: XVI:VII.]

XVI:VIII. People cause their own ailments through sin.

XVII:II. Diseases afflicting a house and the sin of the owner.

XVII:IV. God penalizes first property, then the person.

XXII:VI. Thievery is tantamount to murder.

XXII:X. For each prohibition there is a release.

XXIII:X-XI. God rewards those who avoid sin.

XXIII:XII. Adultery may be in one's mind.

XXIV:VI. Sanctification is through avoiding sexual misdeed.

XXIV:VII. Israel must remain holy if God is to be in its midst. [Also: XXIV:VIII.]

XXV:III. People are like God when they plant trees.

XXVI:II. God's pure speech versus humanity's gossip.

XXVII:I. God seeks justice, but it may be fully worked out only in the world to come. [Also: XXVII:II.]

XXX:V. One cannot serve God with stolen property. [Also: XXX:VI.]

XXXII:V. Israel keeps itself sexually pure.

XXXIII:I. What people say has the power of life and death.

XXXIV:II. God repays generosity.

XXXIV:V. People should not envy one another.

XXXIV:VIII. God rewards generosity. [Also: XXXIV:IX, XXXIV:X, XXXIV:XI.]

XXXV:VII. If Israel keeps the commandments, it is as if they made them.

XXXVII:I. It is unwise to vow.

First of all, the message to the individual constitutes a revision, for this context, of the address to the nation: humility as against arrogance, obedience as against sin, constant concern not to follow one's natural inclination to do evil or to overcome the natural limitations of the human condition. Israel must accept its fate, obey and rely on the merits accrued through the ages and God's special love. The individual must conform, in ordinary affairs, to this same paradigm of patience and submission.

Great men and women, that is, individual heroes within the established paradigm, conform to that same pattern, exemplifying the national virtues. Among these, of course, Moses stands out; he has no equal. The special position of the humble Moses is complemented by the patriarchs and by David, all of whom knew how to please God and left as an inheritance to Israel the merit they had thereby attained.

Israel's leaders: Priests, rabbis, prophets

I:I. Prophets are messengers to mortals, and Moses was the greatest of them.

I:III. Moses had several names.

I:IV. Abraham, Jacob, David, Moses were recognized by God.

I:V. Moses was humble.

I:VI. Moses' teaching was precious in God's view.

I:VII. God recognized how much honor was paid to him by Moses.

I:VIII. God showed special favor to Moses.

I:IX. As above.

I:XII. After tent of meeting was built, prophecy ceased among gentiles.

I:XIV. Moses was superior to all other Israelite prophets.

[III:VI. Priests have every right to the residue of the meal offering.]

V:VII. The elders sustain Israel through their merits, which they pass on.

V:VIII. David knows how to please God.

X:I. God favored Abraham because he sought mercy.

X:II. The great prophets all loved to justify Israel.

XI:VIII. Israel can do nothing without its leaders.

While we find numerous stories about rabbis in the modern (fourth-century) mold, Yohanan, Simeon b. Laqish, Yudan, not to mention Hillel, they usually exemplify established social policies or virtues. They scarcely exhibit distinctive traits of personality. They do not stand comparison with the scriptural figures and only rarely appear in the same supernatural framework. Such stories do not belong in the present classification at all. When we do find them, we observe that they exemplify such common virtues as are catalogues in the earlier lists.

If we now ask about further recurring themes or topics, there is one so commonplace that we should have to list the majority of paragraphs of discourse in order to provide a complete list. It is the list of events in Israel's history, meaning, in this context, Israel's history solely in scriptural times, down through the return to Zion. The one-time events of the generation of the flood, Sodom and Gomorrah, the patriarchs and the sojourn in Egypt, the exodus, the revelation of the Torah at Sinai, the golden calf, the Davidic monarchy and the building of the Temple, Sennacherib, Hezekiah, and the destruction of northern Israel, Nebuchadnezzar and the destruction of the Temple in 586, the life of Israel in Babylonian captivity, Daniel and his associates, Mordecai and Haman -- these events occur over and over again. They turn out to serve as paradigms of sin and atonement, steadfastness and divine intervention, and equivalent lessons. We find, in fact, a fairly standard repertoire of scriptural heroes or villains, on the one side, and conventional lists of Israel's enemies and their actions and downfall, on the other. The boastful, for instance, include (VII:VI) the generation of the flood, Sodom and Gomorrah, Pharaoh, Sisera, Sennacherib, Nebuchadnezzar, the wicked empire (Rome) -- contrasted to Israel, "despised and humble in this world." The four kingdoms recur again and again, always ending, of course, with Rome, with the repeated message that after Rome will come Israel. But Israel has to make this happen through its faith and submission to God's will. Lists of enemies ring the changes on Cain, the Sodomites, Pharaoh, Sennacherib, Nebuchadnezzar, Haman.

Accordingly, the mode of thought brought to bear upon the theme of history remains exactly the same as before: list making, with data exhibiting similar taxonomic traits drawn together into lists based on common monothetic traits or definitions. These lists then through the power of repetition make a single enormous point. They prove a social law of history. The catalogues of exemplary heroes and historical events serve a further purpose. They provide a model of how contemporary events are to be absorbed into the biblical paradigm. Since biblical events exemplify recurrent happenings, sin and redemption, forgiveness and atonement, they lose their one-time character. At the same time and in the same way, current events find a place within the ancient, but eternally present, paradigmatic scheme. So no new historical events, other than exemplary episodes in lives of heroes, demand narration because, through what is said about the past, what was happening in the times of the framers of Leviticus Rabbah would also come under consideration. This mode of dealing with biblical history and contemporary events produces two reciprocal effects. The first is the mythicization of biblical stories, their removal from the framework of ongoing, unique patterns of history and sequences of events and their transformation into accounts of things that happen all the time. The second is that contemporary events too lose all of their specificity and enter the paradigmatic framework of established mythic existence. So (1) the Scripture's myth happens every day, and (2) every day produces reenactment of the Scripture's myth.

In seeking the substance of the mythic being invoked by the exegetes at hand, who read the text as if it spoke about something else and the world as if it lived out the text, we uncover a simple fact. At the center of the pretense, that is, the as-if mentality of Leviticus Rabbah and its framers, we find a simple proposition. Israel is God's special love. That love is shown in a simple way. Israel's present condition of subordination derives from its own deeds. It follows that God cares, so Israel may look forward to redemption on God's part in response to Israel's own regeneration through repentance. When the exegetes proceeded to open the scroll of Leviticus, they found numerous occasions to state that proposition in concrete terms and specific contexts. The sinner brings on his own sickness. But God heals through that very ailment. The nations of the world govern in heavy succession, but Israel's lack of faith guaranteed their rule and its moment of renewal will end it. Israel's leaders -- priests, prophets, kings -- fall into an entirely different category from those of the nations, as much as does Israel. In these and other concrete allegations, the same classical message comes forth.

Accordingly, at the foundations of the pretense lies the long-standing biblical-Jewish insistence that Israel's sorry condition in no way testifies to Israel's true worth -- the grandest pretense of all. All of the little evasions of the primary sense in favor of some other testify to this, the great denial that what is, is what counts. Leviticus Rabbah makes that statement with art and imagination. But it is never subtle about saying so.

Salvation and sanctification join together in Leviticus Rabbah. The laws of the book of Leviticus, focused as they are on the sanctification of the nation through its cult, in Leviticus Rabbah indicate the rules of salvation as well. The message of Leviticus Rabbah attaches itself to the book of Leviticus, as if that book had come from prophecy and addressed the issue of the meaning of history and Israel's salvation. But the book of Leviticus came from the priesthood and spoke of sanctification. The paradoxical syllogism -- the as-if reading, the opposite of how things seem -- of the composers of Leviticus Rabbah therefore reaches simple formulation. In the very setting of sanctification we find the promise of salvation. In the topics of the cult and the priesthood we uncover the national and social issues of the moral life and redemptive hope of Israel. The repeated comparison and contrast of priesthood and prophecy, sanctification and salvation, turn out to produce a complement, which comes to most perfect union in the text at hand.

The focus of Leviticus Rabbah and its laws of history is upon the society of Israel, its national fate and moral condition. Indeed, nearly all of the *parashiyyot* of Leviticus Rabbah turn out to deal with the national, social condition of Israel, and this in three contexts: (1) Israel's setting in the history of the nations, (2) the sanctified character of the inner life of Israel itself, (3) the future, salvific history of Israel. So the biblical book that deals with the holy Temple now is shown to address the holy people. Leviticus really discusses not the consecration of the cult but the sanctification of the nation -- its conformity to God's will laid forth in the Torah, and God's rules. So when we review the document as a whole and ask what is that something else that the base text is supposed to address, it turns out that the sanctification of the cult stands for the salvation of the nation. So the nation now is like the cult then, the ordinary Israelite now like the priest then. The holy way of life lived now, through acts to which merit accrues, corresponds to the holy rites then. The process of metamorphosis is full, rich, complete. When everything stands for something else, the something else repeatedly turns out to be the nation. This is what our document spells out in exquisite detail, yet never missing the main point.

iv. The Program of Genesis Rabbah and Leviticus Rabbah

A single program of theological conviction unites the two Rabbah-compilations. If we summarize the principal doctrines of each of them, the paramount corpus of shared ideas comes to the fore. Let us begin with the earlier of the two documents, commonly held to have reached closure about fifty years before the other. Genesis Rabbah, ca 350-400, in the aggregate proposes to demonstrate that the very creation of the world testifies to the salvation of Israel. The facts of creation, recorded in the book of Genesis, point toward the coming age. What Adam cast in shadow, Israel illuminates. Where humankind went wrong, Israel will go right. The future now stands revealed through the lives of Israel's founders; even now Israel's holy way of life demonstrates the matter. Just as humanity's sins drove God upward from the world, so Israel's saints, Abraham, Isaac, Jacob, and on to Moses, brought God back down. Israel needs to keep the faith and to hope. Humanity's hope indeed is Israel. God's plan governs, and Israel in its Land compares to Adam in the Garden of Eden.

So reality is formed of two components: humanity, Israel, dark, light, sin, redemption. What changes the rules of history? Love on the one side, hatred on the other other. As to the present, that too contains no secrets. The story of Edom, Ishmael, Esau precurses Rome, and the salvation of Jacob, Israel in the present age. What Rome now does Esau long ago did. But Jacob held the birthright then, and Israel does today. Time and again a single message makes its appearance, a message of courage in the face of despair, renewal in spite of the signs of the times.

The same mode of thought -- turning the one-time narrative of a biblical story into a paradigm of the rules underlying existence -- characterizes Leviticus Rabbah, ca. 400-450, as well. The message goes over familiar ground, but Leviticus Rabbah addresses not event but social laws. Israel is unique, the counterpart of the nation. God so loved Israel as to provide it with rules to sanctify its life, concerning food, cleanness, and the like -- that is, the cultic laws of Leviticus. These mark the sanctification of Israel. True, the four kingdoms have troubled Israel's life, but beyond the fourth, Rome, will come the rule of Israel. Indeed the food laws and the skin diseases of Leviticus serve as metaphors for the nations, and the holy way of life of Israel therefore constitutes an acting out of the paradigm of universal human history. What must Israel do? It must so constitute its social life as to form a holy community. What this means is that Israel must form its moral condition to correspond to God's demands. The Torah supplies the rules that Israel must keep, it therefore serves as source of the laws of Israel's history and salvation. Among the immoral acts to be avoided, one stands out, gossip, the opposite of pure speech. And what people say to, and about, one another surely remains under Israel's control. Sifting and resifting the paradigmatic events of Israel's history, we find the patterns of sin and atonement, warrant for Israel's loyalty to and trust in God. God cares, Israel therefore hopes. Genesis, with its myths about creation and stories about the founders of Israel, Abraham, Isaac, Jacob, and Joseph and his brothers, tells the story of Israel's salvation. Leviticus, with its cultic rules about sacrifice and uncleanness, tells the rules governing Israel's salvation. The difference between Genesis Rabbah and Leviticus Rabbah derives from the character of Genesis and Leviticus. The profound correspondence between the one and the other rests upon the simple fact that the framers of the two documents, living within the same century and in the same crisis of confidence, propose to say the same thing. They affirm that God still loves Israel, so confirming Israel's sanctification here and now and salvation in time to come.

Let me then state the program of both compilations: Genesis Rabbah and Leviticus Rabbah take up Israel's position in creation, hence also among the nations and as part of history, stating that, in the here and now, Israel's life is holy, and, in time to come, Israel will be saved. How do we know it? Because in the very facts of Scripture, as they deal with humanity and creation, in

Genesis, and the distinctive way of life of Israel, in Leviticus, prove it -- when rightly interpreted.

In the context of the system of Judaism presented by the canon of late antiquity, summarized so handsomely by the Talmuds of the Land of Israel and of Babylonia, for example, none of these messages presents surprises. Indeed, all of them will strike the contemporary historian of Judaism as commonplaces, as indeed in later times they became. Yet if we set side by side the points of interest and emphasis, the modes of thought and the specific statements, of the compilers of prior composites and compositions in the canon at hand, the picture would change. Specifically, the powerful interest in history and salvation, the recurring emphasis on the correspondence between Israel's holy way of life and the salvation of Israel in history, the reading of Scripture as an account of the present and future -- these will have struck the compositors of other documents as fresh. The authors of the Mishnah, with its close companion in the Tosefta, the compilers of tractate Abot, the author-compilers of Sifra to Leviticus -- none of these circles of authorship took so keen an interest in the issue of salvation or in the correspondence between the biblical narrative and contemporary history. That fact is particularly striking when we compare the exegesis of Leviticus composed by the authors of the Sifra to the treatment of the same book in Leviticus Rabbah. To state matters simply, there is nothing in common, nothing whatsoever, except the biblical text itself. The points of emphasis, the decisions as to form and style, composition, order, and proportion, characteristic of the Mishnah and its fellows contrast starkly with their equivalents in the two Rabbah-midrashim. So, as we survey the established context for compiling sayings to be preserved, we find it difficult to identify a prior circle of compositors with the same plan and program as those of Genesis Rabbah and Leviticus Rabbah.[4] That simple fact makes all the more striking the agreement of the two groups upon a single theological program, imparting to the simple observations we have just made a significance otherwise lacking. It is when we compare what these compositors wish to emphasize, their points of stress, with the plan and program of their counterpart, earlier documents, that the true character of the Rabbah-compositors' theological and literary concurrence, their agreement on a single program and plan, fully reveals itself.

v.   Conclusion: The Centrality of Redaction in the Formulation and Selection of Exegeses of Scripture

Bases for analysis, comparison, and contrast derive from points of differentiation, not sameness. Comparing what unrelated groups said about the same matter tells us only facts, not their meaning. But the purpose of comparison, including comparative *midrash*, is interpretation. We might as well attempt to differentiate within diverse ages and formulations of Israelite culture

---

[4] The case of Sifre Numbers remains to be investigated.

on the basis of so commonplace an activity as writing books or eating bread. True enough, diverse groups wrote diverse books, e.g., some long, some short, and, we might imagine, also baked their bread in diverse ways, e.g., with or without yeast, with wheat, spelt, or barley. But so what? What else do we learn if we know that some people wrote long books and ate rye bread, other people wrote short books and ate whole wheat bread? Only if we can show that people did these things in a way or for a purpose that differentiated one group from another, for example, as a mode of expressing ideas particular to themselves, their condition and context, can we answer the question, so what? That is why comparing merely what people said about the same thing, whether the weather or the meaning of Genesis 49:10, without regard to the circumstance in which they said it, meaning, in our case, to begin with the particular book and canon in which what they said is now preserved -- that sort of comparison produces knowledge of a merely formal character.

Let me now spell this out, since we cannot understand how *comparative midrash* has been carried on to this time without a clear picture of the prevailing, and false, fundamental premise as to category-formation and classification. *Midrash*, meaning exegesis of Scripture, by itself presents nothing new in Israelite culture. Explaining the verses of holy books, even before the formation of the Holy Book, went on routinely. The activity of scriptural exegesis constituted a prevailing convention of thought, and therefore by itself cannot yield points of differentiation. Why what diverse groups said about the same verse would form a consequential area of comparative study therefore demands explanation, for the answer is not self-evident. Any program of comparing the exegeses of a verse without reference to documentary (therefore social and historical) context will have to sort out the results of millennia of responses to Scripture. But the work of sorting things out in the end may prove unable to conduct other than a merely formal analysis of the diverse results: comparing apples to Australians because both begin with an A.

Let us dwell on the simple fact that exegesis of Scripture was routine and ubiquitous even in the times in which various books of the Hebrew Bible were coming into being. A simple instance of the so-called "internal-biblical" exegetical mode, for example, is given by a contrast of Ps. 106:32-33 and Num. 20:2-13. The former of the two passages supplies a motive for the action described in the latter. We begin with the story, as narrated at Num. 20:10-13.

> And Moses and Aaron gathered the assembly together before the rock, and he said to them, "Hear now, you rebels; shall we bring forth water for you out of this rock?" And Moses lifted up his hand and struck the rock with his rod twice; and water came forth abundantly, and the congregation drank, and their cattle. And the Lord said to Moses and Aaron, "Because you did not believe in me, to sanctify me in the eyes of the people of Israel, therefore you shall not bring this assembly

into the land which I have given them." These are the waters of Meribah, where the people of Israel contended with the Lord, and he showed himself holy among them.

Why then did Moses strike the rock? The foregoing account at best suggests an implicit motive for his action. The author of Ps. 106:32-33 makes it explicit: "They angered him at the waters of Meribah, and it went ill with Moses on their account; for they made his spirit bitter, and he spoke words that were rash." Now what is important in this instance is simply the evidence of how, within the pages of the Hebrew Scriptures, a program of exegesis people now call *midrash* reaches full exposure.

Furthermore, we need not hunt at length for evidence of the work of collecting such exercises in exegesis -- of rewriting an old text in light of new considerations or values. Such a vast enterprise is handsomely exemplified by the book of Chronicles which, instead of merely commenting on verses, actually rewrites the stories of Samuel and Kings. Anyone who without attention to the larger documentary context -- the respective programs of the compilations as a whole -- compares what the compilers of Samuel and Kings say about a given incident with what the compilers of Chronicles say about the same incident then misses the point of the difference between the reading of the one and that of the other. For, as everyone now knows, the difference derives from the documentary context -- there alone. So without asking first of all about the plan and program of the documents, the formal comparison of contents produces facts, but no insight into their meaning. That, in my view, is the present situation of comparative midrash.

Obviously, neither of these two biblical cases -- the one of exegesis, the other of composition or compilation of exegeses -- by itself can prove the point. Both serve merely to provide instances of the antiquity of both making up and also purposefully compiling exegeses of Scripture. They call into question any notion that a distinctive historical circumstance -- that of late antiquity, for example -- frames the context in which we are to read all works of exegesis of Scripture. They further show the futility of comparing bits of information that have not been interpreted as part of their original context, meaning, in the case of Samuel-Kings as against Chronicles, the larger theological program of the later compilation. For when people wished to deliver a powerful argument for a basic proposition, they did so by collecting and arranging exegeses of Scripture -- and, it goes without saying, also by *producing* appropriate exegeses of Scripture for these compilations. That is to say, compilers also participated in the framing or rewriting of what they compiled, so that all we have is what they chose to give us in the language and form they selected. That is why I maintain study of *comparative midrash* must begin with the outermost point of contact, namely, the character of the compilation of exegeses. Comparing one compilation with another then defines the first stage of the comparison of exegeses: compilations, contents, principles of hermeneutics alike.

To gain perspective on this proposition, we now turn to two fairly systematic efforts at compiling exegeses of Scripture specifically in order to make some polemical point. These present us with parallels to what is at hand in the work of the earliest composers of exegeses within the rabbinic movement. We have now seen how the compilers of Genesis Rabbah and Leviticus Rabbah made their collections of exegeses in order to demonstrate propositions critical to their theological program. We detected little that was wholly random in either proposition or proportion, selection and arrangement of exegeses or propositions on the meaning of specific verses of Scripture. All aspects -- mode of exegesis, result of exegesis, purpose of compilation alike -- addressed the point of the document as a whole, carried out the established purpose. The two compilations form harmonious and unified statements. That is the centerpiece of my argument as to both their form and their substance, plan and meaning alike. In Parts I-V, I have attempted to establish that claim as fact.

Let us now broaden the range of inquiry, if only briefly, and ask whether the same fact characterizes other documents. That is to say, on our own.let us conduct a brief exercise in *comparative midrash* . The instances to follow will demonstrate in settings far removed in time and theological context from the world that produced Genesis Rabbah and Leviticus Rabbah how exegetes and compilers carried out their work. They once more demonstrate the unity of form and meaning, of purpose and proposition. The selection of exegeses, the creation of exegeses, the arrangement and compilation of exegeses, the use of a particular formal technique, and the larger polemic or theological proposition that motivated the compilers and exegetes alike -- all of these together join in producing the document as we know it. Therefore we compare document to document, not uninterpreted detail ripped from one document to an equivalent detail siezed from some other.

Recalling the exercises already completed, we ask two questions.

First, what is the formal character of the unit of discourse?

Second, how are the units of discourse put together by redactors into a large-scale composition?

We turn first to two passages of exegesis, one of Hosea, the other of Nahum, found in the Essene Library of Qumran. As presented by Geza Vermes,[5] the exegeses do form something we might call a collection, or at least a chapter, that is, a systematic treatment of a number of verses in sequence. Vermes's presentation is a follows:

---

[5] *The Dead Sea Scrolls in English* (Harmondsworth, 1975), 230-33.

Commentary on Hosea

In this interpretation, the unfaithful wife is the Jewish people, and her lovers are the Gentiles who have led the nation astray.

"[She knew not that] it was I who gave her [the new wine and oil], who lavished [upon her silver] and gold which they [used for Baal]" (2:8).

Interpreted, this means that [they ate and] were filled, but they forgot God who.... They cast His commandments behind them which He had sent [by the hand of] His servants the Prophets, and they listened to those who led them astray. They revered them, and in their blindness they feared them as though they were gods.

"Therefore I will take back my corn in its time and my wine [in its season]. I will take away my wool and my flax lest they cover [her nakedness]. I will uncover her shame before the eyes of [her] lovers [and] no man shall deliver her from out of my hand" (2:9-10).

Interpreted, this means that He smote them with hunger and nakedness that they might be shamed and disgraced in the sight of the nations on which they relied. They will not deliver them from their miseries.

"I will put an end to her rejoicing, [her feasts], her [new] moons, her Sabbaths, and all her festivals" (2:11).

Interpreted, this means that [they have rejected the ruling of the law, and have] followed the festivals of the nations. But [their rejoicing shall come to an end and] shall be changed into mourning.

I will ravage [her vines and her fig trees], of which she said, 'They are my wage [which my lovers have given me]'. I will make of them a thicket and the [wild beasts] shall eat them...." (2:12).

On the Commentary on Nahum, Vermes comments: "For a correct understanding of the interpretation of Nahum 2:12, the reader should bear in mind the biblical order that only the corpses of executed criminals should be hanged (Deut. 21:21). Hanging men alive, i.e., crucifixion, was a sacrilegious novelty. Some translators consider the mutilated final sentence unfinished, and render it: 'For a man hanged alive on a tree shall be called...' The version given here seems more reasonable. The passage is as follows:

"[Where is the lions' den and the cave of the young lions?]" (2:11).

[Interpreted, this concerns]...a dwelling-place for the ungodly of the nations.

"Whither the lion goes, there is the lion's cub, [with none to disturb it]" (2:11b).

[Interpreted, this concerns Deme]trius king of Greece who sought, on the counsel of those who seek smooth things, to enter Jerusalem. [But God did not permit the city to be delivered] into the hands of the kings of Greece, from the time of Antiochus until the coming of the rulers of the Kittim. But then she shall be trampled under their feet....

"The lion tears enough for its cubs and it chokes prey for its lionesses" (2:12a).

[Interpreted, this] concerns the furious young lion who strikes by means of his great men, and by means of the men of his council.

"[And chokes prey for its lionesses; and it fills] its caves [with prey] and its dens with victims" (2:12a-b).

Interpreted, this concerns the furious young lion [who executes revenge] on those who seek smooth things and hangs men alive, [a thing never done] formerly in Israel. Because of a man hanged alive on [the] tree, He proclaims, "Behold I am against [you, says the Lord of Hosts]."

"[I will burn up your multitude in smoke], and the sword shall devour your young lions. I will [cut off] your prey [from the earth]" (2:13):

[Interpreted]..."your multitude" is the bands of his army...and his "young lions" are...his "prey" is the wealth which [the priests] of Jerusalem have [amassed], which...Israel shall be delivered....

"[And the voice of your messengers shall no more be heard]" (2:13b).

[Interpreted]...his "messengers" are his envoys whose voice shall no more he heard among the nations.

Treating the materials presented by Vermes as a document, we simply cannot categorize these several "units of discourse" within the established framework of taxonomy suitable for the Genesis Rabbah and Leviticus Rabbah. For we do not have (1) a word-for-word or point-by-point reading, in light of other verses of Scripture, of the verses that are cited, let alone (2) an expansion on the topics of the verses. The forms serving the two Rabbah-compilations obviously do not apply. What we have is an entirely different sort of exegesis, given in an entirely different form, namely, a reading of the verses of Scripture in light of an available scheme of concrete events. The exegete wishes to place into relationship to Scripture things that have happened in his own day. His form serves that goal.

If the generative principle of exegesis seems alien, the criterion of composition as a whole is entirely familiar. The compiler wished to present amplifications of the meaning of a verse of Scripture, not word-for-word or phrase-for-phrase interpretations. He also has not constructed a wide-ranging discussion of the theme of the verse such as we noted in the more philosophical taxon (III), let alone a mere anthology (A). Let me with appropriate emphasis state the main point.

The framer of the passage selected a mode of constructing his unit of discourse wholly congruent with the purpose for which, to begin with, he undertook the exegesis of the passage.

He wished to read the verses of Scripture in light of events. So he organized his unit of discourse around the sequence of verses of Scripture under analysis. Had he wanted, he might have provided a sequential narrative of what happened, then inserting the verse he found pertinent, thus: "X happened, and that is the meaning of (biblical verse) Y." (Such a mode of organizing exegeses served the school of Matthew, but not the framer of the text at hand. I do not know why). In any event the construction at hand is rather simple. The far more complex modes of constructing units of discourse in Genesis Rabbah and Leviticus Rabbah served a different purpose. They are made up, moreover, of different approaches to the exegesis of Scripture. So we see that the purpose of exegesis makes a deep impact upon not only the substance of the exegesis, but also, and especially, upon the formal and redactional characteristics of the document, the mode of organizing the consequent collection of exegeses.

Obviously, there were diverse ways both of undertaking scriptural exegesis and of organizing the collections of such exegeses. In the setting of examples of these other ways in which earlier Jews had responded to verses of Scripture and then collected and organized their responses, we see that there was more than a single compelling way in which to do the work. It follows that the way in which the framers of Genesis Rabbah and Leviticus Rabbah did the work was not predictable. Their mode of formulation, organization, and composition therefore is not to be taken for granted. It represented a distinctive choice among possibilities others in Israelite culture had explored.

It may now be fairly argued that the rather episodic sets of exegeses presented to us by the Essene library of Qumran cannot be called documents and compared to the sustained and purposeful labor of both exegesis and composition revealed in the earliest rabbinic collections. Accordingly, let us turn, for a second exercise of comparison, to an exegetical passage exhibiting clear-cut and fixed forms of rhetoric, both of the exegetical passage itself, and of the composition of several exegetical passages into a large-scale discourse -- hence, units of discourse to be compared with units of discourse of Genesis Rabbah. We find in the literary composition of the school of Matthew a powerful effort to provide an interpretation of verses of Scripture in line with a distinct program of interpretation. Furthermore, the selection and arrangement of these scriptural exegeses turn out to be governed by the large-scale purpose of the framers of the document as a whole.

To illustrate these two facts, I present four parallel passages, in which we find a narrative, culminating in the citation of a verse of Scripture, hence a convention of formal presentation of ideas, style and composition alike. In each case, the purpose of the narrative is not only fulfilled in itself, but also in a subscription linking the narrative to the cited verse and stating explicitly that the antecedent narrative serves to fulfill the prediction contained in the cited verse, hence a convention of theological substance. We deal with Matthew 1:18-23, 2:1-6, 2:16-18, and 3:1-3.

Mt. 1:18-23

Now the birth of Jesus Christ took place in this way. When his mother Mary had been betrothed to Joseph, before they came together she was found to be with child of the Holy Spirit; and her husband Joseph, being a just man and unwilling to put her to shame, resolved to divorce her quietly. But as he considered this, behold, an angel of the Lord appeared to him in a dream, saying, "Joseph, son of David, do not fear to take Mary your wife, for that which is conceived in her is of the Holy Spirit; she will bear a son, and you shall call his name Jesus, for he will save his people from their sins." All this took place to fulfill what the Lord had spoken by the prophet: "Behold, a virgin shall conceive and bear a son, and his name shall be called Emmanuel" (which means, God with us).

Mt. 2:1-6

Now when Jesus was born in Bethlehem of Judea in the days of Herod the king, behold, wise men from the East came to Jerusalem, saying, "Where is he who has been born king of the Jews? For we have seen his star in the East, and have come to worship him." When Herod the king heard this, he was troubled, and all Jerusalem with him; and assembling all the chief priests and scribes of the people, he inquired of them where the Christ was to be born. They told him, "In Bethlehem of Judea; for so it is written by the prophet: "And you, O Bethlehem, in the land of Judah, are by no means least among the rulers of Judah; for from you shall come a ruler who will govern my people Israel.'"

Mt. 2:16-18

Then Herod, when he saw that he had been tricked by the wise men, was in a furious rage, and he sent and killed all the male children in Bethlehem and in all that region who were two years old or under, according to the time which he had ascertained from the wise men. Then was fulfilled what was spoken by the prophet Jeremiah: "A voice was heard in Ramah, wailing and loud lamentation, Rachel weeping for her children; she refused to be consoled, because they were no more."

Mt. 3:1-3

In those days came John the Baptist, preaching in the wilderness of Judea, "Repent, for the kingdom of heaven is at hand." For this is he who was spoken of by the prophet Isaiah when he said, "The voice of one crying in the wilderness: Prepare the way of the Lord, make his paths straight."

The four passages show us a stunningly original mode of linking exegeses. The organizing principle derives from the sequence of events of a particular biography, rather than the sequence of verses in a given book of Scripture or of sentences of the Mishnah. The biography of the person under discussion serves as the architectonic of the composition of exegeses into a single statement of meaning. This mode of linking exegeses -- that is, composing them into a large-scale collection, such as we have at hand in the earliest rabbinic compilations -- shows us another way than the way taken at Qumran, on the one side, and among the late fourth and fifth centuries' compilers of rabbinic collections of exegeses, on the other.

Elsewhere[6] I have shown that a few stories about the life of Hillel were linked to a sequential set of verses of Deut. 15:1ff. Perhaps someone may have thought of linking events of Hillel's life to a contiguous group of verses. But no "life" of a sage of antiquity forms the base line for a composition, whether made up of exegeses, or (more likely) of legal opinions. There are a few chapters in the Mishnah, e.g., M. Kelim chapter 24, that systematically express the generative principle of a single authority; there are many pericopes (units of discourse) framed around opinions of a single authority, and a great many around disagreements between two or more fixed names. But these are not comparable.

The passages of Matthew, therefore, indicate a clear-cut, distinctive choice on how to compose a "unit of discourse" and to join several congruent units of discourse into a sustained statement, a document. The choice is dictated by the character and purpose of the composition at hand. Since the life of a particular person -- as distinct from events of a particular character -- forms the focus of discourse, telling a story connected with that life and following this with a citation of the biblical verse illustrated in the foregoing story constitutes the generative and organizing principle of the several units of discourse, all of them within a single taxon. The taxon is not only one-dimensional. It also is rather simple in both its literary traits and its organizing principle. We discern extremely tight narration of a tale, followed by a citation of a verse of Scripture, interpreted only through the device of the explicit joining language: This (1) is what that (2) means. What we see so clearly in the work of the school of Matthew is a simple fact. The work of making up exegeses of Scripture, selecting the appropriate ones and saying important things about them, and the labor of collecting and compiling these exegeses of Scripture into a larger composite together express a single principle, make a single statement, carry out the purposes of a single polemic. Let me once more give proper emphasis to this simple result:

---

[6] *Journal of Jewish Studies* 25, 1974:263.

Three things go together: (1) the principles of exegesis, (2) the purposes of exegesis, and (3) the program of collecting and arranging exeges into compilations.

That is the fact of Matthew. It is true of Sifra.[7] Here I have tried to demonstrate that it is the fact of Genesis Rabbah and Leviticus Rabbah as well. In time to come, detailed analysis of the various compilations of biblical exegeses produced at diverse places and times within Judaism, from the fifth century to the eighteenth, will tell us whether or not it is so later on as well.

So we see a simple fact. First, what people wished to say about the meaning of a verse of Scripture and, second, why they then proposed to collect what they had said into cogent compositions -- these two considerations cohere. When we can say in connection with other compilations of scriptural exegeses what we think generated comments on biblical verses, and how composing these particular comments on these selected verses into compilations or compositions made sense to composers, we shall be well on the way to describing, analyzing, and interpreting the context -- the life-situation -- of those documents, hence also to the comparison of document to document, one whole compilation of exegeses of Scripture with another whole compilation, that is, *comparative midrash* the way comparison should begin.

---

[7] Cf. *Purities. VI. Negaim. Sifra,* cited above.

Appendix

TWO PRINCIPAL THEORIES OF
COMPARATIVE MIDRASH

Appendix

The Two Principal Theories
of Comparative Midrash

i. Bloch's New *Ueberlieferungsgeschichte*: *Midrash* as "Tradition"

We now turn to examine two other approaches to *comparative midrash*, allowing the proponents of the established method and also practitioners of it at some length to speak for themselves in their own words. These are Renée Bloch and Geza Vermes. The former made the first systematic statement. But, as we shall see when we examine that statement, by comparative midrash" she meant the study of the varied versions of narratives, tales, comments of various kinds on diverse themes -- this, that, and the other thing; she did not mean by *midrash* what the word ordinarily is taken to mean, which is exegesis. In fact when we are finished, we shall not know precisely what she meant by the word, short of the rather general *aggadah*, that is, story, or, the German *Ueberlieferung*, or the hopeless nonsense-word, *tradition*. So in her connection all of our analyses go to waste. She was not talking about the same thing as is ordinarily meant in the present usage of the words *midrash* and *comparative midrash*.

Still, Renée Bloch's is the first, and remains the single systematic statement of the prevailing approach to the problem of comparing what diverse groups say about, among other things, the meaning of biblical verses. What follows derives from her article, "Methodological Note for the Study of Rabbinic Literature," translated by William Scott Green and William J. Sullivan, in William Scott Green, ed., *Approaches to Ancient Judaism: Theory and Practice* (Missoula, 1978: Scholars Press for Brown Judaic Studies), I, pp. 51-76. I contribute a few expository remarks, to underline what I believe are Bloch's principal points of stress. She says:

> The problem, then, is to determine, by a careful work of historical and above all of literary criticism, as well as by comparative study, the development and the respective antiquity of traditions, the formation, the historical situation, and the interdependence of rabbinic writings....In order successfully to classify and date traditions and documents, in addition to employing the historical indicators of external criticism and the criteria of paleography and philology, we propose to resort to a comparative study comprising two stages: an external comparison and an internal comparison.

What is important here is Bloch's stress on what is at stake in comparison. She wishes to supply far more than the fact that A said X about Gen. 49:10 while B said Y about that same verse of Scripture. So she does specify a "what else."

> 1. The External Comparison. This consists of a comparison between the Palestinian rabbinic, especially midrashic, writings which, along with the traditions they transmit, are not dated, and the texts external to Palestinian rabbinic Judaism which have at least an approximate date and in which the same traditions are found. Thanks to these dated witnesses, one can determine the terminus ad quem of certain Palestinian aggadic traditions and, at the same time, establish some guidelines for the history of the literature.

What Bloch proposes to compare, as I indicated above, are "traditions." What she means is not entirely clear. Indeed, quite how at hand is an exercise in *comparison* is not certain.

It appears to me that what Bloch means to do is to identify a given saying or story or opinion on various matters, including, of course, the meaning of a verse, in a dated document, and, on the basis of occurrence in said document, to determine the point prior to which such a saying or story or opinion ("tradition") circulated. When, then, she finds the same saying or story in a document otherwise not dated, she can propose that that saying or story, in the undated document, itself circulated prior to the formulation of the undated document in which the saying or story occurs. We therefore learn that the undated document contains materials that circulated prior to a certain date. That fact does not tell us anything about the dating of the otherwise undated document. I am not entirely certain what, indeed, we are supposed to learn from the fact at hand. For if we know that a group made use of a saying or story utilized, also, by a prior group, what do we learn about the saying or story -- other than its power to serve a number of different groups, under different conditions, and for diverse purposes? But Bloch never tells us what we learn, other than the matter of "dating." I am not entirely certain what this "date" is meant to clarify, other than the issue of priority of occurrence -- if that. So what is claimed in the foregoing paragraph is simply a rather obvious fact. A story appearing in an undated document can be assigned a *terminus ad quem* because of its appearance in a (prior) dated one. I do not see much in that discovery worthy of celebration. What do we understand that we did not grasp before? Why is it important? To Bloch and her successors the answers to these questions prove more obvious than they do to me. And, it remains to note, that statement bears no relationship to comparison at all. What she wishes to do is not to compare and to contrast one thing with something else, and, in this version of matters, we have no such thing as *comparative midrash* at all. All we have is an exercise of a fairly primitive order in the field of "traditions-history."

In the following section of her paper Bloch proceeds to survey the materials she proposes to comprehend in the comparative study of traditions:

> To give an idea of the material which ought to serve as the foundation of this comparative study, it will be useful rapidly to list the groups of writings which can be taken into account.
>
> a. The Writings of Hellenistic Judaism
>
> There sometimes is too great a tendency to identify Hellenistic Judaism with Philo. ...On the whole, a penetrating, exhaustive study of Hellenistic Judaism and of its exact relationship to Palestinian Judaism is still lacking....We think that the studies like those recommended here will show that Hellenistic Judaism was much more oriented towards Palestine than is generally thought. In this manner, moreover, one can establish a distinct tendency in the Greek versions of the Bible progressively to approach the Hebrew text, which fundamentally remained the norm or basic authority, even for Hellenistic Judaism.
>
> For the proposed study, Hellenistic Judaism offers us a good number of witnesses which either are dated with sufficient precision or have at least a well-determined terminus ad quem....
>
> b. The Apocrypha
>
> Most of these writings can be assigned to a fairly well-determined period. This is especially true for several of the most ancient Palestinian apocrypha, which date back to the pre-Christian era or to the period of Christian origins. This literature could furnish important information...
>
> c. Pseudo-Philo
>
> This sort of biblical history (analogous, for example, to Chronicles), which goes from Adam until the death of Saul, must have played a very important role. Pseudo-Philo dates from the first century of the Christian era, probably from the year following the destruction of Jerusalem in 70 A.D. It is a kind of aggadic commentary on the historical books of the Old Testament which unquestionably bears the mark of the ancient aggadic midrash. One certainly can discern the close points of resemblance between Pseudo-Philo, on the one hand, and the biblical Apocrypha, especially the Book of Enoch, the Book of Jubilees, the Syrian Apocalypse of Baruch and IV Esdras, on the other. But it is more evident that Pseudo-Philo's version of the history of Israel to a great extent is derivative of the aggadic traditions known to us through midrashic literature. At the least, this testifies that these traditions precede Pseudo-Philo.
>
> d. Josephus
>
> Dated with certainty and precision, Josephus naturally is an invaluable witness. Moreover, his work, Jewish Antiquities, reveals an extensive knowledge of the rabbinic aggadah. The problem is the same for Josephus as it is for Pseudo-Philo: since the present forms of the rabbinic writings through which we know the aggadic traditions are of later redaction, from where could these ancient authors have drawn the aggadic traditions they used in their work? (For no one would imagine that these traditions might depend on Josephus or Pseudo-Philo.) It is historically impossible to resort to the hypothesis of a purely oral

tradition. It remains, therefore, to postulate one or several common, written aggadic sources anterior to both Josephus and Pseudo-Philo.

e. Glosses of the Biblical Text and Versions (Septuagint, Peshitto, etc.)

While contributing to the determination or precision of the sense of usage of an already established text into which they were inserted at a later period, the glosses sometimes simultaneously reveal midrashic traditions of this milieu...no study as yet has been devoted to the problem of glosses of the biblical text.

f. The Damascus Document and the Qumran Manuscripts

Since none of the extant ancient midrashic texts were edited prior to the second or third century A.D., and since the majority of these in their present form date from no earlier than the fifth, sixth or seventh century, in the Damascus Document and in the manuscripts of the Qumran sect, we have for the first time writings which date from the initial period of rabbinic literature, very probably from the first half of the first century B.C. These texts also provide us with valuable evidence, particularly about the importance attached to the study of Scripture, about the technique of interpreting it during that period, (already very similar to what will soon become the fully developed midrashic genre) and, finally, about certain specific aggadic traditions.

g. The New Testament Writings

The authors of the New Testament are Jews raised in the Jewish tradition who to a great extent speak to and write for Jews who know this tradition as they do. The fact that the New Testament assumes this entire Jewish tradition cannot be stressed enough. ...Apart from this general climate, the well-dated writings of the New Testament also reveal a certain number of interesting traits of a purely aggadic character. An important example can be found in the account of the "spiritual" rock, which -- according to I Cor. 10:4 -- followed the Israelites in the desert: this passage from St. Paul confirms the antiquity of this theme, which has parallels in midrashic literature. Like the best aggadists, Paul here resorts to the midrash aggadah for an illustration, in order to derive from it a doctrinal meaning: "this rock was Christ."

h. Some Ancient Christian Writers

We already have mentioned Clement of Alexandria and Eusebius of Caesarea, both of whom directly preserved written evidences of certain traditions of Hellenistic Judaism. In their writings, but even more so in those of Origen, one also could find other traces of Jewish sources which they knew directly or indirectly. As we already have noted, the writings of the first Syrian Fathers, especially Aphrahat and Ephrem, offer abundant material, still accessible only with difficulty, for comparative study. As with Origen, it is their biblical commentaries which are most important in this regard. But in Syriac literature the similarities to rabbinic tradition are particularly widespread. Despite the relatively late fourth century date of the major witnesses of Syriac tradition, there is no doubt that this is an important avenue to explore.

i. Ancient Liturgical Sources

Jewish liturgy undoubtedly preserves many very ancient texts; but given the present state of research, it is rare to find one which can be dated with sufficient probability to be used as an object of comparison.

This is the case however, for the Qerobot of Yannai, which are based on the liturgical pericopae read in the synagogue every Sabbath, which follow the order of the triennial cycle, and which constitute, in poetic form, a sort of complete midrash on the Pentateuch.

All that Bloch has now told us points toward a purpose unrelated to *comparative midrash* as the comparison of *midrash* in its contemporary and established sense: exegesis, hermeneutics, compilation and redaction of exegeses. What she discusses is traditions-history -- a completely different matter. So, I cannot overemphasize, when she uses the word *midrash,* it is in sense quite different from the familiar one. And I do not know the warrant for her use of the word. So much for external comparison. We turn now to the second part of her program.

2. The Internal Comparison. This work essentially traces a single tradition through the various stages represented by the different documents. It tries to distinguish the most primitive elements and the variants, the developments, the additions and the revisions; it takes account of the diversity of literary genres and historical situations. It does all this in order provisionally to classify the writings according to the evolution of the observed tradition.

This comparative study, which even could be done with the aid of synoptic tables, begins with the biblical text and follows the selected tradition or traditions through the versions of the Bible (LXX, TO, Pesh., etc., making use of the Hexapla of Origen), the Jerusalem Targum, the different midrashim, the Midrash Rabbah, the Talmud, various rabbinic writings (Sefer ha-Yashar, Sefer ha-Zikhronot, Chronicle of Moses, Yalqut Shimoni, etc.) and concludes with Rashi. In certain cases, of course, this work opportunely can be combined with that of the external comparison.

Everything indicates that the point of departure can only be the biblical text. According to the counsel of the Psalmist, it is on this sacred text that one reflects, prays and meditates night and day. And in the synagogue, the homily, which played an extremely important role in the establishment of the midrashic tradition, was constructed uniquely on these venerable texts.

Now we reach a use of the word *midrash* in a familiar setting: what different people say about the same thing. Whether or not Bloch now would admit that we speak only of *midrash*-exegesis or whether the word *midrash* covers a broader frame of reference, e.g., *aggadah* in general, I cannot say. Perhaps she has in mind the unclear classification *midrash-aggadah,* as distinct from *midrash-halakhah.* But that classification has no bearing on her argument. Still, here we clearly undertake the comparison of what different people say about the same thing. We now ask Bloch to tell us what she makes of the matter of context.

In reality, none of this literature was created in an "ivory tower"; it is neither a collection of personal works nor even, in the first instance, the product of scholars and schools. It is a popular product. It springs from the preaching done in the synagogue every Sabbath and festival day, after the reading of the Torah, on that section of Scripture which had just been read. The preaching centered on Scripture, as did all the religious life of Judaism.

Within rabbinic literature, it is the Palestinian Targum which we propose as a starting point. This text cannot really be considered a version (one need only to read it to realize this!), but belongs to a very different genre; it is much closer to the midrash, properly speaking, than to a version. It even is probable that it originally was a homiletic midrash, or simply a series of homilies on Scripture, read in the synagogue after the public reading of the Torah.

Due to the limited scope of this article, we can consider neither the problem of the Targums, nor that of the Jerusalem Targum in particular, that extraordinary imbroglio of hypotheses, often of the most fantastic sort. We merely wish to indicate here the reason for our choice. During a study of the Jerusalem Targum, it became obvious to us that this Targum lies at the base of later aggadic tradition, that by serving as an immediate extension of the scriptural given, it acts as a sort of hinge, a bridge between the Bible and later rabbinic literature, and that it represents the starting point, not of the midrashic genre as such (which is already present in biblical literature), but of midrash, properly so-called, all of whose structure and themes it already contains. This observation seemed to us important. It is no matter of indifference to have access to a firmly established starting point for the internal comparison.

By context Bloch means situation-in-every-day-life. That situation in her view finds no limits as to place, time, or circumstance -- let alone document. The limitations imposed by the boundaries of the diverse documents play no role in interpreting the contents of the documents. How so? That sayings, stories, and comments on verses derive from the uniform setting of synagogue-worship demands our assent without proof. The axiom and the premise generates all else. The Targumim, assumed both to speak for "the rabbis" and to represent the way in which the Scriptures were read to the community in the synagogue, then take pride of place, as well they should within the present premise. The *Sitz im Leben* of all stories will not demand acute analysis, if it is essentially one: namely, synagogal. Though asserted from the time of Zunz, that proposition still awaits systematic demonstration. Now as to comparative method:

III. A Comparative Method

The problem, then, is to determine, by a careful work of historical and above all of literary criticism, as well as by comparative study, the development and the respective antiquity of traditions, the formation, the historical situation, and the interdependence of rabbinic writings. We already have noted that a systematic work of this sort never has been undertaken, that it is imperative at present if we are to advance on solid ground, and, finally, that there exist sufficient materials with which to undertake it.

At the end I must confess I find myself in total confusion. On the one side, we speak of "traditions," in general, but on the other, "the interdependence of rabbinic writings." Since we have already reviewed Bloch's catalogue of writings that none regards as rabbinic, I simply do not know what Bloch now proposes. The one thing that is clear is this: Bloch uses the word *midrash* to mean *tradition*, not exegesis, and therefore *comparative midrash* in her setting bears no relationship whatsoever to the comparison of exegeses. Whether or not her proposed method serves to establish the history of traditions in any meaningful sense need not detain us; it is not our problem. My sense, as I said, is that when she uses the word *midrash*, she means something like *aggadah*, that is, a story or a statement. But this is a far more general usage of the language at hand than any in common speech, for, ordinarily, when people refer to *midrash*, they do mean exegesis, and hence, *comparative midrash* can only mean comparing exegesis to exegesis, not story to story, let alone (to follow up the complete confusion) *aggadah* to *aggadah*. So, as I said at the outset, in Bloch what we find is a kind of new *Ueberlieferungsgeschichte* : *midrash* understood merely as another word for "Tradition." If my understanding of Bloch is accurate, we shall have to bid a fond adieu to Bloch as the first significant theorist of *comparative midrash* as an approach to the study of biblical exegesis in the Judaic literature of late antiquity. That is simply not what she was talking about.

ii. Vermes and "Historical-Critical" Method in *Comparative Midrash*

Co-worker of Bloch until her tragic death in 1957, and principal practitioner of *comparative midrash*, Geza Vermes has provided in writing two expositions of his views of the enterprise. We review them in the order of their appearance. As before, I make comments on some main points. The first derives from Geza Vermes, *Scripture and Tradition in Judaism* (Leiden, 1961: E. J. Brill), pp. 7-10, *pass.*:

> R. BLOCH investigates the biblical origins of the midrash in the post-exilic books of the Bible. She ascribes the birth of the midrashic genre to the progressive fixation of the text of Scripture during the Persian period, and suggests that most characteristic examples appear in the Wisdom literature; but other examples are included in the exilic and post-exilic Prophets, and in Chronicles, the latter being a midrash on Samuel-Kings combined with the Priestly source of the Pentateuch (genealogies). The evolution of the midrash is followed within the "biblical milieu": The Apocrypha, (Ecclesiasticus, Wisdom of Solomon), Pseudepigrapha (Jubilees, Testaments of the Twelve Patriarchs), the Dead Sea Scrolls, the Septuagint, the choice of Dere (text to be read) to replace

Ketib (written text), the Palestinian Targums, and finally the New Testament, where all the midrashic forms are presented.

The wholly novel element in this synthesis if the systematic effort to situate the problem of the midrash within a proper historical perspective, not only as regards halakhah, but also haggadah. If all midrash, even haggadic, is an historical phenomenon whose origins are to be traced to post-exilic biblical times, the condition sine qua non for its understanding is to consider it within the setting of its evolution, to distinguish the stages of this evolution, and determine the causes of change. The whole significance of a midrashic theme cannot be understood without some knowledge of its history, and possibly of its pre-history. For example, the same interpretation of a scriptural story may be discovered in a mediaeval midrash, in the Talmud, in the Targum, in a Tannaitic collection, in JOSEPHUS, and -- let us say -- in Jubilees or Ecclesiasticus. This would mean that the fundamental exegesis is at least as old as the second century BC. The differences in its application at various periods may result from changes in aims, needs, or even doctrines; but such changes cannot be detected without knowing what exactly has been altered. To phrase it differently, the real significance of a Tannaitic haggadah can only be determined by comparing it with an interpretation of the same text by a pre-Tannaitic author and by an Amora.

Vermes validates my insistence that the word *midrash* must relate to exegesis. He now makes matters turn not on themes in general but on exegesis in particular. He further proves that when I point to the non-contextual comparisons accomplished in the name of *comparative midrash*, I do not argue with an absent enemy. There is a real position, held and worked out by actual scholars in precisely the way in which I have maintained they do the work. Vermes does hold that the same interpretation of a scriptural story may occur in diverse documents. What is important in that fact he states explicit. We therefore can investigate the time, circumstance, even determinant or precipitant of the change. Then when I point out that *comparative midrash* ignores the documentary context, treating all. statements about the same verse without regard to the preferences and distinctive traits and viewpoints of the document in which they occur, I do not set up a straw man. This is a real view, carried on by scholars in their everyday work. And, as I have argued, it is wrong. Vermes proceeds:

In short, RENÉE BLOCH demands that midrashic literature should be studied according to the same principles of historical and literary criticism as is the Bible itself. The aim and method of such a study are expounded in an impressive fashion in her Note [cited above]....

In order to classify and to date traditions, she proposed that, in addition to the employment of historical and philological criteria, etc., analysis should proceed in two stages; by means of external and internal comparison. In her view, external comparison consists in confronting Rabbinic writings recording undated traditions with non-Rabbinic Jewish texts which are at least approximately dated. These external criteria should be sought in Hellenistic Jewish works, the pseudepigrapha, Pseudo-Philo, Josephus, glosses in the Bible, the ancient Versions, the Dead Sea Scrolls, the New Testament, ancient Christian writings deriving their inspiration from Jewish sources, (e.g., Origen, Aphraates, Ephrem, etc.) and in the ancient Jewish liturgy.... Internal comparison, on the other hand, follows the development of a tradition within the boundaries of Rabbinic literature itself. The biblical text must afford the point of departure because it is the object of study, prayer, teaching, and preaching. Does R. Bloch's working hypothesis actually work? And how? Her intuition concerning the importance of the Palestinian Targum has, on the whole, been found exact in a recent study by P. Grelot. This cannot, however, be considered conclusive, and in the present book I mean to carry the test a stage further with four problems of general importance in mind:

1)   the origin and development of exegetical symbolism;

2)   the structure and purpose of the re-writing of the Bible;

3)   the historical bond between the Bible and its interpretation;

4)   the impact of theology on exegesis, and vice versa.

At the same time, each chapter is intended to illustrate various methods by which problems of interpretation may be tackled.

This study is essentially devoted to Jewish exegesis, but the last two sections will also contribute, I hope, towards a sounder understanding of some fundamental questions relative to both Old and New Testaments alike.

Vermes makes explicit the grounds for joining the diverse occurrences of an exegetical program into a single composite. He makes matters explicit when he states, "The biblical text must afford the point of departure because it is the object of study, prayer, teaching, and preaching." I cannot imagine a more specific explanation of what is at issue. The studies that Vermes carries on then move in the directions dictated by his premise about the self-evident choice of the biblical text as the point of departure -- by which he means, further, the point of differentiation, comparison, and analysis -- the exegetical fulcrum. And that yields precisely that ahistorical formalism, that anti-contextual cataloguing of uninterpreted coincidences, that for me yield mere facts, but for him produce information on the topics he lists: "2) the structure and purpose of the re-writing of the Bible; 3) the historical bond between the Bible and its interpretation; 4) the impact of theology on exegesis, and vice versa." Once more, therefore, I point out that my characterization of *comparative midrash* as presently practiced constitutes no mere caricature but an accurate portrait of a field as it is carried on. I find here ample justification for writing a whole book to test the premises of the work and to show why they are wrong.

Let me then ask two questions. Can it be that Vermes really wishes us to ignore the documentary setting in which an exegesis occurs? Does he propose paying attention only to the exegesis and the date of the document in which it occurs, without further attention to what the compilers or authorship of the document wished to accomplish by making use of the saying or exegesis? Indeed so. Here too I have not misrepresented his position that the sole fact *about* the documentary context that matters is the date of the document. In this Vermes remains well within the program of traditions-history enunciated by Bloch. We have yet another statement in which Vermes underlines what he regards as the validity of asking Scripture itself to justify simply collecting and comparing exegeses of Scripture. In "Bible and Midrash: Early Old Testament Exegesis," in P. R. Ackroyd and C. F. Evans, eds., *Cambridge History of the Bible* (Cambridge, 1970: University Press), pp. 228-231, Vermes further states:

> Interpreters of the Hebrew Bible cannot fail to benefit from the work of their predecessors in antiquity. Not only will they discover which biblical texts were thought to demand particular interpretation: they will also notice that the midrashist's problems often coincide with their own, and may be surprised to see that 'modern' solutions to scriptural difficulties are not infrequently foreshadowed in these ancient writings. But beyond any immediate exegetical assistance, midrash is by nature apt to provide the closest historical link with Old Testament tradition itself. Scholars not misled by the analytical tendency of the literary-critical school will fully appreciate the importance of primitive midrash to a proper understanding of the spirit in which scripture was compiled.
>
> The historian of the legal, social and religious ideas of post-biblical Judaism, seeking to make decisive progress towards a reconstruction of their complicated evolution, will in his turn find in Bible exegesis *that precious thread of Ariadne which will lead him safely through the literary labyrinth of Targum, Midrash, Mishnah and Talmud. He will also discover there the unifying bond which ties biblical and post-biblical Judaism together.*

The words that I have italicized vindicate my insistence on what is at issue. But Vermes proceeds to state his larger theological program, and it turns out to derive from New Testament scholarship [!]:

> There, too, lies the answer to a great many real problems confronting the New Testament scholar. Since the Christian kerygma was first formulated by Jews for Jews, using Jewish arguments and methods of exposition, it goes without saying that a thorough knowledge of contemporary Jewish exegesis is essential to the understanding (and not just a better understanding) of the message of the New Testament and, even more, of Jesus.

Comparative midrash indeed! In this statement, Vermes reveals the underlying program that he, Bloch and others attempted: a restatement of the theological situation of the foundation of Christianity, an insistence upon the Judaism of Christianity. That point of insistence, full of rich opportunities for contemporary religious reconciliation, bears no scholarly motive whatsoever:

why, in descriptive terms, should anyone care? In fact *comparative midrash* in its present formulation forms a subdiscipline of irenics, now extended even to Judaism. In all fairness Vermes does present a more narrowly historical program as well:

> Insistence on an historical approach to midrash, the sine qua non of comparative study, raises the following fundamental questions, a brief discussion of which will provide an appropriate ending to the present study. Since the bulk of the sources of Jewish exegesis belong to rabbinic literature which received its final form between the third and fifth centuries of the Christian era, is it possible to distinguish the new from the old among the traditions incorporated there? If so, can they be placed in precise chronological sequence?
>
> Approached from this angle, the problem of midrash is not unlike that of the Bible, which nineteenth and twentieth-century critics tackled and, to a large extent, solved. It is, in fact, considerably less exacting, owing to the shorter time-gap between the origin of an exegetical tradition and its recording in writing, and to the greater wealth of sufficiently well-dated intermediary material, such as the Septuagint, Pseudepigrapha, Qumran Scrolls, New Testament, Philo, Josephus, etc. Moreover, it is to be borne in mind that in the field of halakhah the major codification, to which the Tannaitic Midrashim and the Mishnah bear witness, occurred within a century of the catastrophe of A.D. 70. The changes necessitated by the fall of the Sanctuary and its related institutions make it possible to distinguish traditions appertaining to the ancient regime from those of a more recent date. From further comparison of the former with intertestamental sources may emerge not only a reasonably clear picture of the line of evolution followed between 200 B.C. and A.D. 70, but also a pointer to the genesis of a given halakhah.
>
> The dating of haggadah is more delicate because this kind of exegesis, concerned with ideas and beliefs rather than with laws and customs, was less quickly influenced by political and social factors. Consequently, in the absence of parallel pre-Christian or first-century A.D. sources, no one can be sure to which historical period any interpretation may belong. From the analyses included in this chapter and in my *Scripture and Tradition in Judaism* -- though admittedly the examples have been chosen in such a way that external comparative material has always been available -- it would appear that in general the Palestinian Targums preserve, untouched or retouched, Bible exegesis in its earliest form. Is one therefore entitled to rely on the antiquity of targumic tradition as a whole? In particular, to what extent may one depend on Pseudo-Jonathan, which is known to have received additions as late as the Byzantine and Arab periods?
>
> The answer to these questions may be illustrated in one final example. Exod. 2:5 informs us that Moses was saved from the river by one of the attendants of Pharaoh's daughter. Despite the Massoretic text, confirmed by the Septuagint and Josephus, Pseudo-Jonathan declares that the child was brought to safety by the princess herself. Was this interpretation created by the targumist, or did he rather borrow it from the Babylonian Talmud, completed at the end of the fifth century, where

in an exegetical discussion Rabbi Judah ben Ilai, who flourished in the middle of the second century A.D., voices the same exegesis?

The answer to both alternatives is no. The targumic view was so much part of common tradition that the artist responsible for the scene depicting Moses' infancy in the synagogue of Dura Europos substituted it for the Exodus account. We see there Pharaoh's daughter standing in the Nile and holding the child on her arm. But this implies that even on the distant shores of the Euphrates the Bible story was seen in the middle of the third century A.D. through the eyes of the Palestinian Targum. If this was so, and remembering that biblical interpretation requires a relatively long time to become tradition, the exegesis in question must have originated not later than the middle of the second century A.D. In truth, however, the haggadah on Exod. 2:5 may be traced as far back as Ezechiel the tragic poet, who lived in the second century B.C. Furthermore, there is good reason to believe that even Ezechiel was not its inventor but merely bore witness to it. How old then can it be?

The student of midrash may deduce that he is entitled to begin his investigation with the following working hypothesis: unless there is specific proof to the contrary, the haggadah of the Palestinian Targums is likely to antedate the outbreak of the Second Jewish Revolt in A.D. 132.

Vermes' treatment of Ex. 2:5 leaves no doubt that at issue is not exegesis in any literary sense but traditions-history in a far more general context.

iii. Fraade Versus Fraade: (1) Comparative Midrash as Traditions-History. Enosh and His Generation.

The confusion characterizing the field of comparative midrash finds poignant illustration in two articles by a younger scholar, who manages to join together contradictory approaches to the analysis of exegesis of Scripture, its hermeneutics, redaction, and results. In one book Steven D. Fraade follows the path of Bloch and Vermes, ignoring all issues of canon and document. In a long article, he announces his discovery that redactional considerations have affected the shaping of an exegetical passage, claiming as his own an approach that has served as a commonplace for biblical studies for several generations. Anyone who knows that Matthew's reading of a lemma will reflect Matthew's larger polemic, as will Mark's, Luke's, and John's, or that Chronicles rewrites Samuel-Kings, will wonder at Fraade's wonderfully simple pleasure -- announced in a prolix and overabundant article of nearly sixty printed pages -- in his new insight. Still, this survey of the state of the question should not limit itself to the great figures of the field, Bloch and Vermes, but should invite to give testimony also the tyros and the ambitious youngsters. In this way my claim to analyze how things really are done will find ample justification. Hence the urgency of the book at hand. On to Fraade.

In his dissertation, *Enosh and His Generation. Pre-Israelite Hero and History in Post-biblical Interpretation* (Chicago, 1984: Scholars Press/Society of

Biblical Literature Monograph Series No. 30), Fraade surveys the interpretation of Gen. 4:26, "It was then that men began to invoke the Lord by name," in Jewish and Christian exegesis. He surveys pre-rabbinic Jewish interpretations, found in Jewish Greek Scriptures, Ben Sira, Jubilees, 2 Enoch, Philo, and Joseph; Samaritan and Mandaean interpretations; Greek and Latin traditions; sources; rabbinic interpretations, divided among rabbinic Targumim, Tannaitic sources, Amoraic sources, post-Amoraic sources, *piyyut*; then presents a chapter on rabbinic method and motivation. All of these materials are surveyed as only an ambitious graduate student can cull them, with extensive comments on this and that, and the panoply of academic chitchat on every sort of issue. But the purpose that dominates never loses Fraade's final concern. To state his results, we turn then to him (pp. 229-234, *pass.*):

> The Interpretations we have examined can be reduced essentially to two varieties: (a) those that understand Gen 4:26 as a positive statement concerning Enosh the individual (all non-Rabbinic traditions), and (b) those that view this verse as a negative statement about Enosh's contemporaries (Rabbinic traditions alone).
>
> The first interpretation is clearly the more widespread, being evidenced in several groups, from earliest through modern exegesis.
>
> We have seen that in early extra-Rabbinic Jewish, Samaritan, and Christian exegesis Enosh is regularly included as a link in the chain of image and/or messianic seed. In this regard, the interpretation of Enosh is not very different from that of other pre-Israelite righteous figures. These communities wished to trace their own descent back to the first man through an unbroken line of righteous ancestors, bypassing other less savory biblical figures, who were instead identified as the progenitors of the "other nations," and as the originators of worldly evil. By so doing, these group were establishing their pedigrees in sacred history. The earliest ancestors in such lists of righteous ancestors, naturally, were particularly venerated as ideal figures, and any scriptural comment that could be construed as praise of these figures was fully exploited....
>
> Enosh's significance is most pronounced in the writings of certain Church Fathers, who, beginning in the mid-fourth century, interpret Gen 4:26b to mean that Enosh was the first, on account of his righteousness, to be called "God" and "son of God," prefiguring Jesus, who was similarly called. They view him as standing at the head of the righteous Sethite branch of humanity, who (a) initially remain apart from the evil descendants of Cain, (b) following Enosh, prophetically place their hope (i.e., trust) in the Lord Jesus, and (c) like Enosh, bear the name "sons of God." Enosh and his descendants, then, bear witness to Jesus before his incarnation, serve as models of steadfast faith for later Christians, and typologically prefigure and genealogically antecede the Christian sectarian concern not only for grounding the Church's origin in Scripture, but also for tracing it back typologically, as well as genealogically, to the earliest period of human history (or prehistory), thereby strengthening its universal, messianic claims....

Rabbinic exegesis, which views Gen 4:26 as a negative statement about the idolatrous Generation of Enosh, when viewed within the larger context of Rabbinic interpretation of pre-Israelite history, likewise reveals exegetical concerns of a sectarian nature. The de-emphasis of Enosh and other pre-Israelite righteous, the tracing of the origins of idolatry to the Generation of Enosh, as of the other cardinal sins to pre-Israelite society, and the depiction of the steady, unabated degeneration of the pre-Israelite generations (often depicted as beginning with the radical sin and punishment of Enosh's generation) highlight the redemptive role of Abraham and his descendants down to the rabbis and their followers. For the rabbis, it is against the background of progressive, universal human decline that the beginnings of Israelite history, and therefore the origins of the Jewish people, must be viewed.

Enosh the individual is of little concern to the rabbis, their interest lying rather in what Scripture is thought to say of prepatriarchal humanity in general. They would not deny that the Jewish people traces its genealogy ultimately back to Adam through Enosh and Seth, but, then again, so could all peoples. What distinguishes the Jews, from the Rabbinic perspective, is the covenant initiated by God with Abraham, who alone in a sinful age turned to the pure worship of the one God. It is through the fulfillment of this distinctive covenant, as formally contracted with the whole Jewish people at Sinai, that the "golden age" will be regained, and even surpassed. The Rabbinic interpretation implies that had it not been for this covenant, human history would have continued its steady decline, with little hope for redemption. Pre-Israelite, universal history prepares for and necessitates Israelite history, the advent of which now appears to change history's course radically. The prepatriarchal righteous can hardly compare with such Israelite figures as Abraham, Jacob, or Moses, to whom the rabbis trace the "chain of tradition" of which they consider themselves the sole guardians.

Once again, although not as decidedly as for Christian exegesis, antecedents to aspects of Rabbinic exegesis can be found in pre-Rabbinic Jewish sources: (a) Philo's view of Enosh and the other pre-Israelite righteous as being inferior and preparatory to their Israelite successors, (b) Josephus' depiction of a widespread moral and spiritual decline several generations before the Flood. Still, there is little in pre-Rabbinic Jewish exegesis of Gen 4:26 that prepares us for the radical use to which the rabbis put that verse. However, if vertical roots are hard to find, some important lateral ones have become apparent, as Rabbinic exegesis of Gen 4:26 is nourished by contemporary motifs in Greco-Roman historiography of earliest times: Cultural and Chronological primitivism linked to stories of recurring cataclysms....

The Christian Fathers, employing allegory and typology, treated pre-Israelite and antediluvian history as a paradigm, claiming that the Church's election and travail was like that of the righteous Sethite "sons of God," at whose head stood Enosh, true man, and the first "son of God." Such righteous figures as Enosh, preceding the Flood and the "failed" covenant of the law, provided a Scriptural foreshadowing and grounding for the contested claims of the Church that they alone, apart from those who had not accepted Jesus, were "sons of God" awaiting final redemption.

The rabbis, employing what might be called "etiological exegesis," treated pre-Israelite history as a foil, tracing the origins of humanity's sorry state to the pre-Israelite generations. Such universal righteous figures as Seth, Enosh, Enoch, and Noah were denied significant redemptive and revelatory functions since their righteous deeds were unable to prevent the disastrous sins and punishments of their contemporaries. For the rabbis, sacred, redemptive history began with Abraham and the covenant of law contracted with his descendants, but only after universal history had, despite several divine attempts to tame it, run amok. It was the steadfast adherence to that covenant, and to the rabbis as the interpreters of its terms, which would guarantee the redemption of Israel, and ultimately of universal history.

Fraade's statement of his final conclusions presents us with what is both hopeful and disappointing in the anti-canonical approach to comparative midrash. On the one side, Fraade quite persuasively differentiates rabbinic-Judaic from Christian exegesis of the passage at hand. He also accounts for the difference. But Fraade does not even pretend to undertake an analysis of his capacious category, "the rabbis," who all together and all at once lay down their uniform and unanimous judgments. Accordingly, he does not ask at what point in the history of "the rabbis" did the particular position at hand take shape. Why were the issues urgent when they turned up? He in other words has not learned to ask the simplest historical question. The reason he failed to do so is that he did not choose to read the documents one by one, but precipitately joined them all together. So "*the* rabbis," a unity as to time and document, through "*the* rabbinic literature," form a single undifferentiated category. Then simply collecting everything *they* say gives us the rabbinic view.

Now let me suggest a possibility for further investigation. This will suggest why differentiating by documents and their redactors' plan and program may make a difference. What would we say, if we were to discover that the distinctive picture of Enosh that "the rabbis" presented, which Fraade correctly interprets, were to turn up in documents redacted in the fourth century in particular?[1] And how would we interpret matters, if it were to become clear that it is in those documents -- the Yerushalmi, Genesis Rabbah for example -- that the negative view of Enosh in the pattern of redemption turns up. We might wonder, then, why in that century in particular the figure of Enosh and other

---

[1] In "Amoraic sources," pp. 131-156, Fraade surveys a whole group of documents, and, at the end: "Let me briefly summarize the Amoraic traditions we have examined ...These sources..." and on and on. I see no point at which Fraade has differentiated among "the sources." He does not find it necessary to analyze other motifs or points of polemic in the documents in which his materials occur. That is simply not a matter of interest for him. It is an exercise in collecting and arranging, with endless observations about one thing and another -- but no clear point or purpose, other than the one I cited as his concluding remarks. And, as I observed, he seems not to draw much of a conclusion there.

universal, as distinct from Israelite, redeemers or righteous figures attracted particular interest among the compositors who put together the documents at hand. What else happened in that century, and from whom else did the compositors of those documents hear messages? Reflecting on the triumph of Christianity at the time of the formation of the documents at hand, on the broader concerns of the authors of Genesis Rabbah for the interpretation of israelite history in the encounter with the question of salvation, we might reach interesting hypotheses. These hypotheses will, by contrast, entirely escape our attention, if to begin with we do adopt the premise that all rabbis, and all rabbinic compositions and compilations, say the same thing in the same way everywhere all the time. So much for Fraade's *the rabbis* and *their* doctrine. What is the upshot? In the issue before us Fraade finds himself able to make an interesting observation of facts but unable to explain them or ask any important questions. I discern no "so-what" or "what else" that follows the collection and rough-and-ready analysis that he does conduct. In my view by failing to ask about documentary context Fraade misses the point of his own observation about the facts.

iv. Fraade Versus Fraade: (2) Midrash in Documentary Context. Sifré to Deuteronomy 26

In his other study, "Sifré Deuteronomy 26 (ad Deut. 3:23): How Conscious the Composition? (*Hebrew Union College Annual* 54, 1983, pp. 245-302, Fraade treats the canonical context as critical. First (p. 245) Fraade presents a resume of his article:

> The critical study of rabbinic midrash collections needs to take seriously the possibility that whoever redacted these texts did more than simply collect pre-existent traditions of exegesis, but gave new meaning to such traditions in significantly reshaping and recombining them to form running commentaries on the text of Scripture. Consequently, the proper contexts (literary, cultural, social, and historical) in which these collections need to be understood may be as much those of the texts' redactors as those of the putative authors of the contained traditions of interpretation. The discrete case of one small section of Sifre Deuteronomy is here chosen in order to test through application this methodology: To what extent is this text and its communicated meaning the product of self-conscious composition through the selection, shaping, and combination of traditions originating in other literary (whether written or oral) contexts? The conclusion reached is that such traditions have been subtly but significantly reshaped in being combined to form a didactically effective, if not yet polished, introduction to the earliest extant commentary on Deut. 3:23-4:1: Moses in petitioning God to be allowed to enter the promised land stands in complete humility, as if without merit, and in recognition of the gratuitous favor which God bestows equally upon all humanity.

Fraade's statement of his "possibility," as noted earlier, will surely present no surprises to generations of biblical scholars. But in asking whether redaction plays any role in the formulation of exegeses of Scripture, Fraade certainly presents an approach uncommon in the field at hand. For that much he wins our praise. Of particular interest is his framing of his question (p. 251):

> How heavy a hand does the redactor display in his combining of exegetical traditions? Does he simply compile or does he significantly revise? What literary and linguistic conventions does he employ in encapsulating inherited traditions in literary form? Is there any method in his linking or juxtaposition of discrete units of interpretations? Does he superimpose structural or thematic unity? To what extent is the meaning and rhetorical impact of an exegetical tradition determined by its particular textual embodiment? The greater the degree of redactional activity displayed in a text the more will we have to assume that the text reflects, at least in significant measure, the world and world view of its redactor(s).

These questions seem to me right on target. Whether or not Fraade finds answers to them will depend upon the framework in which he pursues his inquiry. The answer, alas, is that here, within the limitations of a single pericope, he is unlikely to discover large-scale points of emphasis in the document as a whole. So what he gains by asking the right questions he loses by answering them in a clumsy way. That is to say, if we ask about redaction, then the entirety of what is redacted forms the arena of first confrontation. Only a thesis formed on the foundation of the entire production of a redactor will serve to clarify the bits and pieces of what is redacted. Fraade cannot answer the first question, so all the other questions and their answers prove mere curiosities, exercises in academic formalism. He further (p. 256-7) states:

> Our fundamental question, then, is how and to what end have the extant commentaries been put together? What is the process of redaction by which exegetical and non-exegetical traditions have been encapsulated in literary form and combined to form Bible commentary? Rather than seeking first to extract pre-literary midrashic traditions and to identify their Sitz im leben, we need to begin with the texts in the redacted forms in which we have them, and attempt to locate them in appropriate literary, historical, and social contexts. Did their editors simply collect traditions, perhaps for the sake of preservation, using the order of Scripture as their organizing principle, but without significantly reshaping what they collected? Or, were these compilers themselves interested in commenting on Scripture through the manner in which they combined traditions, reshaping and embellishing them as they fit them into new literary and historical contexts? If the latter, then they are as much exegetes of tradition as of Scripture. Until such questions are answered, not in general but for each midrashic collection, the mining of these collections, particularly for historical purposes, is fraught with danger.

The methods for seeking an understanding of rabbinic redactional activity as reflected in the early midrash collections are at a primitive stage of development. They are of two types. The first looks at factors internal to the text itself. How are discrete interpretive traditions combined? Are there introductory, connecting, or concluding phrases which are telling? Are there repeated phrases, patterns of expression, or rhetorical conventions which may give a sense of unity to a series of otherwise disjunctive statements? Are there signs of the creation of formal or thematic unity, even if relative, which overarch the atomistic interpretations of individual words and phrases? The second method looks outside the text for parallels, or near parallels, in other rabbinic collections, preferably of roughly the same period. How do such parallels found in different literary settings compare and contrast? Are there signs that they have been variously shaped to fit the different contexts, or do identical traditions assume different meanings simply by virtue of their different surroundings? Does such analysis, when systematically pursued through an extensive section of commentary, reveal a pattern of reworking of tradition for particular didactic purposes? If so, does such a pattern correlate with anything in the historical, social, or cultural context in which the commentary might have circulated?

Let me restate the problem. There can be little doubt that the rabbinic compilers of the early midrashim desired (perhaps felt compelled) to preserve and give authority to existing exegetical and even non-exegetical traditions by attaching them to the order of biblical verses. At the same time they themselves were interested in commenting upon, or what was for them unlocking, Scripture's message in such a way as to effectively inform the practices and perspectives of their followers. How do these two concerns meet at the redactionary level?

I cannot imagine a more perspicacious program of inquiry, when done right. And since Fraade is -- in my view, self-evidently -- right in what he says here, we see that the approach of collecting what "the rabbis" said, without analyzing the traits of the documents in which those statements are now preserved, leads to mere information, not to knowledge of worth. Not answering Fraade's correct question yields no "what else," and no "so-what." I should propose the preceding paragraph as the final judgment on the worth of Fraade on Enosh -- but not Fraade on Enosh alone. Finally (pp. 289-90) he says:

To the extent that it is possible to isolate the component traditions combined in this text they may be said to fall into the following three categories:

1. Traditions taken from other contexts, whether exegetical or not, which appear to have been significantly reworked so as to fit the new context of commentary on Deut. 3:23. Based on comparisons with their early parallels sections B, C, and the introduction to fit this category. In transforming these traditions to fit the context of commentary on Deut. 3:23 the redactor creates certain internal incongruities, a further indication that these traditions are not original in their present context.

For example, in section C the figure of the eating of unripe figs of the seventh year does not fit comfortably in the transformed king-. Similarly, David's request not to have his sin recorded in section E does not accord with God's response, and the basic thrust of the , that people should not think that God forgave David out of love or special favor. Some of these rough edges are eliminated in subsequent developments of the tradition as evidenced in later collections.

2. Traditions which appear to have been created specifically for this midrash. This is not to say that they are created ex nihilo, but simply that they do not have parallels in other contexts (admittedly an argument from silence), and that they seem to be particularly well suited to the present context of commentary on our verse. Sections A and F would fit this category. They both comment, the first explicitly and the second implicitly, on the word wacethannan.

3. Traditions which appear to have been transferred from other contexts to the present one without signs of significant revision or adaptation. Such traditions may acquire new meanings simply by virtue of the new company they now keep. Section D seems to fit this category. Unfortunately, since we do not have early parallels to this tradition it is impossible to know its original context and how it may have functioned therein.

Since Fraade's article is prolix, presenting all manner of information on every conceivable topic, it is appropriate that, in the end, he proves himself unable to answer his original questions clearly and distinctly. But the rather shapeless conclusion, lacking the force of the original proposal, should not obscure the genuine step forward Fraade has taken since his dissertation. In repudiating his earlier methods, Fraade demonstrates that the future of comparative *midrash* lies in precisely the approach advocated by many before him and now also by him as well.[2]

Fraade manages to fill up fifty-seven pages one hundred twenty-nine footnotes, and two excurses, to have his say on no more than two dozen lines of Hebrew. At that pace we shall be answering Fraade's quite proper questions for about five centuries -- and who by then will remember what questions we started off to answer, or why they ever mattered? It looks a bit like busy work for young professors. So, true enough, the present approach proves tedious. At the end Fraade can offer us no clear statement of the point and purpose of the compilers of a document. Not only so, but can Fraade imagine he has made a statement on redactors' interests in an analysis of so trivial an example of redactional work? If we wish to understand compilers, we must examine all that

---

[2] As noted earlier, the questions Fraade presents will produce no surprises for biblical scholars. In my *Midrash in Context* (not cited by Fraade), recast and paraphrased above in Chapter Six Section v, I made exactly the same points with reference to Matthew, the Essene library of Qumran commentaries on Nahum and Habakkuk, and the like. So any implication Fraade wishes to convey that he has found something new is unfounded.

they seem to have compiled. No mere "exemplifying" a program of compilation proves anything. To make the point stick, the entire document demands analysis. Alas, Fraade makes up for his tiny sample by puffing up his footnotes with vast quantities of irrelevant information. So, in all, the article proves tedious. Nonetheless, I look forward to Fraade's and others' successes not only of laying out a solid program but also of executing it. Certainly Fraade may be expected to follow up on his discovery of the well-known approach of redaction-criticism, as it applies to the study of *midrash*-exegeses, *midrash*-compilations, and *midrash*-hermeneutics. When he and others move forward in comparative *midrash* done right, then Bloch's and Vermes's pioneering efforts will take up their honored place in a museum of intellectual oddities.

Index

BROWN JUDAIC STUDIES SERIES

Continued from back cover